The
STEAM
TRACTOR
Encyclopedia

Glory Days of the
Invention that Changed
Farming Forever

John F. Spalding
and Dr. Robert T. Rhode

Voyageur Press

Dedication

I dedicate this book to my mother, Peg Spalding, who has been my inspiration, my conscience, and my guiding light for 51 years. She is, quite simply, Love. I also dedicate this book to my beautiful wife, Marian, who makes my life complete. Seeing her smiling face makes each and every day a holiday. Thank you, Babe . . . love ya! Finally, I dedicate this book to my two children, Alexis and Zachery, who turn the adage "wait until you have children of your own someday" into reality. I couldn't love anyone more, and remember: if the Good Lord came down and let me pick from all of the children in the world, I would still pick you, without hesitation. Last, but never least, I thank the Good Lord for all of His many, many blessings.

—John F. Spalding

I dedicate this book to Timothy W. Lyons, who made many suggestions that improved my writing.

—Robert T. Rhode

First published in 2008 by MBI Publishing Company and Voyageur Press, an imprint of MBI Publishing Company, 400 First Avenue North, Suite 300, Minneapolis, MN 55401 USA

Copyright © 2008 by Dr. Robert T. Rhode and John F. Spalding

Voyageur Press titles are also available at discounts in bulk quantity for industrial or sales-promotional use. For details write to Special Sales Manager at MBI Publishing Company, 400 First Avenue North, Suite 300, Minneapolis, MN 55401 USA.

To find out more about our books, join us online at www.voyageurpress.com.

Library of Congress Cataloging-in-Publication Data

Rhode, Robert T.
  The steam tractor encyclopedia : glory days of the invention that changed farming forever / Robert T. Rhode and John F. Spalding.—1st ed.
    p. cm.
  Includes bibliographical references and index.
  ISBN 978-0-7603-3473-7 (hb w/ jkt)
  1. Traction-engines—History—19th century. 2. Tractors—History—19th century. I. Spalding, John F., 1956– II. Title.
  TJ700.R46 2008
  629.225'2--dc22
                        2008012395

Designer: Helena Shimizu
Editor: Amy Glaser

Printed in China

On the cover:

Background image: Two threshermen proudly touch their Buffalo Pitts steam tractor as if to boast, "This is my engine!"

Color image: This 1911 Case steam engine is a 110, which was the largest steam engine Case built. There are approximately 25 of these engines left in the world today. The serial number of Murray Johanson's engine is 24532. *Murray Johanson*

On the frontispiece: Kids in knickers join in a boxing match in front of this Rumely steamer.

On the title pages: They didn't call it the steam age for nothing. What a thrill it must have been when farm steam engines lined the streets of town for a celebration!

On the back cover 1: The bevel gear of early Aultman & Taylor engines, licensed under the Rogers patent of 1876, was nicknamed a "sunflower gear" for reasons that may be obvious.

On the back cover 2: A center-crank Case is shown pulling 3,350 feet of logs.

On the back cover 3: One complete outfit headed down the road is being pulled by a large Minneapolis Threshing Machine Company gasoline tractor.

A Nichols & Shepard steamer with a Minneapolis Universal Farm Motor gas tractor are busy plowing and seeding.

Contents

Firms Represented by Photographs in This Book

Name by which photographs are indexed in the part of the book devoted to manufacturers of steam traction engines	Names of manufacturers that built steam traction engines (The names that are most often cited in agricultural research are presented here without giving all historical variations of companies' names.)
Advance	Case & Willard, Advance Thresher Company
Advance-Rumely	Advance-Rumely Company
American-Abell	American-Abell Engine & Thresher Company
Ames	Ames Iron Works
Aultman	C. Aultman & Company
Aultman & Taylor	Aultman & Taylor Company
Avery	Avery Company
Baker	A. D. Baker Company
Best, as well as Remington	Remington Company, Daniel Best Agricultural Works
Birdsall	Birdsall and Company, New Birdsall Company
Blumentritt	Blumentritt Company
Buffalo Pitts	Buffalo Pitts Company, Buffalo Road Roller Company
Case	J. I. Case Threshing Machine Company
Colean	Colean Manufacturing Company
Cooper	C. & G. Cooper
Doan Steam Wagon	Roberts & Doan
Fairbanks Lobo	Fairbanks Steam Shovel Company
Farquhar	A. B. Farquhar Company
Frick	Frick Company
Gaar-Scott	Gaar, Scott & Company
Geiser Peerless	Geiser Manufacturing Company
Greencastle	Crowell Manufacturing Company
Groton, as well as Conger	Groton Bridge and Manufacturing Company, Groton Manufacturing Company, Conger Manufacturing Company
Harrison	Harrison Machine Works
Heilman	Heilman Machine Works
Holt	Holt Manufacturing Company
Huber	Huber Manufacturing Company
June	D. June & Company
Keck-Gonnerman	Keck-Gonnerman Company
Kelly, as well as Springfield	Rinehart, Ballard & Company Threshing Machine Works; Springfield Engine and Thresher Company; O. S. Kelly Company; Kelly-Springfield Road Roller Company; Buffalo-Springfield Company
Kitten	Kitten Machine Shop
Lane & Bodley	Lane & Bodley Company
Lang & Button	Lang & Reynolds, Lang & Button
Leader	Marion Manufacturing Company
McLaughlin	McLaughlin Manufacturing Company
Minneapolis	Minneapolis Threshing Machine Company
Nichols & Shepard	Nichols & Shepard Company
Northwest	Northwest Thresher Company (Minnesota Giant, Stillwater, Giant, New Giant)
Port Huron	Upton Manufacturing Company, Port Huron Engine and Thresher Company
Price	Jacob Price (built for Price by J. I. Case Threshing Machine Company)
Reeves	Reeves Company

Continued . . . .

Ritchie & Dyer, as well as other engines built in Hamilton, Ohio	Owens, Lane & Dyer Company; Hooven & Sons; The Hooven, Owens & Rentschler Company; Ritchie & Dyer Company
Robert Bell	Robert Bell Engine and Thresher Company
Robinson	Robinson & Company
Rumely	M. Rumely Company
Russell	Russell Company
Sawyer-Massey	Sawyer-Massey Company
Scheidler, as well as McNamar	Scheidler Machine Works, John H. McNamar, Julius J. D. McNamar
Spence	Lavosier Spence
Stevens	A. W. Stevens Company
Twentieth Century	20th Century Manufacturing Company
Waterloo	Waterloo Manufacturing Company
Waterous	Waterous Company
Watertown	Watertown Engine Company
Westinghouse	Westinghouse Company
White, as well as Cornell	MacPherson & Hovey Company, Haggert Brothers, George White & Sons Company
Wide-Awake	J. O. Spencer, Son & Company
Wood	S. W. Wood Engine Company
Wood Brothers	Wood Brothers
Wood, Taber & Morse	Wood, Taber & Morse Steam Engine Works

Firms Not Represented by Photographs in This Book

Manufacturer names	*Names most often cited in name variation*
Atlas	Indianapolis Car and Machine Works, Atlas Engine Works
Burdett & Webb	Burdett & Webb, James Means & Company
Byron Jackson	Byron Jackson
Davidson & Rutledge	Davidson & Rutledge
Eagle	Eagle Machine Works
Empire	Hagerstown Steam Engine & Machine Company
Fishkill Landing	Fishkill Landing Machine Company
Goodison	John Goodison
Illinois	Illinois Thresher Company
Lansing	Lansing Iron & Engine Works
MacDonald Decker	MacDonald Thresher Company
Merrit & Kellogg	Merrit & Kellogg Company
Messinger	Messinger Manufacturing Company
Morris	George W. Morris (several built for Morris by J. I. Case Threshing Machine Company)
Napoleon	Napoleon Manufacturing Company
New Hamburg	New Hamburg Manufacturing Company
Ohio	Ohio Thresher & Engine Company
Paxton	Harrisburg Car Manufacturing Company; Harrisburg Foundry and Machine Works
Peterson	N. C. Peterson & Sons Company
Union Iron Works	Union Iron Works

Additionally, several of the earliest builders that experimented with steam plows or hauling engines are not represented.

Preface

John F. Spalding's love of the North American steam tractor began in 1959 when he was only three. His mother, a photographer for a rural, central–Illinois magazine in the 1950s and 1960s, reported on the Central States Threshermen's Reunion in Pontiac, Illinois, every year. This event hosted the steam tractors, gas tractors, automobiles, and farm implements that revolutionized agriculture. John's mother roamed the park taking pictures, and he followed her, absorbing this fascinating new world of antique farm equipment. Eventually, he was allowed to roam on his own. From sunup to sundown every September, he spent five days with the owners and operators of steam engines.

John began collecting steam tractor photographs and ephemera in the late 1980s. For nearly two decades, he has been searching garage sales, estate auctions, flea markets, the Internet, and eBay for those elusive vintage photographs of the North American steam tractor. Each photograph is more than a picture; it is a portal back in time.

In June 2003, Richard Backus, editor of *Steam Traction*, an international magazine devoted to the restoration and preservation of agricultural steam engines, invited John to submit a regular column. Entitled "Spalding's Corner," John's contribution was a staple in each issue until *Steam Traction* ceased publication. His column now appears in *Engineers and Engines Magazine*. It features one of his photographs of a steam tractor and asks readers to guess the model, make, and manufacturer of the engine depicted. Because of the renown of "Spalding's

Corner," John has been asked time and time again if he could come out with a book providing a historical photo documentary of the American steam tractor. When Dr. Robert T. Rhode, one of the nation's leading historians regarding American steam tractors, contacted him with an interest in co-authoring a steam tractor book, he knew that the book's time had come.

Bob owns a 65-horsepower Case steam traction engine and has demonstrated it at shows of historic agricultural equipment in Illinois, Indiana, and Ohio. Bob's great uncle ran a Reeves steam engine in the threshing era, and his parents introduced him to steam shows when Bob was a child. During their boyhood, both Bob and John were to be found taking in the sights at the reunion in Pontiac. Because Bob grew up on a farm in Indiana, it comes as no surprise that his principal field of study focuses on the literature and history of the steam power era. He published the award-nominated book *The Harvest Story: Recollections of Old-Time Threshermen*, and the award-winning *Classic American Steamrollers 1871–1935: Photo Archive*, co-authored with Judge Raymond L. Drake. Bob also wrote the entry for "Tractor" in *American Icons: An Encyclopedia of the People, Places, and Things That Have Shaped Our Culture*. He has published more than 100 articles in books and magazines covering the subject of agricultural history and literature. In 2005, Bob was one of a select group of leading American authors chosen to contribute essays on rural topics to the acclaimed book entitled *Black Earth and Ivory Tower: New American Essays from Farm and Classroom*, edited by Zachary Michael Jack.

When John agreed to work with Bob on a project featuring John's exceptional photographic record of one of the most fascinating eras in North American history, their collaboration produced this book that showcases vintage iron in a way that it has never been seen before.

A Buffalo Pitts that was named "Alice" by its owner has sadly become mired in the mud.

This Buffalo Pitts is hauling a train of loaded wagons.

Acknowledgments

The authors offer their most profound thanks to the generous people who made this book possible: Warren Bellinger, for providing early Advance–Rumely photos; Travis Brown, for assisting in the search for Heilman images; John Davidson, for permitting inclusion of his photograph of a Jacob Price steam engine; Raymond L. Drake, for sharing his expertise on North American steamrollers; Amy Glaser, for editing this book with extraordinary talent and consummate skill; Dan Greger, for explaining many mysteries of steam history; John Haley, for helping to identify builders; Ron Harris, for offering his photo of a Ritchie & Dyer steam engine; Tom Hart, for making several Keck-Gonnerman photographs available; Scott Maynard, for tracking down Blumentritt pictures; Ed McLaughlin, for providing photos of McLaughlin steam engines and historical details about the firm; Wayne Metzger, for supplying Heilman images; Jack C. Norbeck, for pioneering encyclopedic knowledge of farm steam engines; Deborah Pope, for lending her computer expertise; Eleanor Stewart, for proofreading and commenting on the company histories; Charlie Thoma, for discussing agricultural history; Scott L. Thompson, for conveying his understanding of the history of the various Rumely firms and for emailing Advance-Rumely photographs; William U. Waters, Jr., for imparting his thorough knowledge of many steam companies and for sharing numerous rare pictures; John H. White, Jr., for discovering information about Lane & Bodley; and Gary Yaeger for volunteering his Reeves photos and his wisdom.

Here is a rare glimpse of a 20th Century at the factory in Boynton, Pennsylvania.

Introduction

John F. Spalding's collection of historic photographs depicting steam engines and gasoline engines is nothing short of amazing. Unless another source is acknowledged in the caption, all of the photos in this book are from John's incredible archive. With John's help and encouragement, I have had the distinct honor and privilege of placing these images in their historical context. While the romance of the railroad has spawned numerous books about steam locomotives, no book has presented a complete photographic record of steam traction engines until now. John's extraordinary collection invites readers to step back into the age of farm steam power.

The development of photography coincided with westward expansion on the North American continent. The names of many of the photographers who captured the swelling tide of American agriculture may have been lost, but their views have miraculously survived. Through their lenses we see the lumbering steam engines in wheat fields, on country roads, in barn lots, and on railroad cars. Such steamers mechanized agriculture, ensured population growth, and transformed the United States and Canada into contenders in world economic markets. Freshly painted or coated with dust, the machines of a bygone era bear testimony to the genius of technological invention.

In 1910, a Department of Agriculture survey found that 100,000 farm steam engines were in use in the United States. Steam traction engines truly revolutionized farming. It is a small wonder that canny photographers recognized the need to chronicle such a golden age of American agriculture! Devoted to the task of preserving the past for the benefit of future generations, John has rescued a comprehensive and unparalleled archive of images. He and I are delighted to share his collection with an audience likely to be surprised by the quantity, quality, and significance of these photographs of the great North American agricultural steam engine.

When the steam era came to the North American farm a little more than a decade before the Civil War, small factories to build threshing machines that were powered by steam engines began to spring up in such states and provinces as New York, Ontario, Pennsylvania, Maryland, Ohio, Indiana, Illinois, Wisconsin, and Minnesota. While many shops soon faded from view, others expanded and eventually became large plants that helped support the cities in which they were located. In all, some 50 factories that built farm steam engines in North America were prosperous. Most of the first steamers for farms were equipped with wheels or skids and were pulled by horses. Steam traction engines later came with chain, bevel-gear, or gear-train drives and could pull themselves along the open road. These earliest steam traction engines usually had a seat for a driver near the front of the unit, and horses were employed to steer the traction engine.

In the decades after the Civil War, steering mechanisms became fully developed and ushered in the heyday of the agricultural steam engine. Just after 1900, more and more firms turned to the gasoline engine as a power source. The first gasoline and kerosene tractors were as large as the largest steamers. When the tractor industry recognized that farmers would buy small tractors in vast numbers, the gasoline tractor entered its full glory. Additional gasoline engines, including both the throttled and the hit-and-miss varieties, provided a long list of services from pumping water to shelling corn to washing clothes.

To coherently present this history, this book is divided into four sections: portable steam engines, steam traction engines, gasoline and kerosene tractors, and gasoline engines. The bulk of the book is devoted to steam traction engines. John and I have arranged that section in alphabetical order by manufacturer, and we have included detailed histories of the companies that built such machines. Spotlight essays feature in-depth examinations of firms for which extraordinary records have managed to escape destruction.

Common knowledge about the general history has bred several misconceptions. One is that the steam traction engine replaced the horse. In fact, the vast expansion of tilled land that was made possible by steam power greatly increased the need for horses, especially for pulling wagons. Another misconception is that in 1876, C. & G. Cooper & Company of Mount Vernon, Ohio, built the first traction engine in North America. Many traction engines predated Cooper's. On November 4, 1858, in Jefferson County, Ohio, Joseph McCune ran a gear-driven traction engine built by the Newark Machine Works a distance of 46 miles. A dozen companies in California manufactured traction engines in the 1850s and 1860s. In Cooper's own state, the Owens, Lane & Dyer Company of Hamilton won the Ohio State Fair's gold medal for a traction engine in 1874, almost two years before the Rogers patent, number 173,498, gave Cooper a bevel-geared traction engine. For that matter, successful experiments with traction engineering go far back in American history. Nathan Read, a Harvard graduate who briefly taught at his alma mater, developed a working steam carriage in Warren, Massachusetts, in 1790. Sources claim that Apollos Kinsey invented and drove a steam carriage in Hartford, Connecticut, in 1797. In 1804, the well-known inventor Oliver Evans constructed a steamboat on wheels. He drove it through the streets of

Philadelphia, launched it on the Schuylkill River, paddled along to a portage, crossed on land to the Delaware River, and put the vessel to work cleaning a dock. Agricultural historian F. Hal Higgins called Evans the first to invent a traction engine in America.

Another misconception is that traction engines replaced portable engines. Throughout the production of steam traction engines, manufacturers advertised and sold portable steamers, which were adaptable to many purposes, notably sawmilling. There is also the misconception that all steam traction engines were called *steam tractors*. The term "tractor" slowly began to be used in advertising steamers after 1905 and did not become widespread until much later. Yet another misconception is that gasoline tractors first appeared after the steam era had all but faded into history. Dr. Reynold Wik's timeline in *Steam Power on the American Farm* (University of Pennsylvania, 1953) establishes the synchronous development of steam traction engines and gasoline tractors (see chart at right).

Despite such misconceptions, the public has a deep and lasting appreciation for vintage iron. North America hosts more than 1,000 annual shows exhibiting machines bearing testimony to a great agricultural-industrial heritage. Thousands of spectators witness steam traction engines and gasoline tractors powering threshers or sawmills, and demonstrations of plowing are greeted enthusiastically. John and I share that excitement as we invite you to view a once-in-a-lifetime collection of photographic images.

—Dr. Robert T. Rhode
Springboro, Ohio
March 1, 2008

1876–1902	*Experimental state of tractor development*
1902–1913	*Manufacture of large gasoline and kerosene tractors*
1913–1924	*Development of the small gasoline tractor to the advent of the all-purpose row-crop tractor in 1924*

Steam tractors did not get much larger than this enormous Geiser engine. The photograph gives the location as Fullerton, North Dakota.

One of Geiser's largest engines pulls a train while a portable steamer rests in the distance.

Main photo: *This is an exceedingly rare glimpse of a Treadwell portable steam engine that was manufactured in San Francisco, California.*

Right: *A portable engine is the power source for this Globe rock driller.*

Chapter 1
Portable Steam Engines

This crew works for Will Hull of Whitcomb, Wisconsin.

This portable steamer provides the power for drilling.

This old steamer is a precursor to the great Sawyer-Massey engines of later years. It is called an LDS and is named for L. D. Sawyer.

A Westinghouse cutting silage is pictured here.

An old Buffalo Pitts portable threshes small grain.

This is a product of the John Best & Son Company of Lancaster, Pennsylvania.

A pre-Geiser Landis Peerless portable engine is shown here. This photo probably dates back to the 1870s.
Courtesy William U. Waters, Jr.

This Brandon steam portable was manufactured at the Brandon Machine Works Company in Brandon, Manitoba.

The engineer is adjusting this portable steamer's governor to achieve the ideal speed.

Dogs and children are often found in conjunction with a steam engine, such as this old portable.

This photograph of an Aultman & Taylor portable dates to 1904.

Seldom does a photograph of a hemp mill appear in the historic record, but here is a Case engine helping process a hemp crop for making rope and twine for binders.

Here a Geiser portable pops off while powering a sawmill.

This is a Geiser skid engine.

This portable was built in Springfield, Ohio, by the Leffel firm, which is best known for the manufacture of steam turbines.

Perhaps the Farquhar is burning barrel rings in its firebox while it is crushing and grading stone.

A skid engine scene in a sawmill is pictured here.

This is an example of a Hench & Dromgold portable steam engine performing barn threshing.

Minard Harder made a success of the Empire Agricultural Works in Cobleskill, New York.

A. E. Olmstead was the proprietor of the Safe Steam Engine & Boiler Company of Pulaski, New York, when this photograph was taken at the 1910 New York State Fair.

While pitchers toss the bundles, or sheaves, from the top of the stacks, the clean grain is sacked.

Convicts are working the stone crusher and grader powered by this portable steamer.

This Russell portable powers a veneer mill.

A buzz saw and barrels of water complement an Oil City engine that has a star on the steamchest.

Main photo: *The custom threshermen overseeing this Advance engine wear matching hats for a professionally uniform appearance.*

Right: *The Advance firm built a number of tandem-cylinder engines such as this one. The cylinders are separated in the Advance, as in the Russell's tandem compound.*

Chapter 2
Steam Traction Engines

Advance Thresher Company

Many old-timers with firsthand memories of steam threshing pronounce this company's name, "add vance," emphasizing each syllable equally. The Advance Thresher Company was located in Battle Creek, Michigan, which was named for an 1824 altercation between two Native Americans and two government surveyors. During the half century after the conflict, the town became a booming industrial center. The Advance Thresher Company grew from the Case & Willard Thresher Company, builders of the Advance threshing machine. In 1881, Constantius G. Case, Lovett J. Willard, and Frank M. Rathbun formed Case & Willard.

Willard contributed his sound business sense to the firm, while Case brought his mechanical acumen. When Elon A. Marsh and Minard LaFever became disenchanted with the Nichols and Shepard Company, they went to work first for the Upton Manufacturing Company and then for Case & Willard. Marsh is well known for the valve gear named for him and for a steam pump that likewise bears his name. LaFever is best remembered for the Upton steam engine and for the Advance steam engine, both of which he is credited with having designed. The factory expanded in 1883, and the business was renamed the Advance Thresher Company in 1884. LaFever became the superintendent and a director of the Advance factory. In 1902, the elderly John Abell sold

This Advance steamer boasts an elegant cap on the smokestack.

Here is an Advance engine of the Case & Willard design.

Barefoot youngsters enjoy the threshing season that many called "Christmas in July" because of the camaraderie and good food.

James H. Jinkins of Berrien Center, Michigan, is the proud owner of this Advance engine.

A large crew was needed to keep up with this Advance steamer, built in Battle Creek, Michigan. Courtesy Robert T. Rhode

American-Abell of Toronto to both the Advance Thresher Company and the Minneapolis Threshing Machine Company. The joint owners built American-Abells at the Ontario plant. In late 1911, the M. Rumely Company under Dr. Edward Rumely (son of Joseph Rumely and grandson of Meinrad Rumely) took over Advance, and in early 1912, Rumely snapped up American-Abell. LaFever left Advance and took his family to California. Rumely continued the production of Advance engines and related machines in Battle Creek even after the M. Rumely Company entered into receivership in 1915. While the passage of time has obliterated the records of various steam engine manufacturers, researchers have fortunately traced the beginning serial numbers of Advance steam engines for each year of production from 1885 through 1917, when a steamer with serial number 14,638 rolled from the factory.

An Advance steam tractor sports a front water tank.

A brand-new, early Advance-Rumely poses for a catalog photograph. Note the short smokebox and the robust smokestack.
Courtesy Scott L. Thompson

Note that this Advance engine is equipped with twin steam gauges and possibly a new, as yet unpainted, smokebox ring.

The differences between the early Advance-Rumely steam engine in this publicity shot and its counterpart catalog photo attest to the steam era's spirit of innovation. Courtesy Warren Bellinger

Advance-Rumely Company

After Dr. Edward Rumely spent the winter of 1911 and 1912 taking over the Advance Thresher Company, the Gaar-Scott Company, and the Northwest Thresher Company, he sold Rumely, Advance, Gaar-Scott, and Northwest engines from a consolidated Rumely Products Company. A brilliant business plan? Perhaps, but Dr. Rumely began to feel a financial pinch as early as 1914. On January 19, 1915, the M. Rumely Company and Rumely Products went into receivership. The receiver, Finley P. Mount, masterfully directed the subsequent reorganization, which concentrated OilPull tractor manufacturing in La Porte, Indiana, and steam-powered thresher production in Battle Creek. The Advance-Rumely Company was launched on September 7, 1915.

A rumor of considerable standing among steam aficionados has long held that Mount's mechanical engineers examined a 65-horsepower Case steam engine—a model developed less than three years earlier—while designing the new Advance-Rumely steamer. Although many discount such a possibility, there is at least superficial resemblance in the silhouettes of the two engines.

When a mismanaged Aultman & Taylor Company began to suffer financial difficulties, Advance-Rumely bought the Mansfield, Ohio, firm on December 28, 1923. Advance-Rumely immediately discontinued production of Aultman & Taylor products and moved the Aultman & Taylor repair business to Battle Creek. Advance-Rumely met a similar fate in 1931, when Allis-Chalmers became the owner of Advance-Rumely assets. The decade of the 1920s witnessed a series of economic depressions in various farming communities. Overextended companies like Aultman & Taylor and Advance-Rumely often teetered on the brink of financial disaster. The Great Depression pushed Advance-Rumely over the edge.

An American-Abell strawburner is shown in all its glory.

An extra-fancy American-Abell is dolled up for a show.

American-Abell Engine & Thresher Company

John Abell exchanged his company's trademark of a dragon slayer for a rooster when he heard that the Gordon Highlanders' Lance Corporal Findlater, shot through the legs, had bravely played the song "Cock o' the North" on his bagpipes during the battle of Dargai Hill in India on October 20, 1897.

Abell, an immigrant from England to Toronto, initially followed the British boiler-making practice of forgoing a steamdome. He manufactured portable engines for more than a decade before he built his first traction engine in 1886. His early steamers sported a water-filled, bulbous spark arrester at the base of the smokestack. One of Abell's later domed, straw-burning boilers extended the tubes halfway across the top of the firebox. Less charitable descriptions depict Abell as a mercurial showman who was all too quick to take credit for others' inventions. Kinder portrayals paint him as a savvy inventor alert to the demands of the market. Perhaps he was a combination of both. By 1902, Abell was an octogenarian without an heir. He decided to sell his firm, and the Advance Thresher Company and the Minneapolis Threshing Machine Company took joint ownership. The emergent

manufacturing concern was named the American-Abell Engine & Thresher Company and its products were known as the Cock o' the North line. Smokebox doors boasted a casting of a proud rooster standing on a stump. Toward the end of production, American-Abell built rear-mounted plowing engines. The front wheels were close together within a yoke extending downward from the smokebox. The Rumely takeover of Advance at the end of 1911 began the denouement of American-Abell.

This behemoth dwarfs the men in the foreground.

This American-Abell was located near Scott, Saskatchewan.

This is a rare look at an Ames steamer.

Here is an equally rare glimpse of an Ames in the field.

Ames Iron Works

In 1855, Henry "Harry" Ames, a miller, bought an iron works established two years earlier by Talcott & Underhill in Oswego, New York. The foundry was renamed Ames Iron Works. Leonard Ames, Harry's brother, who was also a miller, and Arthur Merriam were involved in the business. Leonard served as a delegate to the 1860 convention that nominated Abraham Lincoln for president, and Lincoln named Leonard a federal assessor. In 1872, Leonard and Merriam purchased Harry's interest in the Ames Iron

Works. The company manufactured boilers, portable and stationary steam engines, machine tools, sawmills, and gristmills. Ames' western agent was A. S. Petticrew of St. Louis. In 1882, the Ames Iron Works was passed to Allen Ames, Alfred Howlett Ames, and Leonard Ames, Jr., a half brother of Allen and Alfred. The Ames partnership ran the firm until 1893. Allen and Alfred continued with the business until 1919. Ultimately, the Skinner Engine Company bought the Ames engine rights.

C. Aultman & Company and the Aultman Company

Professor Lorin E. Bixler, who published the definitive history of C. Aultman & Company in 1967, wrote that "both of the writer's grandfathers were close friends of Cornelius Aultman, and as a small boy he listened to these men relate their experiences with Mr. Aultman. . . . Their praise of the sterling qualities and magnanimous spirit of the man made him something of a hero to one small boy."

Aultman was born near Canton, Ohio, in 1827. Having served in the millwright and wheelwright trades, Aultman built and sold Obed Hussey reapers in Illinois in 1849. In 1850, Aultman was a partner in Ball, Aultman & Company, a machine shop in Greentown, Ohio. In December 1851, Ball and Aultman moved their reaper and thresher business to Canton for improved manufacturing and shipping opportunities. Ball left the partnership in 1858. C. Aultman & Company was incorporated in Canton in 1859. In 1863,

This is a rare photograph of a chain-driven Canton Monitor, built by C. Aultman.

An exceptionally rare photograph of a pre-production C. Aultman vertical-boiler engine with a double cylinder is shown here.

This C. Aultman Mogul was caught on film at James Mathews' farm in North Dakota. Courtesy Robert T. Rhode

This early 10-horsepower C. Aultman Star dates between 1889 and 1891.

This C. Aultman is equipped with a seat for a driver if pulling the engine by horses is desired.

Children look on in this nostalgic scene of a C. Aultman Double Star, threshing machine, and crew.

A man pretends that his coal shovel is a guitar in this old-time photograph of a C. Aultman Double Star.

A man smoking a pipe sits comfortably on a disc plow pulled by a
C. Aultman Double Star steam engine.

The whole family has come out in their
Sunday best clothing for this photograph of a C. Aultman Mogul.

Two C. Aultman Star steamers are belted back-to-back for work in this
sawmill operation.

Aultman and three other incorporators established the
Buckeye Mower and Reaper Works in Akron. Aultman
lived in Mansfield, Ohio, in 1865 and in 1867 joined Henry
H. Taylor in founding Aultman, Taylor & Company, which
eventually produced its own distinctive steam engine
designs. Aultman returned to Canton in 1867.

The Canton Monitor, which was arguably C. Aultman
& Company's most successful engine, began production in
the nation's centennial year of 1876. Aultman had sold most
of his interest in the firm in the preceding year. His motivation to concentrate his efforts in the Aultman & Taylor firm
remains unclear, but two events may have contributed to his
decision to do so. In 1875, Henry Taylor died, and shortly
thereafter, the Aultman & Taylor Company developed an

Note the chain looped over the smokebox of this C. Aultman Star. Engineers frequently carried chains in this way.

This C. Aultman Star has built a huge straw stack with a webstacker.

With bright new paint, this C. Aultman engine on a railroad car is truly a Star!

engine with a drive system based on the Rogers patent of 1875 and 1876.

Aultman often went hunting and fishing with John Nichols and David Shepard of Battle Creek, Michigan. On December 26, 1884, Cornelius Aultman died. At the time of his death, he was president of the Aultman & Taylor Company, the Nichols & Shepard Company of Battle Creek, the Canton Glass Company, and the Akron firm of Aultman, Miller & Company (which was absorbed by International Harvester in 1908). C. Aultman & Company lasted until 1893, when the firm went into receivership. The closing of C. Aultman & Company coincided with the panic of 1893, which continued through 1895. After the company was reorganized, it emerged as the Aultman Company, which produced the Star, Phoenix, and Mogul engines, as well as the Double-Star, an undermounted engine. The Aultman Company went bankrupt in 1904 and was placed in the hands of a receiver. The firm was reorganized as the Aultman Engine & Thresher Company for the purpose of liquidating the plant and assets in 1905, and the last machines were built and sold from inventories by the end of 1906. A repair firm existed from 1907 until 1925.

The bevel gear of early Aultman & Taylor engines, licensed under the Rogers patent of 1876, was nicknamed a "sunflower gear" for reasons that may be obvious.

The brand-new wood lagging around the boiler of this Aultman & Taylor return-flue engine was intended to diminish heat loss from the boiler.

Three generations of a family posed with this Aultman & Taylor bevel-gear steamer.

This photograph could be an advertisement for the various forms of headgear appropriate during threshing season.

A woman watches the scene from a window of the nearby house.

Aultman & Taylor Company

Professor Lorin E. Bixler wrote the definitive history of the Aultman & Taylor Company in 1977 but did not publish it in his lifetime. Dan Greger was helping Bixler revise his manuscript when Bixler died. Dr. Robert T. Rhode rescued Bixler's work from obscurity and serialized his book beginning in 2000.

Henry Hobart Taylor was born in Durhamsville, New York, in 1835. When Taylor was 10, his father opened a general merchandise store in Chicago, where Taylor later clerked. In 1854, the family moved to Freeport, Illinois. Taylor studied pharmacy in Cincinnati, Ohio, but never became a pharmacist. In 1856, Taylor returned to Freeport to establish an agency for Ball, Aultman & Co. of Canton, Ohio. Taylor's association with Cornelius Aultman lasted 19 years.

With the cultivation of the prairies, trade in agricultural machinery rapidly increased. In 1864, Taylor became a stockholder in the company of John Nichols and David

An Aultman & Taylor sunflower-gear engine pulls a load down a highway of yesteryear. Courtesy William U. Waters, Jr.

Shepard of Battle Creek, Michigan. Nichols and Shepard had perfected a new thresher that was distinct from the old "endless apron" type. Nichols coined and copyrighted the term "Vibrator" for the innovative machine. Taylor had opened a dealership in Chicago for the distribution of equipment manufactured by C. Aultman & Company and Nichols, Shepard, and Company. Taylor and Aultman recognized the advantages of vibrator-style threshers and formed a company to perfect the mechanism. Aultman, Nichols, and Shepard were friends who enjoyed hunting and fishing

together. The exchange of ideas and patent rights flowed smoothly between the inventors. The Aultman and Taylor threshers were built under license to Nichols and Shepard. They both held stock in Aultman and Taylor, who located their vibrator thresher factory in Mansfield, Ohio, to take advantage of its excellent railroad facilities. Beginning in 1865, Aultman spent four years in Mansfield to supervise the erection of buildings and the installation of machinery. In 1867, Aultman, Taylor & Company had become a reality. Having established the factory, Aultman returned to Canton in 1867 and lived there until his death.

Taylor did not live to see the glory days of the firm that bore his name. He died in 1875 at age 40. Aultman gained the controlling interest in Aultman & Taylor when he purchased Taylor's holdings in the Mansfield firm. Aultman died at the age of 57 in 1884. His daughter, Elizabeth, inherited the bulk of her father's interest in the company, which made her the largest stockholder.

The Aultman & Taylor Company adopted an unusual trademark: a starved rooster. According to Lyle Hoffmaster, a Nebraska thresherman noticed an emaciated rooster vainly searching for grain around an Aultman & Taylor threshing machine. The fellow shipped the fowl to the Aultman & Taylor headquarters with a note stating that the rooster had been "fattened" on an Aultman & Taylor

A boy with a manure fork poses near an Aultman & Taylor engine complete with canopy.

With its cylinder oil can propped on the preheater, this Aultman & Taylor is pulling a building.

strawstack. The rooster became a factory pet and company writers penned a widely circulated verse about him: "This is the cock that crowed in the morn, with features deranged and look forlorn; For scratch where he might and roam where he may, he found not a grain his labor to pay. Aultman-Taylor's thresher had been that way."

A nameless hobo once strayed into the Aultman & Taylor offices and asked for employment. When he confided that he was good with a paint brush, he was put to work painting a four-story rooster on both ends of the warehouse. The hobo's art greeted thousands of rail passengers, who remembered Mansfield as the home of the starved rooster. The huge warehouse burned in 1896.

Early Aultman & Taylor engines used a sunflower gear, for which Rogers filed in 1875 and received in 1876 a patent. Famous collector "Steam Engine" Joe Rynda of Minnesota owned a 10-horsepower Eureka engine with the sunflower gear and wooden wheels that was built around 1877. Rynda acquired two such engines at different times. Near the end of 1906 or the beginning of 1907, Aultman & Taylor built a mammoth 45-horsepower steamer that attained a maximum indicated horsepower of 171. The

One trademark of the Aultman & Taylor firm incorporated portraits of the company's founders. Another trademark was a starved rooster—starved because the thresher dropped no grain.

behemoth was used around the factory and yards until 1909, when it was shipped to Faulkton, South Dakota. It remained in that vicinity for several years.

The Aultman & Taylor Company developed a full line of agricultural implements and, for a time, enjoyed a brisk business in Cahall water-tube boilers. Around 1906, the Aultman & Taylor Company became interested in building a gasoline tractor. The 30–60-horsepower tractor achieved immediate success. In 1918, the company announced a smaller 15–30-horsepower tractor. A new manager named E. L. Brunger, whom the Advance-Rumely Company was happy to have gotten rid of, attempted to model the 15–30 after the Rumely OilPull. Not until 1920 did Aultman & Taylor overcome the problems with the 15–30 design. By then the firm had lost the market to other companies' small tractors. Lethargic and inflexible, the management of the factory failed to keep up with the rapidly changing world of agriculture. On December 28, 1923, Advance-Rumely bought the crumbling Aultman & Taylor firm and quickly liquidated most of its assets while transferring the Aultman & Taylor repair business to Battle Creek.

This Avery is hauling an Erie City Iron Works boiler for the Des Moines pumping station.

With a girl on the bunker, this Avery is trimmed with a fancy canopy.

This return-flue Avery with an extra bunker has helped to create two perfect straw stacks. Courtesy Robert T. Rhode

Avery Company

An oft-repeated anecdote about the founding of the Avery Company states that R. H. Avery, a Union soldier in Andersonville Prison, sketched his design for a corn planter in the sand. Back in Kansas after the war, he refined his ideas. By 1874, he created a working model, which was later housed at the Ford Museum. J. P. Carroll of the Caterpillar Tractor Company told this story as early as 1951. Carroll continued by saying that three years later, R. H. and his brother, C. M., established a company in their names in Galesburg, Illinois. The inventive R. H. and the business-minded C. M. produced corn planters, stalk cutters, and cultivators. In 1882, they moved their business to a new three-story building east of the intersection of North Adams and North Jefferson in Peoria, Illinois. During the following year, they renamed their firm the Avery Planter Company.

The production of steam engines did not begin until 1891. Before long, the company was manufacturing not only return-flue models, which were discontinued in 1915, but also top-mounted, locomotive-style engines that were discontinued in 1917. During the next year, R. H. died,

Here is a rare look at a return-flue Avery without a water tank. Her crew nicknamed this engine "Big Bess."

A top-mounted Avery is shown with lantern and oil can on the preheater and with the ubiquitous water wagon.

The bulldog trademark of the Avery firm bore threshing-machine teeth, not the canines found in the mouth of a real dog.

A very busy scene includes a Geiser Peerless in back, an Avery gas tractor, and an undermounted Avery on a railcar.

The crew takes a moment for a photo op on the road with a Yellow-Fellow threshing machine and a straw carrier.

C. M. became president, and J. B. Bartholomew, a relative, became vice president. Bartholomew embodied talent for invention and skill in business.

The firm was incorporated as the Avery Manufacturing Company in 1900. During the opening years of the new century, the factory rapidly expanded. In 1905, C. M. died and Bartholomew became president. The firm's name was changed to the Avery Company in 1907.

Avery became well known for its Yellow Fellow threshers that were appropriately painted a bright yellow. The company developed the undermounted steam engine that most people associate with the Avery name. Bartholomew won a case against the A. W. Stevens Company for infringement of the Avery-patented undermount design. Avery also built an

undermounted steamroller. Avery products were known as the Bull Dog Line, and a dog with teeth shaped like those in a threshing drum became the firm's trademark.

As John Ruff has shown, the company began producing gasoline tractors that resembled trucks around 1909. Within a few years, the firm relinquished the notion of having a truck that could pull farm machinery and the company made its truck only a truck. In 1910, Avery withdrew a more conventional but poorly designed 65-horsepower gasoline tractor from competition. In the following year, Avery contributed a smaller 20–35-horsepower tractor, which assumed a customary form by 1912, the same year that the 12–25-horsepower model was introduced. A 40–80-horsepower tractor

Steam engines and gas tractors are born inside the Avery factory in Peoria, Illinois.

appeared the next year. By 1914, Avery had brought out a 25–50-horsepower model and an 8–16-horsepower size. In 1916, the 18–36-horsepower model replaced the 20–35. By World War I, Avery's outmoded 8–16-horsepower and weak 5–10-horsepower models could not compete effectively with the 10–20-horsepower tractors of other firms. Avery produced a 14–28-horsepower tractor in 1919, but the decline of the company was at hand. By 1920, companies were submitting their tractors to the Nebraska tests. Under the close scrutiny of the Nebraska engineers, several Avery tractors initially did not attain their rated horsepower. Avery consequently gained a bad reputation for having failed the Nebraska tests, even though the firm corrected most of the problems that the tests had exposed.

An agricultural depression shocked Avery in 1921. The firm sustained production of the 8–16, 25–50, and 40–80

until 1922. Although Avery strove to design new models in 1923, the company went bankrupt in 1924 and was placed in receivership. In 1925, Bartholomew died. Later that year, a group of former Avery employees organized the Avery Power Machinery Company. This small firm attempted to compensate for the difficulties that had plagued the larger company. Business proceeded to falter until 1931, when the Great Depression could no longer be ignored. The firm dwindled. Two businessmen purchased the parts business in 1938, changed the name to Avery Farm Machinery Company, and produced the Ro-Trak. Ultimately, the plant was sold to the earth-moving machinery manufacturer R. G. LeTourneau. In 1949, the corporation that had sustained the parts inventory was dissolved, and a man by the name of Earl K. Smith purchased the parts-manufacturing rights. (The B. F. Avery tractor built in Louisville, Kentucky, bore no connection to the Peoria firm.)

A. D. Baker Company

In 1898, A. D. Baker built his first agricultural steam traction engine in Swanton, Ohio. He went on to manufacture approximately 1,800 more before 1928, when the age of steam was coming to a close.[1] Today's vintage-iron restoration movement has placed nearly 200 Baker steam engines in preservation.[2] Each summer, more than 100 Baker steamers appear at thresherees. While many of Baker's steam engines have survived, details of his life and times have begun to vanish. This essay reclaims the biography of Baker, an entrepreneur who, like William Heilman, kept a low profile. Baker lived a generation after Heilman and faced stiffer competition in the marketplace. He compensated by being more inventive than Heilman. Here is a portrait of A. D. Baker, the quiet genius.

A Long Lifetime

The man who preferred to be called A. D., not Abner, was born the son of Samuel and Lydia Baker near Fredericktown, Knox County, Ohio, on March 17, 1861, the first year of the Civil War.[3] He died on June 17, 1953, the final year of the Korean War.[4] During the 92 years in between, Baker established himself as one of an elite group of industrialists who brought steam power to America's farms, thereby helping America become the world leader in agricultural production. His mechanical inventions included a valve gear that enhanced his farm engines and, in a modified form, became a success story in the railroad locomotive industry. Baker watched

his business crest to an impressive height, only to see it recede with the end of the threshing era when combines replaced threshers in the late 1940s.

Lillis Baker Cort, Baker's granddaughter, remembered her grandfather as "very quiet—very quiet."[5] Rosabelle Krauss, owner of the P&G Grill in Swanton, Ohio, and a housekeeper who worked for Baker for 15 years said, "He was a very intelligent man."[6] During the Baker company's busy seasons, when Krauss finished her work at Baker's house, usually at 2 p.m., she crossed the railroad tracks to the factory and spent "a couple of hours" in the parts department. Krauss recalled, "In the center of the factory he had a machine with different saws. He told me, 'If I'm working at that machine, don't talk to me. I'll lose concentration if you talk to me. If I'm needed, just walk by, and I'll see you. When I can stop what I'm working on, I will.' At those times, he was working on a new invention to be patented."

Louis Abner Carson, Lillis Baker Cort's son and Baker's great-grandson, who is vice president of Scottdel Incorporated located in the former Baker factory in

This engine was only the sixth Baker to leave the factory.

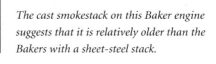

The cast smokestack on this Baker engine suggests that it is relatively older than the Bakers with a sheet-steel stack.

Swanton, said, "When A. D. really got going on an idea, nobody would see him for weeks. He'd disappear."[7]

This quiet genius served as plant superintendent "for the life of the company."[8] Chauncey E. Berkebile, Baker's brother-in-law, worked alongside Baker as assistant superintendent.[9] Baker and Berkebile spent their time in the factory and not in an office cut off from the action. Horace Levengood of Jackson, Michigan, wrote, "About 1916, my brother had to go to Swanton, where the Baker plant is located, to get some repair parts. . . . While he did the business I went out in the back and ran into an old man in overalls sweeping the floor. He took me all around and even showed me a steam tractor they had built. They were using it to pull freight cars around the yards. . . . On the way home my brother asked me if I knew who the old gentleman was. I said no. Then he told me it was Mr. Baker."[10] Krauss said, "He was as common as you and me. Fame didn't go to his head."

Once, Krauss asked her employer if she was doing anything wrong. Baker responded, "If you weren't doing what you were supposed to do, I'd suggest a way to do it."[11] As long as A. D. said nothing, his employees knew that their boss approved of the job they were doing.

The Early Years

Baker was 15 years old when he moved with his parents to a farm east of Swanton.[12] There, long before he stood at the head of a widely acclaimed manufacturing company, he developed a lasting appreciation for agriculture and the people engaged in its pursuit. Like Henry Ford, a later friend of Baker's, A. D. aspired to invent machines to make farming easier. According to Catalog Number 27 of the A. D. Baker Company, the mechanically gifted Baker built his first steam engine in 1884.[13] At age 23, Baker traveled to

This Baker engine is equipped with a kerosene lantern for travel at night. Henry Ford often visited his friend A. D. Baker. The two of them liked discussing failed inventions.

Akron, Ohio, where he served for three years as a machinist at the Empire Reaper Works. In April 1886, he married Ella Berkebile. Then he spent a few months working at Erie City Iron Works in Pennsylvania, followed by a 90-day stint at the Frontier Iron Works in Detroit, Michigan. After his useful apprenticeship in iron, Baker came back to his father's farm.

In 1888, A. D. opened a shop on a farm that specialized in the repair of agricultural machines. Seven years later, he moved his business to Swanton. He was fascinated with the steam engines he studied. Within three years of the transfer of his business to Swanton, Baker felt prepared to build a steamer of his own design. A. D. suffered a temporary setback when a Toledo bank rejected his loan application, but his friend F. E. Pilliod came to the rescue and co-signed the note to get the money for Baker's experiment. Baker built his engine on a boiler purchased from a boiler shop. The money from the sale of Baker Number One repaid the loan and gave A. D. enough profit to plan more engines.

A. D. eventually bought Baker Number One back from the first owner, and it "was used as a yard engine to pull threshers and engines around the shop,"[14] said Louis Carson, A. D. Baker's great-grandson. As Carson's mother, Lillis Baker Cort, pointed out, "It always sat out to the east of the factory."[15] Carson added that "Henry Ford [had] once offered A. D. a blank check to buy Baker Number One, but A. D. turned him down."[16] Baker Number One was frequently under steam at the National Threshers Association show in Wauseon, Ohio, and at other area steam rallies where Carson worked the throttle of the remarkable 16-horsepower engine handcrafted by A. D. Baker. A few years ago, John Schrock of Osseo, Michigan, restored Baker's first steamer to running order.

The Baker Company's Growth from 1898 through 1909

After building Baker Number One in 1898, A. D. built two more engines in 1899 and again in 1900. In December 1900, the A. D. Baker Company incorporated with $150,000 capital.[17] A. D.'s unobtrusive manner inspired trust in customers.

On March 3, 1903, Baker received U. S. Patent Number 721,994 for his center-hung radial reverse valve gear.[18] It proved so successful that it was widely imitated. According to Frank L. McGuffin, "William H. Miller took the Baker gear idea and mounted it on the engine instead of the boiler and was granted a patent . . . on January 19, 1915. This valve gear was used on the Keck-Gonnerman single engines and was as good as the Baker gear—in fact, it was the Baker gear, engine-bed mounted."[19]

The Baker firm painted the name and hometown of the company on the edge of the canopy.

In 1905, the MacDonald Thresher Company Limited of Stratford, Ontario, reached an agreement with the A. D. Baker Company that licensed MacDonald to build a Canadian version of the Baker engine. MacDonald first built an 18-horsepower engine and later added a 20, 22, and 25.[20] Perhaps as few as 500 MacDonald engines were built.[21]

In 1905, the Baker company was building engines in sizes 16, 18, 20, and 25 horsepower. By the end of 1907, the firm had produced more than 500 engines.[22] Baker first used Brennan boilers, then Brownell and Broderick boilers.[23]

In 1907, A. D. was granted a patent for an adaptation of his valve gear that made it suitable for locomotives. Two years later, the rapidly increasing demand for the gear necessitated the creation of a separate firm, the Pilliod Company. New, red wooden threshing machines with green framing, yellow striping, and the Baker name joined the popular Baker engines in the firm's 1908 catalogs of products for the thresherman.[24]

In 1909, the Baker company added road rollers to its list of manufactures.[25] A. D. anticipated that the building of more good roads required steamrollers, and he adapted his traction engine to roadwork. From 1909 through 1927, the firm sold 157 road rollers.[26]

Wichita and Other Contests

In April 1907, A. D. Baker used a large fan he had invented to test the power of engines at a competition held in Wichita, Kansas.[27] Representatives of the Huber Manufacturing Company of Marion, Ohio, claimed that their 16-horsepower engine turned the fan faster than the 16-horsepower Baker engine. Ordinarily, no engine could defeat a Baker engine pulling what came to be known as the Baker fan. In fact, at Wichita, the 16-horsepower Baker triumphed over an 18-horsepower Avery. Someone asked A. D. why the lower-rated Baker engine beat the higher-rated Avery engine and A. D. replied, "The Avery was not designed right." Learning of Baker's remark, J. B. Bartholomew, president of the Avery Company, demanded an apology, but A. D. asked, "Our Baker engine did turn the fan faster, did it not?" Bartholomew answered in the affirmative. A. D. replied, "Well, then, I told the truth and do not owe you an apology."[28]

Once, when Baker employees took their fan to the Ohio state fair, representatives of the Advance Thresher Company asked A. D. if they could belt their engine to his fan. He told them they would do well to wait until the crowd had gone home, unless they wanted to be embarrassed. The larger Advance engine turned the fan far below the speed achieved by the smaller Baker engine. Perplexed, the Advance employees asked A. D. to explain the difference. He said they "should know better than to try to turn the fan as fast with an engine with their large flywheel compared with the 36-inch diameter on the Baker."[29] The engineers' skill and the design of their engines had much to do with the degree of success experienced in running the Baker fan;[30] however, A. D. hinted at the clever principle behind his famous fan. Essentially the fan's power consumption varies as the cube of its rotational velocity. In other words, a more powerful engine creates more resistance and fails to turn the fan faster than a less powerful one.[31]

Easily Recognizable Features of Older Baker Engines

Throughout the Baker company's history, the steam engines underwent changes. An obvious difference between older and newer Baker engines may be seen in the design of the smokestack. The older stack is straight with a bell-shaped top. The tapered Venturi stack came later. An older drive-wheel lug traces a zigzag pattern while a newer lug runs straight. The hubs of the newer drive wheels were made up of removable wedges, and each wedge supported two spokes. Tightening the bolt in each wedge tightened the two spokes by placing them under compression rather than elongation tension, as was the case in the older wheels that used threaded spokes with nuts in the hub to draw the spokes tight. Another feature of the older engines was the installation of a crosshead pump and cast-iron water heater on the engine's left side—a feature that was discontinued with serial number 1229.[32]

The Baker Standard and the Baker Special

The Baker Standard engine had either one water tank or two side-by-side water tanks underneath the platform. The Baker Special engine had contractor's fuel bunkers with extra tank capacity. Customers could order the Special bunkers with either counterflow- or uniflow-cylinder engines. They could also request boiler jackets and canopies. Around 1915, a wide canopy with offset corners for better coverage of the bunkers became available. Besides the contractor's tanks on the Baker Special and the tanks beneath the platform on the Baker Standard, an optional water tank holding an additional 65 gallons of water could be mounted on brackets in front of the engine's left drive wheel on all 16-, 18-, 19-, 20-, 21-, and 23-horsepower models.[33]

The Big 25-Horsepower Engines

The Baker Company built 70 25-horsepower engines.[34] The last one was manufactured in 1920.[35] Kim Besecker of Arcanum, Ohio, owns the engine and he exhibits it at several steam shows.

The Baker Uniflow Cylinder

In 1915, the Baker company built its first uniflow-cylinder engines.[36] Raymond H. Fork, who threshed with Baker equipment, said, "The original uniflow cylinder combined auxiliary poppet-type valves and a slide valve with a steamchest located below the cylinder. This did not prove out to be completely satisfactory. It was reported by engineers that in going down a steep hill and using the reverse gear for braking, the auxiliary valves would malfunction with a loss of reverse control."[37] Baker eventually took back most of the initial uniflow cylinders and replaced them with the piston valve uniflow familiar to steam engine enthusiasts. Fork stated, "I have seen only one engine with the original uniflow cylinder. Apparently a very limited number of them were produced. They were discontinued on the 19-horsepower after serial number 1419, on the 21-horsepower after number 1417, and on the 23-horsepower after number 1420. Uniflow engines ordered after these serial numbers got the piston valve uniflow." An immediate exhaust, a sharp return stroke, and consequent economical operation characterized the new uniflow cylinders that worked at a maximum boiler pressure of 180 psi. The boilers of engines equipped with counterflow cylinders customarily popped off at 150 psi. The 16-horsepower counterflow engine became a 19-horsepower uniflow engine. The 18-horsepower counterflow became a 21-horsepower uniflow, and the 20-horsepower counterflow became a 23-horsepower uniflow. When the company installed a uniflow cylinder on a 25-horsepower counterflow, Baker called it a 29-horsepower engine. In a brake test, one attained a horsepower of 114.87. While the firm listed the 29-horsepower engine in a 1916 catalog and in parts books, probably none were sold and the behemoth was later dropped from production.[38]

Heavy-Duty Engines

Baker engines wore red and green livery through 1920. Blue Baker engines decorated with yellow striping entered the market in 1921. The new paint scheme was introduced concurrently with the advent of heavy-duty steam engines. The traces of red and green paint that have been found on heavy-duty engines suggest that buyers could request either color scheme. After 1921, all 21–75- and 23–90-horsepower engines were heavy-duty, but the Baker company never upgraded the 19-horsepower model to the heavy-duty class. The firm continued to produce lighter models, designated simply as 23 and 21, without reference to the higher horsepower figures. A heavier crankshaft, crank disc, crank pin, connecting rod, gearing, heavier crankshaft bearings and brackets, a higher pedestal, more staybolts to support a deeper firebox, the addition of a full-length cannon bearing to support the rear axle, and a support rib in the crosshead casting were among the improvements that enhanced the heavy-duty engines.[39] Interestingly, bull gears on heavy-duty engines were 4 3/4 inches wide, whereas bull gears on the earlier style of 23 were 5 1/2 inches wide. The road speed of the 23–90 was 2.6 mph, whereas the road speed of the 23 was 2.3 mph. The bunker tanks on the 23–90 were 28 inches wide, whereas the tanks on the 23 were 32 inches wide. The grouters on the driver wheels of heavy-duty engines were staggered and not evenly spaced as on earlier models.

A Few Intriguing Variations in Model Specifications

Today, Baker aficionados enjoy speculating about differences in specifications from model to model. For example, why is the piston stroke of the 19-horsepower engine 10 1/4 inches, when the stroke of the 21- and 23-horsepower engines is 10? Why is the 21-horsepower boiler greater in diameter but shorter than the boiler of the 19-horsepower engine?

A Tornado Menaces Swanton

In 1920, a tornado struck Swanton and caused severe damage to the Baker company's buildings, but the last 25-horsepower engine survived the devastating winds.[40] Baker asked his employees to bring hammers and saws to work the next morning. Repairs to the factory soon were completed. The workers also helped rebuild other structures throughout Swanton.

Diversified Interests

Baker built and ran the electricity-generating plant for Swanton. He also owned the feed mill in town. His company produced feed mixers, corn shellers, and a hammermill to grind corn.[41]

Baker Serial Numbers Change

Beginning in 1921, the Baker company changed its method of assigning serial numbers. For example, instead of 1633, the number 16133 was given, with the "1" in the middle of the number reflecting the year "1921." At the time of this writing, a Baker belonging to Herb E. Beckemeyer carries serial number 16389 and was built in 1923.

Rosabelle Krauss' Memories of Her Association with the Baker Company[42]

Krauss remembered that from the last of April through early May, men from faraway states such as Idaho, Wyoming, Nebraska, Kansas, and Arkansas came to Swanton to purchase parts for steam engines and threshers. They saved freight expense and avoided delays by driving to the factory. "Many times they arrived in the middle of the night," Krauss said. "They often had an extra driver to help them drive such long distances." They rang the doorbell at Baker's house and relayed their requests to Krauss. George Dick, head of the parts department, was "a man of few words," she said. Together, Dick and Krauss provided the needed supplies. Krauss said, "When A. D. sat down to breakfast, there would be the bill of sale on the table waiting for him. A. D. would be just as grateful in the morning as the customers had been in the night.

"One of A. D.'s favorite guests was Henry Ford, Krauss said. "I cooked many a meal for Henry Ford." At one time, Ford was considering Swanton as a possible location for an automobile manufacturing plant. When Ford came to A. D.'s house, he "was not dressed in a suit but in a blue denim shirt with a red handkerchief tied around his neck. Nobody in town knew it was Ford," Krauss said. "After I had served dinner, they had me sit in the dining room with them and I listened to their conversations. Ford and A. D. talked about their inventions. They also seemed to enjoy talking about inventions that had fizzled—their own and those of others," Krauss said. "I once asked A. D. how many patents he had. He said, 'There should be at least 129.' I don't know how many more he received after that.

"A. D. and Ford were people that were not too proud to wear mended socks," Krauss commented. "One time, Henry Ford forgot one of his socks. After he left, I found it under the bed. I noticed that it had a little hole in it so I mended it. The next time he came, I returned it to him. He gave me five dollars for mending that sock. He said he knew of no other young person who could do work that beautiful.

"The only time I saw A. D. wear a suit and tie was when he left to visit his farm in Michigan. He had a farm near Marlette. He thrived on going up there, especially at harvest time," Krauss said.

A. D. seldom ventured far from Swanton, but his valve gear "was shipped all over the world," Krauss stated. "Walter Smith in Chicago and Walter Brown in New York were A. D.'s agents. When they were in Swanton, they'd stay only one night. They're the ones who put the valve gear on locomotives in Australia, Europe, and South America. They sent parts everywhere. They were in touch with the rest of the world." Krauss continued, "A. D.'s son, Louie, worked at the plant after he had gone to college at Ohio State." He eventually became vice president of the firm.

"Whenever an old engine would come back to the factory," Krauss said, "they would have the flues rolled. They'd clean the engine and paint it. Oftentimes, you couldn't tell the old ones from the new ones. The paint back then would spread a lot easier. It was thicker. It covered very nicely. The painters brushed it on. They used big brushes when they needed to." During slack times, painters practiced their art by elaborately striping the engines.

"A. D. threw a threshermen's dinner each spring in the middle of May," Krauss remembered. "He served baked beans, potato salad, ham, buns, pickles, mustard, and ketchup. It seems like it was cake and ice cream both for dessert. On that special day, all the employees were there with a book to take orders. The factory was closed down. Three-hundred people attended. It was discontinued after the steam era ended and A. D. was only selling parts.

"My father was a thresherman by trade," said Krauss. "He wore out two Baker engines and two Baker separators. He bought the first one in 1914, the second one in 1921. He had six men on the payroll. Threshing started around the fourth of July and ran through August. My father had a Blizzard ensilage cutter, a husker-shredder, and a sawmill. He kept those steam engines going the year 'round. From about two miles south of Swanton, it was all forest to the Maumee River. My father cleared farm ground by sawing the lumber. He would clear land, and it would be time to start planting oats and buckwheat.

"I'm the oldest of six. The farmers wanted boys to work in the field. Because I was born first, I got to help my father. I was a tomboy. I was just a little girl when my father got the second engine. They fired it up at the factory and drove it out. Ooh! That new engine was exciting! It had a wildcat whistle. The first thing my father had me do was blow the whistle, and I've always remembered that. Whenever my father's crew would pull out to go to another job, he would throw off the governor belt and make the engine go like greased lightning. We kids thought that was great sport.

"My uncle bought a Baker steam tractor," Krauss continued. When the steam age was coming to an end, A. D. experimented with what he called a steam tractor, as opposed to a steam engine, that employed a condensing engine, coal stoker, and other devices not customarily found on steam traction engines. He hoped that his tractor could successfully compete with the gas-fired tractors that were becoming more popular. "My uncle always had a problem getting the steam tractor started. It didn't pan out very well for A. D."

Baker introduced the less-than-successful 16–30-horsepower steam tractor in 1921. In the latter part of the decade, the firm's first gasoline-powered tractors, the 22–40- and the 25–50-horsepower models, appeared. They resembled contemporary mainstream designs.

A Thresherman Who Knew A. D.[43]

"Yes, I knew A. D. Baker," said Raymond H. Fork of Gibsonburg, Ohio. "My father was a custom thresherman who used Baker equipment since 1910. I was the oldest boy out of six. My father took me along to Swanton to get

This panoramic view depicts E. H. Wilson's Baker outfit at Charles Weigle's home near Greenhill, Indiana. Picture by Lighty Photo Company, Williamsport; Courtesy Berry's Camera Shop

parts. We lived about thirty-five miles from the factory. We often went to Swanton at night because Dad didn't want to stop working while it was light. It would be seven or eight o'clock when we arrived at A. D.'s house. He'd take us across the railroad tracks to the plant. He knew where to find everything, and when he found the part we were looking for, he jotted down the part number or the casting number on an old piece of paper. He threw that paper on a desk all full of papers. I used to wonder how we ever got a bill, but we eventually did get one. I always thought A. D. was very accommodating."

Fork recalled, "A. D. came out to our farm one time. He was always interested in how well you liked the Baker equipment. My father had told A. D. about a new idea for the Baker separator and A. D. wanted to see it work. Dad had improved the arrangement of the deflector board, which directs the blast from the fans. A. D. came right out to the threshing lot."

The Forks had long experience with Baker products. "Dad bought a new engine and separator in 1910," Fork said. "They were an 18-horse counterflow and a wooden 33–56 Baker separator. The separator had babbit bearings. You had to grease them all the time because you might get hot boxes. Dad used that engine until 1920. In that year, he got a 21–75 uniflow, one of the last engines that was not heavy-duty. In 1929, he bought a new separator. It was all

steel with Hyatt roller bearings and a Heineke long feeder. A few Bakers in the earlier years had the Ruth feeder. Then for a long time they had the Garden City feeder."

A company threshing crew in the vicinity of the Fork residence had a Baker engine with a superheating device. The superheated steam, Fork said, "caused premature wear on the piston rings and the rings of the piston valve. The quality of the oil wasn't as good back then. After two years, they took out the superheater."

A. D. must have been confident that the steam tractor would sell. Fork explained, "He experimented with, and built, both a 20–40-horsepower fire-tube model and a 35–70-horsepower water-tube model. Records indicate the first steam tractor was built in 1922 and about seventy-five were built. For whatever reason—the timing, the switch from steam power to gas- and oil-powered tractors being already on the way, the extra work connected with furnishing coal and water—the steam tractor did not prove to be very successful. It was said that Mr. Baker would take any of the steam tractors back in trade for a Baker steam traction engine or a Baker gas tractor. I remember seeing what seemed like several dozen of those returned steam tractors lined up in rows along the roads around the plant buildings. I often wondered what they did with all those they took back. I know of only two surviving steam tractors, one in the Henry Ford Museum at Greenfield Village in

This Baker steamer is dual-belted.

Dearborn, Michigan, and another at one time owned by the Murphy brothers in Michigan and shown at the National Threshers reunion at Montpelier, Ohio."

At the time of this writing, Fork has a collection of Baker equipment including both regular and heavy-duty 21–75- and 23–90-horsepower models. He also has the 33–56 all-steel Baker separator his father bought new in 1929, and the 21–75-horsepower Baker uniflow steam engine his father bought new in 1920. Fork saw A. D. Baker for the last time at the National Threshers Association reunion held at Montpelier, Ohio.

A Satisfied Customer in the Twilight of the Steam Age[44]

Herb E. Beckemeyer's father, Fred W. Beckemeyer, had four threshing runs at one time. They were located within a 12-mile radius of the Beckemeyer home near Carlyle in southwest Illinois. Even though he liked Russell engines, Fred bought the make of engines that his engineers wanted. For instance, in 1918, he acquired a new 25-horsepower Gaar-Scott engine at the request of one of his engineers. "He got the Gaar-Scott just a few days before it had to go in the belt," Herb remembered. "It was shipped from Fargo." In 1923, he purchased a 21–75 Baker that Herb still shows at threaderees. "That engine was a snappy engine and still is," Herb said.

Engineer John Montague, who ran the Baker engine, once made an analogy to help Fred better appreciate the peppy Baker: "What do you do with a racehorse? You let her run," Montague said. And that's what Montague did, Herb recalled. "The Baker used less water and coal per day than any of the rest of the engines," he added.

At the age of 14, Herb said, he ran an Advance-Rumely engine. "That engine was kept at home for the home threshing run. That way I could be home at night," he explained. He remembered when the Advance-Rumely was brand new: "In 1924, they were out there after him to

buy an engine. They sold him that Advance-Rumely for $2,500. One morning at church Dad said, 'I'm gonna drive down to the depot to see if that engine is in,' and there it was—a new engine!" It made quite an impression, and Herb remembers the significance of the new engine from a financial perspective. "Father milked cows," he said. "He always had a couple of hired men around. In those days, hired men got $25 a month. An engineer and a separator man got $5 a day."

On Beckemeyer threshing rings, "we ran balers and cleaned up around the straw stack," Herb recalled. "We earned one cent a bale. At the rate of three-hundred bales a day, you made three bucks."

One of the engineers who worked for Fred "was a doggone good mechanic and a good sawmill man. If he sawed a two-by-four, you could be sure that two-by-four was a two-by-four from one end to the other. He was a one-armed man; he had his arm taken off in a husker-shredder. He'd have me help him hammer the saw. In the days before interchangeable teeth, the saw blade was solid and you'd have to swage the teeth. You had to do it by hitting the swage with a hammer. Sometimes I'd hit the swage too hard, and other times I wouldn't hit it hard enough. He'd criticize the hammering, but I didn't run. My butt would've been red for a month."

Herb was never out of work. In the late 1930s and 1940s, Herb operated a bulldozer and other heavy equipment in the fall and winter. "It seemed like whenever anybody wanted anything done, they'd say, 'Go talk to Herb.' I was out in days not fit for a dog." Still, he had no regrets.

Herb was proud to have witnessed the age of steam power and describes the steam era's twilight years like this: "In the late 20s, I went with my father to Belleville to the Harrison Machine Works to have governor work done. There was an engine or two sitting out there in a lean-to shed—brand new! I can remember when we parked our own engines for the last time. Along about 1935 or 1936 was the final season a steam engine threshed on our runs. I used the Advance-Rumely. I finished the run that year with a 40–62 Huber tractor purchased in 1933 or 1934. I came home from World War II in 1946 and stood on a cliff to look down on a flood. The water was halfway up on an undermounted Avery engine, which my father had used in a sawmill for two years before selling it. They'd put a new boiler on it and the engine would wear it out. My father had let the Advance-Rumely go for scrap to help the war. The boiler was as brand new as any boiler could be. About 1948 or 1949, I came across the river into East St. Louis and there were several railroad cars with brand-new Keck-Gonnerman threshing machines. They were going to Nebraska or somewhere. In 1952, they were announcing there'd be a threshing demonstration up by Springfield. I told my wife, 'Get the boys! Don't wear good clothes—it's out in the country.' When I saw that engine there, I got the bug. I wanted the Baker engine we had down at a sawmill. My father said, 'Go get it! Go restore it!' I said, 'I want something to show it's mine.' My father said, 'Give me a dollar, and I'll write up a bill of sale on it.'" Herb's mint-condition Baker drew compliments at threshing reunions in Illinois summer after summer.

Herb said, "If we could bring A. D. Baker back to life, I think that about the first question I'd ask him is why he put a longer boiler on the 19-horsepower and 23-horsepower engines than he put on the 21-horsepower. The tubes in the 19 and 23 are 84 inches long, but the tubes in the 21 are only 6 feet long. The next question I'd ask him is why he built the kind of wheels he put on his engines. On rough terrain or rocky roads, those wedge-shaped sections want to come apart." Herb pointed out that the 22-horsepower Advance-Rumely engine has 46 flues, 2 inches in diameter, but the 21-horsepower Baker engine has 54 flues, of the same diameter. "The Baker got steam up fast and kept it up," Herb said. "Even though my father was a Nichols and Shepard man for threshing machines, if I were going to start threshing tomorrow, I'd have a 36-inch Keck-Gonnerman thresher and a 21–75 Baker engine or maybe a 23."

A. D. Baker and the End of the Threshing Era

A. D. loved steam. His doomed efforts to perfect the steam tractor attest to his faith in steam power. To continue in business, the Baker company had to build a gas tractor and a steel thresher. Two sizes of Baker tractors emerged (22–40 and 25–50), as well as a line of steel threshers.[45] The combine gradually became more popular, edging out the threshing machine and signaling the end of the Baker company's prominence. Krauss said, "I suggested to A.D. that he build a combine—put Swanton on the map—but he thought the combine would be too heavy" for the area's soil. "After I started my restaurant," Krauss continued, "A. D. once said to me that one of the biggest mistakes he made was not listening to me."[46] There was, apparently, some sentiment in the family toward Krauss' idea though, based on what Lillis Baker Cort said: "My father [Louis, A. D.'s son] was all ready to manufacture combines. He was all set to advance with the times. But they needed an engineer over at the Pilliod Company. He went to the Pilliod Company in 1933. They were manufacturers of big railroad engines. My father was president of the company at a later date. He never complained about his father not doing

The Baker in this scene has a uniflow cylinder and extra grouters to permit travel on asphalt roadways, the surfaces of which were protected by severe laws.

the right thing. A. D. worked until there were only two employees left. His heart would skip a beat now and then, and they would catch him before he fell."[47]

The Baker company sold seven traction engines in 1927 and two more in 1930; it sold its last traction engine in 1936.[48] A. D. "had witnessed the rise, zenith, and the fall of his beloved steam power in agriculture."[49] In 1945, he attended the first threshing reunion on LeRoy Blaker's farm near Alvordton, Ohio, and became one of the first organizers of the National Threshers Association. He brought Baker Number One to shows, and he donated his Prony brake, a machine for testing an engine's power, to the NTA in 1948.[50] A. D. lived long enough to see the advent of the old-iron restoration movement.

"The whole town of Swanton mourned twice," according to Krauss.[51] The first time was for Ethyl, Louie's wife and A. D.'s daughter-in-law, who was killed on the railroad tracks in front of the factory. It was early spring in the days before automatic gates. The watchman who was supposed to crank down the gate and hold a stop sign had fallen asleep. A freight train passed, and Ethyl was first in line to drive her automobile across the tracks. A passenger train struck her car.

The whole town mourned a second time when the quiet genius A. D. Baker was laid to rest in 1953. His legacy lives on in the steam engines that bear his name and proudly parade across America's show grounds.

Remington Company and Daniel Best Agricultural Works

Marquis de Lafayette Remington was born in 1847. Lafayette was named in honor of the beloved French aristocrat who aided the American Revolution. According to F. Hal Higgins, in 1844 Virgilius Elmore Remington, Lafayette's father, was in charge of the Carthage Jail near

Peak Production Years

As the accompanying chart illustrates, the Baker company's peak production years occurred from 1905 to 1907 and again from 1913 through 1916.

Baker Production Totals Per Year

Year	Engines Built	Year	Engines Built
1898–1900	50	1918	42, including 6 road rollers
1901–1902	23	1919	75, including 1 road roller
1903	46	1920	69
1904	84	1921	52
1905	118	1922	27
1906	120	1923	31
1907	103	1924	14
1908	80	1925	26
1909	71, including 1 road roller*	1926	19, including 2 road rollers
1910	85, including 13 road rollers	1927	10, including 2 road rollers
1911	83, including 16 road rollers		
1912	78, including 8 road rollers		
1913	90, including 13 road rollers		
1914	106, including 22 road rollers		
1915	126, including 31 road rollers		
1916	113, including 33 road rollers		
1917	59, including 9 road rollers		

From the A. D. Baker Company Traction Engine Book,**courtesy of Louis Abner Carson.

*Almost all early road rollers were 16 horsepower, but later ones were 21 horsepower.

**The traction engine book lists each engine built by the A. D. Baker Company. In contrast, the sales books show the engines sold each year. The Carsons have complete records of Baker engines built and of Baker engines sold.

Nauvoo, Illinois, when violence broke out and Mormon leader Joseph Smith and his brother Hyrum were martyred. At least one biographical account has theorized that Virgilius' slow-growing fear that Mormons would avenge Smith's death led Virgilius to leave Illinois, but Virgilius may also have felt gold rush fever. Whatever his motivation, Virgilius moved his family from Illinois to California in 1849. In 1858, Virgilius died and Lafayette's mother, Esther Doud, and the siblings moved to Oregon and arrived there in 1859. Until 1870, Lafayette farmed near Silverton. He was a blacksmith in Woodburn in 1872 and

by the 1880 census was listed as the owner of a sawmill. A decade later, he had begun a foundry and machine shop.

Daniel Best was born in Ohio in 1838. Best's father ran a sawmill in Missouri before he moved to Iowa to farm. In 1859, the year when the Remingtons were relocating in Oregon, Best guarded a wagon train on the Oregon Trail. He patented a thresher and entered into a business partnership with Nathaniel P. Slate of Albany, Oregon. Best & Slate established a branch in Oakland, California. Best eventually purchased the San Leandro Plow Company from Jacob Price and renamed it the Daniel Best Agricultural Works.

A towering Best steam engine pulls a massive load.

A majestic Best is doing what so many Bests did: hauling on the road.

This photograph is rumored to depict the very first Remington.

Note the sighting arrow on the front of this Best steamer.

Best Serial Number 268 and Holt Caterpillar Serial Number 1325 of the Newmark Grain Company are pictured here.

Production was then centered in San Leandro and pulled out of both Albany and Oakland.

As early as the late 1860s, Best and Slate were experimenting with steam engine design. According to anecdotal evidence, Marquis de Lafayette Remington accepted Slate's first steamer in payment of a debt. In turn, Remington developed and patented a steam engine for heavy work in 1888. His first model pulled six plows and hauled pipe to a reservoir at Mount Hood. He demonstrated the machine at Daniel Best's farm in California, where it ran a combined thresher. Best marketed the Remington

Company machine through the Daniel Best Agricultural Works in San Leandro. Best sold Remingtons for plowing, harvesting, mining, and logging, and he improved Remington's design. For a time, Best advertised both Remington and Best steamers. Eugene Remington, Lafayette's son, eventually assumed control of Lafayette Remington's business.

Holt bought out Daniel Best in 1908. In 1925, Clarence Leo Best, Daniel's son, merged his firm, the C. L. Best Gas Traction Company, with the Holt Manufacturing Company of Stockton, California, to form Caterpillar.

Behind this Best steamer is a combined harvester-thresher from which the agricultural implement term "combine" was derived.

Two Bests can span a vast space.

A Birdsall with two Nichols & Shepard steam engines and yet another steamer lurking in the background are shown here.

The fellow with a broken finger is holding his painkiller while posing before a Birdsall steamer and Case threshing machine.

The Birdsall engine provides an occasion for everyone to turn out for this photograph.

New Birdsall Company

Hiram Birdsall, who was briefly associated with Abram Stevens, and Edgar M. Birdsall founded an agricultural implement company in Penn Yan, New York, around 1861. The Birdsall company began the manufacture of portable steam engines in 1874. By 1881, Birdsall and Company had outgrown its quarters and, in September of that year, moved to the Cayuga Chief Company's former plant in Auburn, according to Geoffrey Stein. Birdsall produced its first traction engine after the move. Then, in 1886, the company was reorganized. As Steve Davis has shown, the firm's name had become the New Birdsall Company by 1899. In 1917, the firm relocated to a spacious new factory in Newark, New York. Across its history, Birdsall built threshers, horse powers, traction engines, portable engines, sawmills, mowers, and other agricultural implements.

This is a Birdsall with a belly tank for water.

In a time when bicycle clubs were popular, people would ride bicycles from all around to witness a steam engine in operation.

This Birdsall keeps going in a circle while largely unattended during the 1910 New York State Fair. Behind it is a Monarch steamroller built in Groton, New York.

By the end of the nineteenth century, Birdsall engines were using a steering apparatus called an automobile steer. Elmer Ritzman, founding editor of *The Iron-Men Album Magazine,* reported that early automobile manufacturers paid Birdsall a royalty for the steering patent. Birdsall invented an open zigzag pattern of drive wheel face known as the lattice wheel, and was one of the few traction engine firms to offer open-faced wheels. Essentially, iron lugs in reversed diagonals were riveted to two iron tires to form the lattice face. Many of the firm's traction engines used lattice wheels, which were designed to cut through soft ground. Birdsall also built a solid drive wheel face. The company's steamrollers employed the solid-faced wheels. Birdsall sold a heavy roller engine that had two front wheels rather than a front roller and could perform roller work or heavy haulage with equal ease.

Here is a Birdsall that was owned by the town of Springfield, New York.

This Birdsall engine and thresher were the property of the Duesler brothers of Fort Plain, New York.

This Birdsall and its train of wagons have special wheels to run on tracks.

Blumentritt

Joseph Blumentritt was a German immigrant who built a 6-horsepower portable steam engine in LaCrosse, Wisconsin, in 1870. When he moved to Winona County, Minnesota, he continued to experiment with steam engine production. To power a turbine in the shop on his farm, he built an earth dam on a nearby creek and redirected the water. He manufactured 22 steam engines, which came in sizes of 6, 12, and 24 horsepower and were of the return-flue design but fired from the front!

This photo was taken on Charlotte Happel Braniff's farm. Her father, Wesley C. Happel, contracted the threshing with this Blumentritt engine. Courtesy Charlotte Happel Braniff and Scott Maynard

Here is a photograph of the very rare and highly unusual Blumentritt steam traction engine. The Blumentritt was fired from the front and steered from the side. Courtesy Scott Maynard

Buffalo Pitts Company and Buffalo Road Roller Company

On June 2, 1799, twin brothers John Avery and Hiram Abial Pitts were born in Winthrop, Maine. They are towering figures in agricultural history. They first built tread powers to run groundhog threshers. In 1830 and 1831, the brothers experimented with designs of threshers that would also clean the grain. Hiram eventually invented a thresher that included a mechanism for separating and cleaning. The brothers patented and sold the thresher as early as 1834. In 1837, they patented their improved thresher, which introduced an apron conveyor that became the model for various early threshers.

By 1847, the Pitts brothers were selling threshers in Illinois. John left Illinois to sell threshers in Ohio. In 1851, Hiram was marketing threshing machines known as Chicago Pitts threshers in Chicago. Meanwhile, John left Ohio and traveled to Buffalo, New York, where he began to produce Buffalo Pitts threshers in 1851. The implement firm of Pitts & Brayley was in existence in 1859. John passed away in July of that year. In 1860, the company sold steam engines that were made portable by attaching wagon wheels to a frame beneath the boiler. Hiram passed away in September 1860. By 1866, the company was known as the Brayley and Pitts Works, named for John B. Pitts, the elder John's son, and James Brayley, the elder John's son-in-law. In 1877, the Pitts Agricultural Works was incorporated, and beginning in 1897, the firm was called the Buffalo Pitts Company.

The Buffalo Pitts Company built a wide variety of steam engines. The firm had already sold several of the Buffalo Pitts double-engine steam road rollers by 1901. In 1910, Marquis J. Todd assigned his patent for a front roll with a center section that could be removed, thereby converting the three-wheel roller into a road locomotive, to the Buffalo Steam Roller Company. The plant built traction engines designed to be road locomotives, along with road freight cars.

Evidence indicates that Buffalo Pitts developed a lively Australian trade. In the first decade of the twentieth century, the International Harvester Company (IHC) served as agent for Buffalo Pitts products. IHC ensured that many Buffalo Pitts steam tractors made their way down under. Buffalo Pitts also marketed a number of kerosene and gasoline tractors, including a three-cylinder model introduced in 1910.

The company began its expansion as early as 1895 by adding several product lines. In the 1890s, the Waterous Company was laying the groundwork for integrating Buffalo products into their lines. They began building traction engines that used the same gearing and controls as Buffalo Pitts engines. The first of these were mounted on the New Economic Boiler. The Pitts engines were of the open-bottom, top-mounted locomotive type. Most of the firm's engines were double-cylinder models by 1904.

During the decade of the 1890s, Waterous also began using Buffalo Steam Roller Company gearing in their steamrollers. In 1910, the Waterous firm constructed

This is a product of the Pitts Agricultural Works.

its own rollers using Buffalo gearing and also imported Buffalo steamrollers from the United States to help to meet demand. The Buffalo Steam Roller Company was quick to supply Waterous with rollers, as Buffalo Pitts and the Buffalo Steam Roller Company sought rapid expansion.

Even though Buffalo Pitts continued to advertise such steamers as its special plowing engine in the 1912 *Threshermen's Review*, Buffalo Pitts was headed for bankruptcy. The panic of 1907 had lasted through 1908, and for the intervening four years, business had been cautious and jittery. A receiver had to seek ways to divest the firm of collateral lines. Between 1910 and 1912, the company had been financing Charles Olmsted in the design and production of an airplane. Unfortunately, just when the success of the airplane was assured, Buffalo Pitts had to cut off funding.

Could that be Teddy Roosevelt seated on the Buffalo Pitts engine?

Due to its long-standing sales territory agreements with O. S. Kelly in Springfield, Ohio, Buffalo Pitts began selling steamroller components to Kelly. The first roller built in Springfield with Buffalo Pitts components came

continued on page 65

Buffalo Pitts' return-flue model is shown here.

Pictured here is a Buffalo Pitts steamer from the mid-1800s.

A return-flue engine with the smokestack near the engineer could be an advantage in cold weather.

A Buffalo Pitts is equipped with both a large lamp and a small coal-oil lantern.

A man and his dog watch a Buffalo Pitts and a thresher parading down their street.

continued from page 61

from the factory in early 1913. The Buffalo Steam Roller Company merged with the Kelly-Springfield Road Roller Company in 1916. A frequently reprinted anecdote holds that because a Buffalo stockholder refused to endorse the merger, Kelly-Springfield and Buffalo Pitts road rollers were built under the same roof in Springfield until 1921, when the stockholder relinquished his stock. Only then could the production of new Buffalo-Springfield steamrollers begin in earnest. Indeed, batches of steamrollers that were finished in Springfield in 1921 bore the name Buffalo Pitts on the rollers that were completed first and the name Buffalo-Springfield on the rollers that were completed last.

After the 1916 merger that led to the Buffalo-Springfield firm, steamroller production in Buffalo sharply declined. No new farm engines were built in Buffalo after 1916 because in 1915 Buffalo Pitts had sold its steam tractor business to Toledo, Ohio's, Banting Manufacturing Company. It was reorganized on the foundation of the Banting Machine and Supply Company, which had long been an agency for Buffalo Pitts equipment. Banting gave the product name Greyhound to the Buffalo steam tractors assembled on Ohio-built boilers.

Two threshermen proudly touch their Buffalo Pitts steam tractor as if to boast, "This is my engine!"

A Buffalo Pitts gets ready for a rest toward the end of a work day.

J. I. Case Threshing Machine Company

The industry giant in the manufacture of agricultural steam engines was the J. I. Case Threshing Machine Company. Serial numbers for Case engines reached 35838 in 1926, when the last Case steamer, an 80-horsepower portable, was built. The biggest year for production of Case steam engines was 1911, and 1912 witnessed the highest sales. Case also built nine legendary 150-horsepower road locomotives. The boiler from one still exists.

The Case chronicle begins in 1842, when Jerome Increase Case, who lived from 1819 until 1891, bought six groundhog threshers. They were hand-cranked threshing

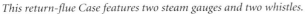

Here is one of the earliest Case traction engines, but without a driver's seat. This picture probably dates to 1879.

This return-flue Case features two steam gauges and two whistles.

A water barrel, as opposed to a tank, graces the platform of this Case.

An early 1880s Case traction engine is shown here. Note the curved flywheel spokes that are often called "dog-leg" spokes. They were believed to be stronger than straight spokes.

Boys and men from age 5 to 60 gather around this old Case return-flue steamer.

This Case, with its elaborate grillework, poses with a Russell Massillon Cyclone threshing machine and crew. Courtesy Robert T. Rhode

machines so named because the wheat was thrust down a chute vaguely reminiscent of a groundhog's earth hole. Case left Oswego, New York, traveled by steamship to Chicago, Illinois, and journeyed to Rochester, Wisconsin, marketing the machines. Between Chicago and Rochester, he sold five of the threshers, which he had purchased on credit. He did custom threshing with the sixth thresher. By 1844, Case had perfected a design of a threshing machine that cleaned the grain, and he decided to become a manufacturer rather than a thresherman. Because Case could not secure rights to build a millrace in Rochester, he established his factory in Racine. His first threshers were built under license from brothers Hiram and John A. Pitts, who held the patent for the apron design, and from Jacob V. A. Wemple, a partner of George Westinghouse and the inventor of a patented threshing mechanism similar to that of the Pitts brothers. Soon the Case firm began a virtually uninterrupted growth cycle that lasted throughout Case's lifetime. Enthusiasts attribute Case's dominance of the agricultural steam market to sophisticated designs and excellent workmanship.

A Case is rigged to run a sawmill as a one-man operation. Note the ornate grillework on this model.

A center-crank Case is shown pulling 3,350 feet of logs.

A one-of-a-kind photo shows a pre-production, tandem compound, spring-mounted Case engine from 1895.

Detractors claim that easy credit terms then combined with these traits to create the Case hegemony.

Throughout its long history, the Case firm manufactured a full line of agricultural equipment, automobiles, and well-received designs of gasoline tractors too numerous to describe in a brief account. Among the many notable achievements of this firm was the all-steel thresher that Case unveiled in 1904.

Case also built steamrollers. David Erb's research has found that the first 10-ton Case steamroller was serial

A Case tandem-cylinder engine boasts a cab. A large straw stack attests to the machine's propensity for hard work.

Two-wheel tenders were popular accompaniments for many Case traction engines.

Three boys pose with a bobtail Case loaded on a railcar. The word bobtail *implies a short platform with relatively small bunkers.*

Evidently not all farmers were starving out there on the prairie.

number 15901, which was built in 1905. The first 12-ton roller appeared as serial number 20649 in 1908. The smaller size proved more popular. Case built 678 10-ton steamrollers and 29 12-ton rollers for a combined total of 707. Case rollers could be converted to traction engines by removing the four front roller sections, installing a different axle wide enough to support regular front wheels outside the roller yoke, and attaching grouters to the drive wheels. Case manufactured rock crushers, elevators, stone graders, special plows for breaking up rocky roads, grading plows, road drags, road graders, dump wagons, spreader wagons, scrapers, barrows, steam-lift scarifiers pulled by the engine, and scarifiers attached to the roller.

With a Case standing guard on the precipice, a steam shovel and a Master truck of the Halpin-Dwyer Crushed Rock Company work down below.

A Case steamer is shown wedded to a Keystone drill.

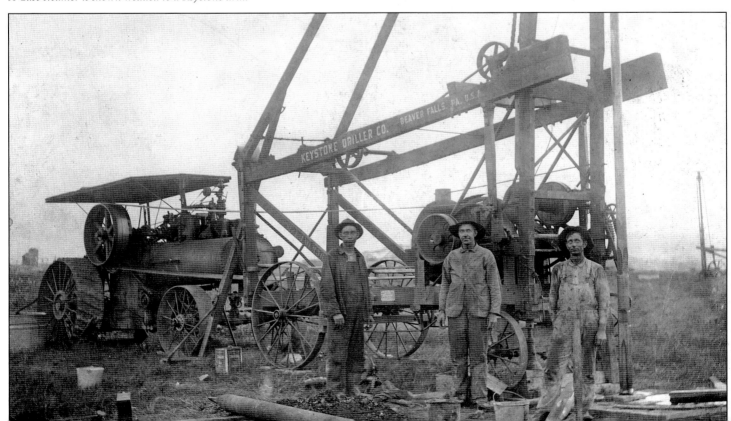

A full Case outfit of steam engine, water wagon, and threshing machine is pictured.

This is a 32-horsepower Case steam engine.

Old Abe, the Case trademark, deserves special mention. Richard H. Zeitlin has traced the history of this famous eagle that served as mascot of the Eighth Regiment of Wisconsin Volunteer Infantry during the Civil War. By flying above siege lines, Old Abe inspired the regiment in battle. The Wisconsin monument at the Vicksburg National Military Park honors Old Abe with a statue of the bird perched atop a tall column. J. I. Case was so impressed by Old Abe that the industrialist featured the eagle in company literature and in countless castings.

The Case firm was well known for a daredevil stunt repeated at fairgrounds across the nation. Intrepid engineers would run steamers up steep inclines to demonstrate the superior hill-climbing capabilities of their machines. According to Case historian Chady Atteberry, the first Case incline performance occurred in 1901 on a hair-raising

75-percent grade. The grade was reduced to 45 percent at the Wichita threshermen's reunion in 1903, but a Reeves engine and a C. Aultman Double Star called Case's bluff and mastered the incline. For the Louisiana Purchase Exposition in 1904, Case increased the incline to 57.2 percent, thereby discouraging further competition. Crowds were thrilled to see Case engines scaling the sky.

Jerome Increase Case has become legendary as stories involving Case have been told and retold. C. H. Wendel relates the following anecdotes descriptive of Case's character:

"A man near Marion, Indiana, refused to make further payment on a Case thresher, claiming it to be incapable of threshing more than thirty bushels a day, and terming it 'a Yankee humbug.' Case personally went to Marion. . . . Getting the

Girls peer out from Mr. Irish's Case steamer.

Has the boy in the cab of this 110-horsepower Case worked the steamer so thoroughly that a mound of ash has been raked outside the ashpan?

machine ready by noon of the appointed day, Case himself fed the bundles into the machine. In about six hours they had threshed 177 bushels of wheat, far more than Case had claimed for the machine in an entire day! That settled the matter, the buyer paid up, and Case returned to Racine.

In later years, perhaps about 1884, . . . [a] farmer near Faribault, Minnesota, had purchased a new Case engine and thresher. The thresher pulled too hard and would not deliver clean grain. He complained to the agent and the latter attempted to make it work. Having no success, the agent contacted the home office at Racine. They sent their best troubleshooter, and after several hours he wired the company, recommending that they either supply a new machine or a refund.

To this wire J. I. Case replied directly that he was heading for Faribault on the next train. Arriving in the afternoon, Case set to work on the thresher. Numerous times during the afternoon the machine was started and stopped. Finally, toward evening the old man asked the farmer whether he might have a sizable can of kerosene handy. Bewildered, the farmer soon returned with the flammable liquid. Without a word, Case doused the machine from one end to the other, and then touched a match to the brand-new thresher. Even while the flames were still bright against the evening sky, Case put on his coat and hat, bowed to those present, and left for Racine. The next morning a new Case thresher was delivered from the nearby Faribault warehouse."

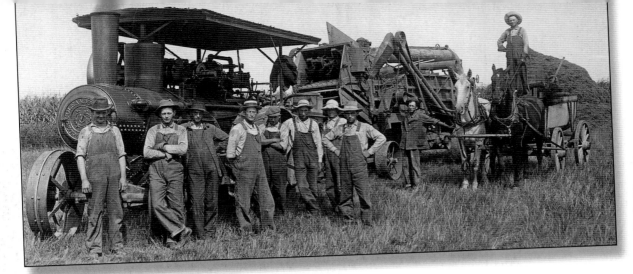

The Hart brothers of Vesta, Minnesota, owned this Colean.

Colean Manufacturing Company

A Colean steamer (serial number 322) was found in Kansas during the late 1950s. It was enshrouded in grapevines with only the top of the smokestack visible, its engine bearing mute testimony to a company that existed from 1898 until 1908.

William H. Colean, who went by "Will," had sold C. Aultman engines and threshers in Illinois. He decided to design and build his own machines in Peoria, where he established a modern plant for the purpose. While launching his new line, Colean distributed Buffalo Pitts steam engines and threshers.

When Colean went bankrupt in 1908, Caterpillar moved into the well-equipped factory and created a dynasty as famous as Colean is unfamiliar. The few Colean engines in preservation are known for their relatively short smokestacks. Had the grapevines had another summer, they could have completely hidden the Kansas Colean.

This Colean serves a custom threshing operation large enough to support at least two cook shacks.

With a tank surrounding the smokestack to heat the water, this big Colean pulls a house.

This Colean is a mobile classroom at an agricultural school that trains engineers.

C & G Cooper

During the steam era, clever writers in the advertising department of C & G Cooper invented a "fact" that persists even today. It stated that Cooper built the first successful traction engine in North America. Cooper catalogs and yearbooks repeated this statement, and a recent history of the Cooper firm makes the same claim. The only problem with this fact is that it is false. Several engine builders in California had mastered traction engineering decades before Cooper, and at least two firms in Cooper's own state of Ohio had produced successful traction engines prior to those Cooper built.

In 1808, before the birth of Charles or Elias, the Cooper family moved from Pennsylvania to Ohio. Charles was born in 1811, and Elias was born in 1813. They were reared three miles south of Mount Vernon on a farm that their father had bought in 1810. The grown brothers began a coal mine in Zanesville in 1832 but eventually became disillusioned with mining. Charles wrote that he felt blue during the summer of 1833. Sitting on a hill above Zanesville, he noticed the smoke curling above the town's foundry and decided he must switch from coal mining to foundry work.

Charles sold one of his three horses for $50 and invested the money in a Mount Vernon foundry during 1833. In November of that year, Charles and Elias hauled their earthly belongings in two wagons from Zanesville to Mount Vernon. Bessie, one of their horses, powered the plant until the Coopers installed a steam engine in 1836. Struggling through the panic of 1837, the brothers kept their foundry going until 1839, when business finally began to improve. The brothers built carding machines and plows using coal and iron that were hauled 25 miles from Newark. The completion of the Baltimore & Ohio Railroad through Mount Vernon greatly aided the effort. The Coopers were manufacturing steam engines by the 1840s and contributed machinery for the Mexican War. In 1848, Elias died and the C & E Cooper name was changed to Cooper & Clark because T. L. Clark had purchased an interest in the business. In 1852, John, Charles' younger brother, joined the firm, which then became known as Coopers & Clark. The business continued to expand. A blast furnace, blowing engines, and cotton gins were added to the product line, which included virtually every form of mill. When Clark retired in 1853, the firm's name changed to C & J Cooper.

In the early 1850s, the company began to manufacture steam locomotives for the western division of the Baltimore & Ohio and other railways. During the panic of 1857, the weak financial condition of railroading nearly spelled disaster for the Coopers, but the brothers kept their firm afloat through careful fiscal management. For a time in the 1850s, the name of the business was John Cooper & Company. F. L. Fairchild joined the firm in 1865, he was made a partner in 1868, and the firm's name changed to C & J Cooper & Company.

In 1868, Cooper hired Julius C. Debes, of the George H. Corliss Works in Providence, Rhode Island, to design Corliss engines. The firm began to manufacture Corliss engines in 1869. By 1886, the Corliss machines became the principal products of the company. In the late 1860s, Debes improved many Cooper product designs. C. G. Cooper, Elias' son, and Colonel George Rogers, Elias' son-in-law, assumed partnerships in the firm in 1869. In November of that year, John Cooper retired and the company's name became C & G Cooper & Company.

Beginning in the late 1860s, Cooper traction engines used a chain drive from a shaft mounted above the firebox to bull gears on the axle of the driver wheels. Rogers designed a bevel-gear drive familiar to steam buffs and highly touted by Cooper's advertisers. Rogers filed his patent on October 6, 1875, and was granted the patent on February 15, 1876, as number 173,498. Cooper licensed other manufacturers, such as Aultman & Taylor, to employ the bevel gear, or sunflower gear, as it came to be known. The Rogers bevel gear was widely employed for a brief interval in history and greatly advanced traction engineering in the United States. It influenced the writers of Cooper ads to exaggerate Cooper's claim to being the first company to produce a successful traction engine in the United States. Cooper traction engines eventually used spur gears. A Currier and Ives painting by Nathaniel Currier beautifully portrays one of the horse-steered 1875 Cooper engines.

Rogers retired in 1881, and D. B. Kirk, son-in-law of Charles Cooper, and C. F. Cooper, son of Charles Cooper, took partnerships in the firm. In 1894, C. F. Cooper died, and the name changed incrementally from C & G Cooper & Company to the C & G Cooper Company the following year. Charles Cooper died at the age of 92 in 1901.

Cooper steamers were not the first traction engines, as often claimed. Many firms built traction engines before Cooper did, but Cooper eventually licensed several companies to build bevel drives under the 1876 Rogers patent. Courtesy Robert T. Rhode

Riley R. Doan invented his steam wagon in 1875. Several of these massive engines were in service for many years in California and Nevada. Courtesy Kathryn Totton, Special Collections, University of Nevada, Reno Library

At ease in their lofty perch, women look on as the photographer captures this scene of the lumber industry and a Doan Steam Wagon of yesteryear. Courtesy Kathryn Totton, Special Collections, University of Nevada, Reno Library

Doan Steam Wagon

Riley R. Doan was an Ohio native who made the adventurous journey across the plains to the Pacific Coast in 1852. For a time, he worked in a sawmill at Sly Park in El Dorado County, California. He then removed to Austin, Nevada, where he was a miner. Doan continued in that line and went to Colfax, Placer County, California. He returned to the sawmill in Sly Park before moving to Sacramento to become foreman of the Harrison Gulch mines run by Captain John H. Roberts.

Roberts was born in Detroit in 1832. As a young man, he caught the gold fever and traveled to Chicago, where he threw in his lot with a company setting out for the Pacific Coast with ox teams and horses. Roberts found mining a disappointment and soon became intrigued with the prospect of running flatboats on the Sacramento River. Many years passed before he could develop his flatboat project, though. He first cut logs and hauled them to a mill. In 1866, he founded the Sacramento Transportation Company, which served Sacramento and towns all along the river with boats running as far north as Red Bluff. Roberts eventually held interests in various gold mines and owned several ranches and orchards.

In 1875, Doan invented a steam wagon, or road locomotive, and secured funding from his former employer, Roberts, who envisioned the machine as augmenting his flatboat business. Doan steam wagons were eventually put to work in the logging industry in California and Nevada. By 1889, Doan and Roberts' partnership had manufactured at least half a dozen of these behemoths. Several of them were in service for many years.

Fairbanks Steam Shovel Company

James G. Fairbanks established a construction company in his name in Marion, Ohio, in 1893. Fairbanks owned a quarry and had served as a superintendent at the Huber Manufacturing Company. He considered return-flue boilers the most economical in the use of steam and fuel. The Fairbanks Steam Shovel Company was incorporated in 1903. A large Corliss engine powered the plant. Fairbanks manufactured steam shovels, ditcher machines, dredges, sawmills, cranes, and the Lobo return-flue traction engine. The Spanish word *lobo* means wolf. Not surprisingly, words like lobo entered the American vocabulary after the Spanish-American War in 1898. After all, many soldiers in that conflict had shipped out from a camp located near Point Lobos Avenue in San Francisco.

This Lobo (a rather unusual engine produced by the Fairbanks Steam Shovel Company) is pulling a thresher to the next job.

A. B. Farquhar Company

A. B. Farquhar's autobiography stands in sharp contrast to the reminiscences of William Heilman, even though both ran businesses on the border between the North and the South and both lived through the Civil War and the financial panics that followed. These nineteenth-century industrialists were equally adept at business but developed opposite styles. Heilman's memoir reflects a quiet man with keen judgment. Farquhar's book portrays a flamboyant man willing to take risks. Farquhar perceived himself as positioned at the epicenter of national politics and culture. He may well have been right. Even today, his autobiography is well received. Many who have not read it recognize its memorable title: *The First Million the Hardest.*[1]

In sketching "prominent figures associated with American locomotive engineering in the nineteenth century," John H. White, Jr., wrote, "Their origins, almost to a man, were humble. Most started as blacksmiths, pattern-makers, or draftsmen and rose to the top by luck and energy.

This idea is currently unfashionable and is dismissed as a 'Horatio Alger' fantasy, yet for the mechanic of the early nineteenth century it appears to have been a common phenomenon."[2] While each new generation attempts to rewrite history according to its prejudices, one nineteenth-century industrialist resists any effort to diminish his success. He is Arthur Briggs Farquhar, and his story echoes those of Horatio Alger's heroes, rising from rags to riches.

Doubleday, Page & Company published Farquhar's autobiography in 1922. The book holds up well even today, although jaded readers might construe Farquhar's unassailable confidence as bordering on egotism. Farquhar's memoirs nonetheless capture the life of a most lively millionaire. Farquhar built a massive factory, which turned out agricultural steam engines and a host of other machines. He kept the plant going despite the obstacles of economic woes and the bloodiest chapter in American history—the Civil War. When he turned to the writing of his memoirs, Farquhar proved a most able author, capable of clever word play, as when he said, "My life, stretching as it has over that eventful period in our national history which began before the Civil War, has been most interesting to lead, and I trust, may be found interesting to read."[3] Farquhar's book opens with a profound thought: "I have always believed that in a normal life one should grow happier with added years. This has been my experience."[4] Farquhar penned those words on New Year's Day in 1922.

When Farquhar was in his 80s, he reflected that he had "known most of the great figures of the nation during the last sixty years."[5] He saw "the change from a farming to a manufacturing country." A self-proclaimed "raw country lad" in his teens, Farquhar journeyed to New York from his home in Sandy Spring, Maryland, in 1858, to ask wealthy New Yorkers the naive question, "How can I make a million dollars?" The trip marked "a turning point" in Farquhar's life.[6]

Farquhar entered a city vastly different from what it would become. "The New York of today would regard that big city as nothing but a fair-sized town. There were no great buildings; few of any kind had more than three stories. They were mostly of red brick and very plain and solid. Some of the streets were roughly paved, but many were not much better than country roads, and many were lined with trees."[7] To find the answer to his question, Farquhar intruded upon the office of William B. Astor, where, he said, an "old clerk glared at me without welcome and growled: 'What do you want?' 'I want to see Mr. Astor.' 'You cannot see him. He is busy,' he growled again, and then made a grab at my coat as I tried to dive past him. I shook him off and landed somewhat ruffled before the desk of the richest man in the country. He had heard the scuffle and looking up from his writing snapped: 'Well, boy, what do you want?'"[8]

Farquhar explained that he wanted to know how to make a million dollars. Astor's answer was: "Do you want to make yourself as miserable as I am and stay up all day and half the night trying to keep people from cheating you?" Astor went on to say, "I do not have enough fun. I am too afraid that people will cheat me and in spite of everything, they do cheat me." Astor looked over a roster of rich New Yorkers' names that Farquhar had penned on a sheet of paper and asked, "Do you expect to see all the men whose names you have on your list?" Farquhar replied, "Yes, I shall tell them that Mr. Astor sent me." "Don't do anything of the kind," he returned, snappishly. "I am going to anyhow," Farquhar said. "It is true, you did tell me to see them." Astor laughed and responded, "All right, go ahead. You'll do."[9]

Farquhar next called on James Gordon Bennett, the tough-minded founder of the New York *Herald*. Before Bennett saw Farquhar, Bennett sent him across the street for breakfast on Bennett's bill. After dining, Farquhar returned to Bennett's office and tried to pay, but Bennett refused and said, "Let's talk about something important. The really important thing for you to know as a young man is that you must bank up a health account. Look at me: I am never sick. I never take a vacation. I am here at the office early in the morning and sometimes late at night. But I always try to be in bed early enough to get a good night's sleep. If you get plenty of sleep and be careful of your diet you will never be sick."[10]

A. T. Stewart told Farquhar that "money is made by saving—saving and investing. You get your profit out of the leaks that you stop."[11] Stewart also said that he hired honest men who had failed in running their own businesses. According to Stewart, such men were willing to take the initiative but knew that they were not competent to manage their own enterprise and should work for someone else.

Once Farquhar had made the rounds of the richest men in New York, he concluded, "They had no shortcuts to suggest, and curiously enough not one of them even spoke of technical or other proficiency. They were concerned only with fundamentals. I gathered from them that if one were scrupulously honest, industrious, and economical, then the other business qualities came almost as of course, but without the fundamentals nothing else mattered."[12] Farquhar also noticed that such men were "elemental; they did not work through others as people do today. They did everything themselves. They did not have secretaries."[13] Farquhar summarized, "What made these men rich and powerful was not only their scrupulous honesty and high

character but also, and this is a point I have never seen dwelt upon, their extraordinary memories."[14] Costs and overhead expenses were not written down; instead, executives memorized them.

"They were despots," Farquhar wrote, "absolute rulers, and they were inclined to be paternal. It was unconscious paternalism that caused Mr. Bennett to give me a meal ticket. The most absolute and stern in demeanor was A. T. Stewart. All of them gave orders where the modern executive makes suggestions. . . . They worked with things while the man of today works with people."[15] Farquhar concluded that the "big men" he met on his trip to New York were less interested in humanity than later "big men" were.

Farquhar eventually came to know Andrew Carnegie. Despite the general belief that Carnegie was of the "old school," Farquhar found him to be a much more "modern" businessman than the wealthy men he had visited in New York. Farquhar once told Carnegie that he made it a practice to be at his office at seven o'clock each morning, to which Carnegie replied, "You must be a lazy man if it takes you ten hours to do a day's work." Farquhar remembered Carnegie's description of his work day: "I never give . . . orders. My directions seldom go beyond suggestions. Here in the morning I get reports from [my workers]. Within an hour I have disposed of everything, sent out all of my suggestions, the day's work is done, and I am ready to go out and enjoy myself."[16] Farquhar regarded Carnegie as a manager worthy of emulation, and "Mr. Carnegie made more than all of the men I have mentioned put together."

Farquhar's boyhood home of Sandy Spring, Maryland, lay only 18 miles from Washington, D.C. He recalled sleigh rides, Maryland biscuits, quilting parties, and the quintessential nostalgic pleasure of chestnuts roasting "in the open fire."[17] The Quaker family lived in a log house that was later weather-boarded. Farquhar had a sister, Ellen, and brothers Hallowell, Edward, Henry I, Henry II, and Allan. Henry I died from scarlet fever before he was four years old. Farquhar thought he was "the real genius of the family," although Edward memorized all of *Paradise Lost* at age seven or eight.[18] Edward went on to become fluent in 13 languages, "including Sanskrit."[19] Farquhar remembered "very distinctly the great bonfires at the barbecues held at the end of the Harrison and Tyler campaign in 1840—although I was then but two years old."[20] He also recalled the booming of the guns in the nation's capital the following year when President Harrison died shortly after his inauguration.

Living in a state where slavery was practiced, Farquhar's father believed that African slaves should be taught to read, which was against state law. Farquhar once read hymns to

This Farquhar steam engine is pulling a boiler manufactured by the Coatesville Boiler Works of Pennsylvania.

a group of blacks in the barn shop and a mob gathered outside. He said, "I was not molested, owing to the great regard that everyone had for my father."[21]

Farquhar enjoyed a strong background in literature. His grandmother repeated Alexander Pope's version of Homer's *Iliad* to the young Farquhar. He liked the writings of Socrates, Plato, and especially Aristotle. He felt that the Trojan horse was a cruel trick and he despised cruelty. "It would break my heart to see a horse struck or a child teased or imposed upon, or any advantage taken of the helpless."[22] In the evenings, his family read aloud such masterpieces as *David Copperfield* and *Jane Eyre*.[23]

Farquhar "was of a philosophical turn of mind."[24] Discussions in his family often turned on ethical issues. "I remember having taken the side that a bad promise was better broken than kept, because if it was bad it ceased to be a promise." Years later, Farquhar encouraged President McKinley to follow the same logic and to break a bad

promise that would have forced the president to fill a ministerial post with an unfit man.

Farquhar's father, who had "mastered Latin at twelve and Greek at thirteen or fourteen" and had attended a prestigious boarding school with Robert E. Lee,[25] often took the boy on a steamboat ride between Washington and Alexandria. "I remember especially the great rocking beam as it swung up and down, driving the side wheels, and I thought it all very wonderful."[26] When Farquhar was 12, his father farmed and also ran a ladies' boarding school.[27] Farquhar's father gave his son the shop in the barn where he could use a lathe and other tools once he had completed his morning chores. Farquhar wrote that he "was always tinkering with machinery or making something, and finally I could make wheelbarrows and other things used about the farm. I started experimenting with a threshing machine when about twelve years old and worked on that threshing machine until I went to York, but I could never get it into practical shape. The anxiety to make a thresher that would work had a great deal to do with my eventually going to York as an apprentice in a shop that made threshers."[28]

Farquhar managed his father's farm for a year, after finishing his course at the same boarding school his father had attended in Alexandria, thereby renewing his enthusiasm for agricultural machinery.[29] Farquhar said that he "wanted to do something at once in a big way, but my father . . . told me . . . that I should have to learn a trade, learn all about the work from the worker's standpoint, before I could even think of directing anybody."[30] His friends laughed at Farquhar's plan to become a mechanic since they perceived him as a student who loved literature.

On the evening of Friday, April 4, 1856, A. B. arrived in York, Pennsylvania, and was greeted by family friend Edward Jessop. Farquhar spent two nights with the Jessops, and then boarded with Mrs. Alexander Immel, who charged $2.50 a week for room, board, and laundry. At 7 a.m. on Monday, April 7, Farquhar became "indentured as a machinist's apprentice" at the agricultural implement shop of W. W. Dingee & Company.[31] The firm employed 10 workmen, yet Farquhar "thought of it as rather a large shop." Back then, workers learned to chisel and file by hand with the accuracy of the machines that came later in history. The workers also made their own tools and hardware. "The employees became my warm friends," Farquhar remembered. "I think I managed to get the worker's point of view and that I have never lost it."[32] In those days, men typically apprenticed with a company and remained there for the rest of their working lives. It was rare to find the worker who expected to run his own business one day.

In the evening or on holidays, workers often walked into the country "to see how a machine they had made was working," Farquhar said. "For when a man made anything, he considered it his own. He felt personally disgraced if it did not work well."[33] Farquhar added this about yesteryear's mechanics: "When we laid out a machine, we drafted to full size on a big wooden board, and the men measured from that and not from a blueprint. We had no blueprints, and I doubt if any of the men could have worked from scale. They had great skill of hand and eye, and while their minds were actively employed upon the work in hand, there was comparatively slight emphasis put upon saving labor or speeding production. There was little planning ahead or thought of sequence of operations, and no idea of saving steps."[34] The work day lasted from seven in the morning until six in the evening, and mechanics earned between ninety cents and a dollar a day.

On the subject of clothing Farquhar commented: "A suit of clothes would serve a man, first as his Sunday best and next as a working suit, for years. On weekdays they did not so much care how they looked, and the ordinary working suit was not discarded until entirely worn out—until there were no places left on which to hang patches. In summer some of the men . . . went barefooted."[35] Women made their own dresses, and Farquhar recalled that the wife of the richest man in York made all of her own clothing.

Farquhar remembered how low prices were in those days prior to the Civil War. He paid $84 a year for a comfortable house. A washer-woman did laundry in the morning and ironed clothing in the afternoon for 25¢ a day. A good Baltimore hotel charged 25¢ a night. Had there been streetcars, no one would have ridden them, for it would have been considered an expensive pleasure. Farquhar wrote that "affairs were conducted on such a small scale that the possibility of even the employer acquiring a great fortune was considered remote. A man who was worth $20,000 or $25,000 in those days was considered quite well off."[36]

Even though a customary apprenticeship lasted four years, Farquhar completed his in a year and a half. He mastered all the business of the shop, studied drafting, and went to a business school in York at night to learn bookkeeping

What's not to love about a Farquhar, a road grader, children, and dogs?

and writing. He was 20 years old. Dingee offered him a partnership as soon as he was ready to leave. Farquhar's father advanced him the small amount of money needed to purchase an interest in the company.

Much of the firm's business was in the South, and Farquhar became a sales agent at a time when there was no separate sales division. Whenever a lull in the work occurred, "one of the partners hitched his horse and buggy and started out for orders."[37] Farquhar frequently was away from home for two or three weeks at a time.

Farquhar wanted to sell equipment to Colonel Ned Lloyd, the largest slave owner in Maryland, who also owned a plantation in Louisiana. The great orator Frederick Douglass had once been one of Lloyd's slaves. Farquhar rented the best team he could find in the county seat for the occasion. When he arrived at the Lloyd mansion, he met Mrs. Lloyd in the drawing room and they talked about music and literature. When the Colonel arrived, he sent Farquhar's team back to town. Farquhar recalled, "We had a delightful evening. The next morning we rode around the estate. I pointed out to him how he could use some machinery to advantage, especially threshing machines . . . [which] were new things then, and he was a large wheat grower."[38] Lloyd ordered "quite a lot of machinery" and "did not seem to be particular about the cost."[39] Nothing was written down. Farquhar always carried his orders in his memory.

All of a sudden, "the Civil War broke out" and cut off business south of Maryland. Farquhar's company carried few credit accounts in the South and the rebellion ended hopes for any new business from that sector of the country. Some Southern bills were secretly paid through Canada, since paying Northern businesses was considered unpatriotic in the South.[40]

Farquhar recalled the old South before the Civil War: "I was driving one evening . . . in Virginia. Night approached. . . . I asked a man I met on the road where was the nearest good house to stop. He gave me the name of a planter, said I should know it by the high pillars and long avenue lined with trees. . . . It was quiet and dark but in the Negro quarters there were music and dancing. I drove down there with the buggy, which was at once taken in charge by one of the servants who told me I should find the doors open, the dining room also open with plenty of refreshments on the sideboard, to help myself, and then go up in the hallway, peep into some room, and if there were nobody in, just make myself at home. This I did. I was warmly welcomed at the breakfast table and spent a

day or two there very pleasantly. They wanted to make me stay longer. . . . I visited them again after the war broke out. The lady of the house said she wished all the Yankees had one head so she could cut it off, even if she suffered eternal punishment. Shortly after she saw some Union officers riding by and notwithstanding her recent words of hatred said, 'We must not let them pass at dinner time. Invite them in.' There was no hospitality in the world like Southern hospitality."[41]

After the outbreak of the Civil War, commerce almost came to a standstill. "Business dropped dead," as Farquhar put it.[42] He returned from a sales trip to find that the factory had burned to the ground the night before. He said, "We carried practically no insurance and therefore our loss was almost total."[43] The partners agreed to dissolve the business. One of the partners moved to Philadelphia. W. W. Dingee, "a gentleman of great ability and the highest character," accepted a position with J. I. Case and Company of Racine, Wisconsin. Dingee "warmly thanked me for taking over the debts of the firm."[44]

Farquhar asked the firm's creditors to "release the property so that I could start up business again without any interference on account of debts and then let me bind myself to pay within three or four years."[45] Farquhar gave assurances that he would pay in full within the stated time frame. The major creditor consented to Farquhar's plan. It was a highly unusual decision in a day when people expected rapid compensation in cash. Farquhar took out a lease on a warehouse and set up shop. The creditors gave Farquhar supplies to get started and essentially became silent partners.[46] Farquhar recalled, "Those were four hard years," but he paid off all claims during that time. Farquhar worked in the office from five until seven in the morning and from six until ten at night,

and he worked at the factory in between. All the same, Farquhar "enjoyed the work," and commented, "It was a kind of play—a great game that forestalled the need for outside recreation."[47] He added, "[A]lthough absorbing, the business life was not so intense as is today's."

Meanwhile, the war raged. Farquhar's town of York "was distinctively Northern but not bitterly anti-Southern."[48] He observed, "It so often happens that the less you know about a subject, the more fanatical you can become. It is hard to hate a man whom you know. The fanatical abolitionists and the fanatical slave advocates did not know each other. Therefore they could hate."[49] Farquhar also commented, "We felt that slavery was a political question and we were more concerned with establishing the principle that all new states admitted to the Union—for then the admission of a new state was as personal a matter to every citizen as the election of a member to a small club—should be free states."

Farquhar remembered Abraham Lincoln as having the "gift of clear thought" and a biblical form of speech.[50] After meeting Lincoln and talking with him, Farquhar felt "that he was one of the few supermen." Farquhar stood near the platform when Lincoln was inaugurated.

Farquhar married Edward Jessop's daughter, Elizabeth, on September 26, 1860. Because he was recently married when the war broke out, Farquhar "provided a substitute" to take his place in the Civil War and joined a home guard unit. When it was rumored that

Note that a Farquhar engine such as this has a support girder beneath the boiler.

the Confederate army was approaching, the guard rode out to defend York. Many became tired during the long journey and turned back. Farquhar was on his own and felt he was in no danger since "men on both sides were mainly of American stock and could not think of playing other than fair."[51] Farquhar said that "outposts of the armies might with perfect safety camp within gunshot of each other; for it was not considered fair to fire on sleeping men."[52] Farquhar encountered a Southern picket and asked if his old schoolmate W. H. "Rooney" Lee, son of General Robert E. Lee, was there. The soldier thought so and gave Farquhar directions to find Commander Fitzhugh Lee's tent. Farquhar met with Fitzhugh, a nephew of General Lee, and asked if the Confederate army was headed through York. Lee said no and gave Farquhar permission to tell the citizens of York that the town was safe.

A year later, a Confederate column did aim toward York: "[F]or several days a steady stream of farmers and merchants with wagons . . . had filled the Gettysburg Pike. . . . To our own people were added others from Adams County and the northern part of Maryland."[53]

On Saturday, June 27, 1863, the Confederate army was expected in York. Farquhar drove his buggy out to parley. "I struck the Confederate lines beyond Abbotstown, eighteen miles out, and was fortunate in meeting an old classmate, Lieutenant Redik, from Georgia, whom I had not seen since school days. He greeted me with the words, 'Hello, Farquhar. What are you doing up here among the Yankees?' I replied, 'I came just to find out what you are doing up here among the Yankees.'"[54] Redik told Farquhar that Generals Gordon and Early were in charge. Farquhar knew Gordon through mutual friends. Redik joined Farquhar in the buggy and the two of them went to see Gordon, who was "exceedingly courteous." Farquhar ultimately secured an agreement that General Early would give York a written request for supplies and money. Early and the army were in town by Monday, and although the supplies had been provided, not all the money had been gathered. Early threatened to burn the Northern Central Railway property, where cars were built for the Union.

Fortunately for Farquhar and York, a dispatch from General Ewell alerted Early to the fact that "troops were concentrating near Gettysburg where they expected to make a stand, and he was ordered to join them."[55] By five o'clock the next morning, the Confederates had passed through York without sacking the town.

Farquhar had passes from Generals Gordon and Early and penetrated the Confederate lines at Gettysburg. On the second day of the battle, he entered the Union lines "in command of General Kilpatrick."[56] Farquhar was arrested because he had been seen coming from the Confederate position, but a friend interceded on his behalf. Farquhar was released and visited Kilpatrick to ask for permission to serve in the medical corps. Kilpatrick said, "If you are an impostor, you are more dangerous than Jeff Davis," but he consented to Farquhar's request.

Farquhar's horse and buggy were pressed into service and he never saw them again. Farquhar described the third day of fighting: "About two o'clock in the afternoon . . . there commenced a tremendous cannonade of some three hundred guns in one great battery to clear the way for a charge on which the Confederates were to stake their all. . . . [T]he cannonade ceased and then began a terrific din—the rattle of small arms, shouts, yells, orders—for Pickett and his men were making their famous charge up Cemetery Hill. I saw the men rushing forward and dropping, wave after wave, each wave gaining a few rods over the last. And then they stopped and seemed almost to clutch, as does a drowning man at a stick, and went down. They were near enough for me to see their faces, and I shall never forget that sight."[57]

Many citizens back in York accused Farquhar of having sold the town to the rebels. To preserve his honor, Farquhar went to Washington to see the president. At the suggestion of John Hay, Lincoln's secretary, Farquhar waited for Lincoln on the front portico of the White House. He noticed that it "particularly needed paint."[58] Lincoln appeared and asked Farquhar, "Well, sonny, what are you after?"[59] Farquhar told him while he and Lincoln walked toward the War Department Building. Lincoln wanted to know if Farquhar was married, if he had any children, what kind of business he ran in York, and if the company was prosperous. They entered a room filled with generals and Secretary of War Edwin Stanton, whose personal secretary was Farquhar's cousin. Lincoln said, "Stanton, I have captured that young chap who sold York, Pennsylvania, to the rebels. What are we going to do with him?"[60] Stanton replied, "We ought to promote him."[61] Lincoln thanked Farquhar for saving millions of dollars' worth of property. When Farquhar returned home, word of Lincoln's respect for him had already reached the town and Farquhar was cordially received.

The ceremony to commemorate the Gettysburg battlefield brought Farquhar back to Gettysburg, where he shook hands with Lincoln. "He remembered me and spoke a half-joking word or two."[62] Farquhar stood near the speaker's stand and listened to Edward Everett's eloquent but long oration. The president "looked very, very weary."[63] According to Farquhar, Lincoln "rose slowly, and as he took his place in the center of the platform, he drew from his waistcoat pocket what appeared to me to be a small, discolored leaf torn from a memorandum book, and glancing at it now and then, delivered slowly, clearly, dwelling on each phrase as though he were pronouncing a benediction," the renowned Gettysburg Address.

During the war, Farquhar nearly fell victim to unscrupulous businessmen that cheated the Union. "In a number of cases an account of the people who sold supplies to the government during the Civil War would be little better than a record of crime," he wrote.[64] With almost no business, Farquhar had gone to Washington to seek government contracts and secured an order with the medical purveyor for chairs and litters. Farquhar's hospital furniture and stretchers were of the highest quality, yet to his astonishment, his goods were condemned. Farquhar then exposed a ring, including inspectors, responsible for approving poor-quality merchandise at a high price and secretly sharing the large profits. General Sutherland thanked Farquhar and gave him a major percentage of the chair and litter business for the duration of the war.

Farquhar attended Lincoln's second inauguration, "and that was the last time I saw him alive."[65] Looking back on Lincoln's life, Farquhar commented, "By the time of Lincoln's second inauguration his position had become more permanent. The personal opposition to him was negligible. But it was not until April 15, 1865, with the war ended, and Abraham Lincoln suddenly dead, that the country began to know what it had had and what it had lost."

After the war, "the country began to hum with business."[66] In Farquhar's assessment, "We had extravagances then, but not on the scale of the present day. I do not know whether that was because there were then not so many things to buy or because people were not so gifted in extravagance."[67] One of the boosts to the economy came from westward expansion. "Men were needed for the building of railways; they were needed everywhere in constantly increasing numbers, for we were beginning that tremendous expansion on inflated money which culminated in the panic of 1873."[68] The production of goods swelled beyond the capacity of distribution systems. Meanwhile, people bought government securities and invested in greenbacks.

Farquhar felt that had Lincoln lived, the South would have joined in the virtually immediate economic recovery after the war. Of President Johnson, however, Farquhar wrote, "although I try to think well of everyone, I never . . . have been able to think well of him."[69] Animosity toward the North developed not from the war so much as from reconstruction, according to Farquhar. Farquhar's former customers in the South nevertheless began to contact him about trying to start up their businesses again. Of course, none of them had any money whatsoever. Many Southerners could not afford shoes. "They had plenty of corn bread and some bacon, but that is all they did have."[70] The plantations had been stripped of tools to provide iron for the Confederate war effort. Immediately after the war, a heavy export tax on cotton, which was later removed as unconstitutional, made Southern farming nearly hopeless. Farquhar took orders on credit with one half to be paid the next fall and the other half a year later. Practically all accounts were eventually paid.

Southern commerce, however, was dismal during the reign of the carpetbaggers. These political criminals used methods that were shockingly unfair, fostering intense resentment against the North. Southern hatred for Northern corruption encouraged the formation of Ku Klux Klan groups. President Grant interceded on behalf of a Ku Klux Klan leader who had been arrested and was to be sent to the Albany Penitentiary. The man had been present at Appomattox and President Grant remembered the man, as well as his horse, which Grant had patted on the neck. Grant pardoned the man, on the condition that he disband his KKK alliance.

Farquhar traced the origin of the American concept of big business to the years following the Civil War. The industrial population at the time was small: "[W]e were a nation of farmers."[71] Most factory workmen had farming experience in their background. With the increased demand for materials brought by railroads, "we simply had to visualize business on a large scale," he said, with each man producing more goods.[72] The new lands under cultivation, the mechanical reaper, and the shortage of manpower created a strong market for threshers. Farquhar remembered that "as soon as steam engines became of practical driving power for farm use, we began to make them."[73] Steamers were in Farquhar's blood. His Uncle John Elgar had collaborated with Ross Winans of Baltimore to turn out the first of the coal-burning railroad locomotives.[74]

The earliest direct foreign shipment that Farquhar recalled consisted of plow parts sent to South Africa in 1866. By the early 1870s, Farquhar had a thriving export trade, with cash paid on the docks. He kept approximately 25 percent of his output going overseas.[75] The Farquhar catalog was published in a Spanish edition to develop trade with Mexico and South America.[76] Like many of the wealthy New Yorkers he had talked with years before, he was a hands-on businessman—one day, for example, pouring the molds to make plowshares early in the morning, personally packing the new plowshares that afternoon, and rushing them to a ship just in time for sailing. Farquhar maintained, "Delays are bad enough in domestic business. In overseas business they are fatal because if you miss a ship, the goods may miss the season during which they were expected to be sold."[77] Farquhar described himself as "one of the first Americans to export agricultural implements."

After the war, Farquhar's factory was producing goods at a rate twice as fast as before the war. Farquhar was "proprietor, superintendent, foreman, office manager, cost accountant, and bookkeeper" of his business.[78] He lived next door to the factory, which was lighted by kerosene torches. Only the main office had gas lighting. Farquhar produced catalogs and trade cards, the wording of which suggests that he wrote most of the copy himself: "Frequently I found, on my sales trips, farm libraries consisting of the Bible, an almanac, and Farquhar's catalog!"[79]

Farquhar said, "We lived buoyantly, and only a very few gave much thought as to what we were really living on or whether the foundations of our prosperity were planted in sand or on rock. The panic of 1873 answered that question."[80] On Thursday, September 18, when Jay Cooke & Company, which had helped finance the Civil War, suspended business, it appeared to most Americans that the financial father of the country had failed. It was unthinkable. By Friday morning, "nearly everyone with a bank account was outside his bank's doors foaming at the mouth for his deposit. No one thought of doing business."[81] By Saturday, all banks had closed, as had the New York Stock Exchange. Farquhar described the mayhem: "A currency panic is not pretty. It is a mad, unseeing, unthinking scramble for money. I saw hundreds fighting tooth and nail to get into banks—fighting as cowards fight their way out of a burning theater. It was a terrible orgy of crude greed when a gold dollar ranked above every sentiment that makes life worthwhile."[82] Farquhar closed his shop and walked about to watch the panic unfold.

The Small family, the richest businesspeople in York, had been keeping gold coins for farmers, who now demanded their money back. The Smalls calmly said that they would be happy to return the money but that they would never again accept coins from anyone withdrawing funds at this time. The Smalls were standing in front of bags of gold piled high in the back of their shop. Some farmers took their gold coins and left, but many thought that since there was so much gold, it was safe. After the last farmer

departed, one of the Smalls tossed Farquhar a "gold" coin from one of the bags toward the back. It turned out to be a newly minted copper penny. As soon as they had learned of the Cooke failure, the Smalls had purchased bags of pennies to swell the number of coin bags in their shop. They bluffed the farmers into thinking they had plenty of gold on hand and thus continued to be solvent.

Speaking of farmers, Farquhar affectionately remarked, "I have always had a good part of my business directly with farmers, and in all these years, trading with thousands of farmers, I have never heard one admit that prices were satisfactory, and only one, in my recollection, admit that he was making money. I should regard a farmer who was not thoroughly dissatisfied with prices and who was not declaring that he ought to stop farming and cease putting out crops to rot in the fields as an exception. I should regard him as even more an exception if ever he did fail to plant to capacity."[83]

Farquhar said that the panic of 1873 arose from unsettling influences—namely the Franco-Prussian War, the Chicago fire of 1871, and the Boston fire of 1872—and from Jay Cooke's over-investment in the Northern Pacific Railway. Farquhar wrote, "The New York financiers could have saved Cooke and could have saved the banks, but they were intensely jealous of Cooke. They let him fail, and then failed themselves."[84]

The panic became protracted. "For a hundred days this coma lasted. The Christmas of 1873 was about as cheerless a festival as has ever been intoned."[85] Farquhar, however, refused to give up hope. His factory stayed closed only four days. It opened again on the Monday after the panic began. As he put the matter, "[I]t occurred to me that the whole world was not involved in the panic, that there certainly must be customers to be found somewhere."[86] Farquhar secured an order at reduced rates from New York commission merchants. He asked his employees to accept a 25 percent cut in salaries on the premise that he could reimburse them when business improved. His workers accepted the plan. Next, Farquhar sent queries to find raw materials. After six months, wages throughout the country had fallen so low that his employees felt comparatively well off and demanded no increase.

Farquhar needed cash. He commented, "One of the several causes for the long duration of the panic was the breakdown of every kind of credit; we cannot do business without credit.... Business is founded on confidence; when confidence is withdrawn, ... then credit stops and business ceases. The man who never extends credit is a greater menace than the man who extends credit too freely."[87] The bank where Farquhar did business extended no credit to him, but a member of the Small family decided to supply credit to Farquhar from the York County Bank. Farquhar's factory was the only one in York that kept going at full force throughout the panic and the slow times afterward.

Farquhar stated, "I made money. I have always made money in panics."[88] During the panic of 1873, he concentrated on his exports "and sold very extensively in South Africa, Cuba, Mexico, Brazil, and in the Argentine."[89]

Soon after the panic began, Farquhar confronted severe difficulties at home. Of the five children born to Farquhar and Elizabeth, two—a daughter and an infant son—passed away. After the deaths of the children, Elizabeth fell ill. Her doctor recommended that she might improve in the fresh air of the countryside. In two days, Farquhar built a simple frame house outside York. His wife's health improved there. She feared returning to the town, and Farquhar decided to spend part of his profit to build a country estate "on a high hill."[90] Building began in September 1874, and by Christmas the Farquhars moved in.

Then came the unexpected. In 1876—the same year that Farquhar attended the Centennial Exposition in Philadelphia, where he spoke for the first time via telephone[91]—the factory "and all I owned were one Sunday completely wiped out by fire," Farquhar said. "I found myself back once more at the point from which I had started years before."[92] It was a Sunday, but the telegraph operator opened his office to help Farquhar. Messages were sent to most of Farquhar's suppliers: he had been burned out and he wanted materials at cash prices and on easy credit terms. Even though credit was tight during the business depression, which lasted until 1879, Farquhar's reputation for paying his bills won the day.

Farquhar acquired a factory that had failed with a $5 down-payment. The new shop opened the day after the fire, and Farquhar's employees accepted a 15 percent cut. Simultaneously, Farquhar negotiated with a contractor to expand the building. Farquhar was back in business and succeeded once again.

Farquhar modeled his business practices on those of Andrew Carnegie, a fellow admirer of literature. "I have always held Andrew Carnegie to be the world's greatest businessman, and I think he became so because he was not a businessman in the sense of knowing nothing but business. That much esteemed 'hard-headed' quality in businessmen comes only from a lack of imagination that really prohibits the growth to the stature of 'big businessmen.'"[93] According to Farquhar, "Carnegie was, perhaps, the first to grasp the ideal business policy—a large output sold at a reasonable price that includes a fair profit, and at the same time permits good wages to workmen and high compensation to managers." Carnegie paid his workers what were then unheard-of salaries. Farquhar regarded Carnegie as a genius. "Many men knew more about iron and steel, but none knew so much about iron and steel and men and business."[94] Carnegie was opposed to speculation; following suit, Farquhar bought excess stock only after "careful study of world conditions."[95]

Farquhar knew every detail of his business. "I could judge with my eye the number of feet of lumber or the weight of pig iron on a railroad car. I could tell whether the amount was short or over the invoice.[96] Of course, it took longer to do our work then than it does now. Remember that we had no stenographers or typists and had either to write our own letters or dictate them to good penmen who transcribed as we talked. It was an easy matter to keep two men thus going."[97]

In 1879, commerce started to improve, payments in gold were restored, and in turn, an era of prosperity began. Looking back on 1879, Farquhar remembered, "Steel started up in June 1879. That was the time when the age of steel began, and ever since steel has constituted an important barometer of business."[98] Farquhar took the opportunity of a brightening commercial outlook to visit New York's National Park Bank, where he made his first New York banking connection by accepting a line of credit. He also prudently expanded his factory. He remained opposed to tariffs, however, "observing that a policy of high protection follows every depression and usually forms part of a prosperity-hindering program to restrict production."[99] The brisk sales lasted until the depression of 1884. Business rebounded and sales were lively until the panic of 1893. From then until 1897, during a lull in domestic trade, Farquhar depended largely on his export business.[100] Eventually, his exports went to Russia, Bulgaria, Serbia, Greece, and Turkey.[101] After the Bolshevik Revolution, Farquhar wisely prophesied, "The chapter on American trade with Russia will have to remain suspended until the mass of the Russians find Communism less amusing."[102]

When exporting machinery to South America, Farquhar had to take extraordinary measures. "In many cases where the goods have to be taken over the mountains, the limit of weight for each package is 125 pounds, and since they are carried on mule back, we sometimes have had to send a boiler in such small parts that they could not even be riveted, yet the native labor satisfactorily put the boiler and engine together."[103]

The age of big business had arrived, and Farquhar credited the expansion of railroads with introducing the corporate model into American commercial enterprise. In 1889, Farquhar chose to enter into "a limited partnership under the name of A. B. Farquhar Co., Limited. We had been known before as the Pennsylvania Agricultural Works, with my name as proprietor."[104] His aims were "to facilitate the distribution" of his estate and to give his sons "some present interest in the business." He conservatively capitalized at $500,000, even though his property was worth much more. While Farquhar appreciated the comparatively easy acquisition of new partnership capital under laws of incorporation, he worried that corporate organizational schemes permitted corruption at the expense of a public unaware that a par value of $100 does not make "stock worth $100 or worth anything beyond the earning power of the property it represents."[105] Corporations did, however, foster larger and more efficient production. When corporations began to join together as trusts, Farquhar favored the trend. "[T]he tendency was to eliminate waste, and in spite of the attempts at monopoly or interference with competition, the real growth of the

witness, thinking that he would complain about his inability to compete. On the stand, Farquhar expressed his belief that International was "a public benefactor because . . . the farmer was able to buy a better article for the money than he was able to buy from me."[108] A government attorney said, "I do not want to hear another word from that witness." Farquhar told the attorney that he should have checked ahead of time to see what Farquhar might be likely to say. The judge permitted Farquhar to continue. Farquhar told the court that he always believed in the greatest good for the greatest number and that such a credo had helped him in his own business.

Farquhar's principal contribution to government originated in his desire to preserve peace throughout the world. "I regard war as the greatest enemy to business as well as to moral and intellectual advancement."[109] Farquhar attended the Hague Conference in 1907. He was on the same platform with Britain's Lloyd George at an arbitration conference in

On a winter's day, this Farquhar steamer is pulling a boiler built by the Ames Iron Works of New York.

truly big corporation was due to the fact that it could manufacture and sell goods more cheaply than could the less efficient small producer. And the more goods we get at low prices, the better off is the country."[106]

In keeping with his philosophy on corporations and trusts, Farquhar discontinued machinery lines that the International Harvester Company could produce at less expense.[107] When International was sued under the Sherman Anti-Trust Law, the government brought in Farquhar as a

London. In June 1914, the government sent Farquhar to Germany to study municipalities for the purpose of adopting their best practices in America. While in Germany, Farquhar remained blissfully unaware of impending military action.[110] The declaration of war with Serbia came as a complete surprise and nearly trapped Farquhar in war-torn Europe. He escaped to Constantinople, which was in wild commotion, and with the help of the American embassy, departed aboard a freighter bound for the United States.[111]

His trunk was lost and it miraculously reappeared seven years later with none of its contents missing.

Farquhar earned many honors over his lifetime. In 1892, Farquhar was appointed to be a commissioner to the Columbian Exposition in Chicago. He was in charge of practically all of Pennsylvania's participation in the fair, and his fellow commissioners elected Farquhar to preside over the board.[112] In addition, he was the recipient of an honorary LL.D. degree from Kenyon College in Gambier, Ohio.[113] His friends included Presidents Garfield, Cleveland, Roosevelt, and Taft; and his acquaintances included many more men in the country's highest office.[114] President Taft called Farquhar "an adviser of presidents."[115]

Farquhar set eight rules for himself: to trust human beings, to consider troubles as steps toward progress, to work for success and happiness while not putting dollars ahead of people, to keep faith with yourself, to keep God's laws, to remember that you can be your own worst enemy, to regard friends as assets and to get friends by being one, and to give value for anything you seek, thus avoiding "the disposition to speculate—which is one of the greatest dangers that beset the businessman."[116] Farquhar concluded that by following the eight rules, he found the world to grow in interest and life to become happier over time. Thus ends the autobiography of A. B. Farquhar, a nineteenth-century industrialist who, through confidence, hard work, perseverance, and intelligence, attained the American dream.

Afterword

According to the *York Daily Record* (a newspaper Farquhar had owned for a time), a car struck Farquhar and weakened his constitution. He died in 1925 and was honored with the largest funeral York had ever seen. Ironically, an unemployment office operates on the site where his great factory once stood.[117]

Frick Company

The history of the Frick Company is intertwined with that of the Geiser Manufacturing Company and the businesses of the Landis brothers, which were all ultimately based in Waynesboro, Pennsylvania. Abraham Frick brought his son George to Quincy, a town north of Waynesboro, in 1835 when George was nine years old. His father ran a water-powered vertical saw. In 1843, George was apprenticed to Martin Kendig, a millwright in Ringgold, Maryland. George opened a repair shop near Quincy two years later. He eventually moved to a gristmill and sawmill on Antietam Creek, a short distance south of Waynesboro.

Franklin Frick Landis was born in 1845. When he was three, his family moved to the same mill where George

This early Frick steam engine has a chain drive.

Here's a young crew with an old engine. Perhaps the bent whistle can be attributed to the free spirits of youth.

The boiler of a Frick engine such as this could slide independently of the support above the front axle by slowly expanding while being fired.

Anyone of any age who drove the team hauling the water wagon could be nicknamed "water boy," but sometimes he was a boy! The rod controls the spark arrester.

The members of the crew appear to be ready for a good nap in this exceptionally fine side view of a Frick Eclipse steam tractor.

Frick was working. In 1854, Franklin's brother Abraham B. was born. When the boys' father, Benjamin, died in 1855 at the age of 33, their mother returned to Lancaster County with her seven children.

A motto attributed to Franklin Frick may help explain his energetic pursuit of improved machinery and enhanced sales: "Be sure you are right, then do it quickly!" In 1850, Frick began building his first steam engine on his farm in Ringgold, Maryland. Frick erected a shop in Ringgold in 1851 or 1852. He was soon manufacturing portable steam engines to power threshers built by Peter Geiser. He rented a larger building north of Ringgold in 1857. In 1861, Frick moved his business from Ringgold to Waynesboro. Frick built sawmills along with his steam engines. Frick's apprentices lived with him and his family in a large house adjoining his shop. Confederates commandeered all leather belting from Frick's shop at the time of the Gettysburg campaign, and Frick's manufactory was closed for a month. Frick historian and editor-in-chief of *Engineers and Engines Magazine*, Brenda Stant, reports that after the Civil War, the South was in such dire need of saw-mills that patrons provided leather belting for Frick's shop. Customers often paid for sawmills in lumber so Frick could build additional mills and threshers. In 1867, Frick's eight-year-old daughter died when she was caught in a spinning shaft that ran between two buildings of the factory. After the war, Frick had begun to erect new brick shops across the street and sold his thresher business to Geiser, Price & Company. Frick's former shop became part of Geiser. The Frick firm occupied its new site until 1881.

In 1872, the Frick family was struck by typhoid fever. Frank, the eldest son, died from the illness. In 1873, Frick relinquished his interest in his company while continuing to serve as treasurer, manager, and superintendent.

Here is a close-up view of a Frick chugging along.

This Frick steamer has seen hard service.

A spy in a tree overhead watches a Frick steamer pulling a train of wagons loaded with green lumber.

The camaraderie of the crew helps explain why most people who lived during the threshing era had such positive memories of those times.

Thirteen men, including Frick's son A. O., formed a partnership to bring the company safely through the panic of 1873 and were thereafter known as "the lucky 13." In the 1870s, the Frick firm named its portable engines Eclipse. The firm outgrew its facilities and moved to the western side of Waynesboro in 1881 to be near the new railroad that was being built. Frick added Corliss stationary engines to its line in 1883.

In 1876, Franklin and Abraham Landis founded F. F. and A. B. Landis to manufacture portable agricultural steam engines. In 1879, the Landis brothers sold their engine plant to the Geiser Manufacturing Company and began working for Geiser. Franklin designed steam engines and Abraham ran the machine shop. When Geiser began to compete with Frick in the steam engine business, Frick resumed the manufacture of threshers.

In 1882, Frick's firm became interested in refrigeration, which relies on the same scientific principles that govern steam technologies. In 1883, A. O. began full production of the company's first refrigeration machines, which soon were in demand around the globe. The Frick firm was incorporated in 1885. George Frick retired at the age of 62 in 1888 and died in 1891. Around 1894, Franklin Landis joined the Frick firm and built roller threshers for Frick. A. O. served as president of the company from 1904 to 1924, and his brother Ezra took his turn at the presidency from 1924 to 1942.

By 1918, Frick had developed a gasoline-powered tractor. Frick wanted to expand its product line, which now included balers, spreaders, silo fillers, and eventually peanut pickers. The last Frick traction engine was shipped in 1927. (At the time of this writing, Brenda Stant owns it.) In that same year, Frick ended gasoline tractor production and distributed tractors built by the Minneapolis Threshing Machine Company. After the merger that formed Minneapolis-Moline, Frick became the eastern distributor for the new firm. Frick steam engine production ended in 1945 with the shipment of the company's last two portable engines. After World War II, half of America's ice rinks used Frick refrigeration units. Frick sold its sawmill business in 1973, and in 1987, York International purchased Frick.

A Frick engine is on the road again.

An early engine of Gaar, Scott & Company is shown with a webstacker-equipped threshing machine.

Gaar, Scott & Company

Because Jonas Gaar's Bavarian ancestors were weavers, his 1835 announcement that he and Job W. Swain would build carding and spinning machines came as no surprise, according to Gaar descendants Joanna Hill Mikesell and Annette S. Warfel. Jonas (born in 1792) employed his sons Abram (born in 1819) and John Milton (born in 1823) in his Richmond, Indiana, shop. The venture ended after less than a year, however, and Jonas went to work at a nearby stove factory known as the Spring Foundry, named for a nearby spring. Nevertheless, the Gaar family always listed 1836 as the founding year of their vast company. John Milton Gaar, a machinist, officially joined the factory in 1841. Abram Gaar, a patternmaker, joined the company in 1843. In 1839, brothers Jesse M. and John H. Hutton bought the Spring Foundry from Isaac E. Jones and Ellis P. Coale. Jonas Gaar and Elkanah Hully shared foundry space to manufacture machinery for the woolen trade and became partners with the Huttons to build engines and farm implements. By 1843, Jonas was superintendent of the shop, which produced such equipment as pickers and power looms, as well as machines for shearing, napping, and carding. Stoves, mills, and threshers also proliferated. The foundry had experimented with the small threshing machines called "groundhogs" around 1841. Then, in 1845, the Gaars invented threshers that could remove chaff from the grain. In 1849, the Gaars sold a single thresher—that they would later call "utterly worthless"—in exchange for grain and horses. That same year, though inexperienced, John Milton and Abram bought out the Huttons. A. Gaar & Company had become a reality. Jonas Gaar and William G. Scott (Jonas' son-in-law, a bookkeeper, and a molder) played major roles in the firm. The fledgling company was financially on weak feet. John Milton had only $10, which paid for a load of coke brought from Cincinnati in a wagon. The firm miraculously persisted. A mainstay of Gaar family stories is that the company began with John Milton's $10.

This photograph could well depict a scene familiar during the farm steam era: a manufacturer's representative ready to show threshermen how to run the engine in the field

A brick addition to the factory appeared in 1851, and an expanded machine shop was built in 1856. Gaar's closest competitor was the nearby Robinson Machine Works. In 1870, the firm was incorporated as Gaar, Scott & Company. Jonas died in 1875. One year later, Abram built a large and well-appointed home, which still stands at the time of this writing. Mike McKnight has found that the Gaar firm began building traction engines around 1878.

The plant enjoyed a further expansion by 1879. Joe Park and Lawrence Porter have reported that during that year, a 44-inch Gaar thresher and a 25-horsepower Gaar engine in California broke a widely publicized record by threshing 6,183 bushels of wheat in one day. Agricultural publications carried the news, and the census of 1880 noted that the threshing crew on that historic day had included 36 header wagons, four men filling bags, and another four men sewing the sacks of wheat.

The firm survived the panic of 1893, but only by scaling down the workforce. Although the firm had a long history of growth greater than anyone had the right to expect, the company experienced the occasional economic downturn.

continued on page 96

A wood-burning steam engine carries two jugs: one on the platform, and the other on the water tank.

This Gaar, Scott & Company rig struts before J. E. Dafler's distributorship in Brookville, Ohio. Courtesy Brookville Historical Society

A water cup dangles from the driver's seat on this straw-burning return-flue steamer.

This product of Gaar, Scott & Company is headed through town, which is the straightest path to the next farm!

continued from page 93

The entire plant was closed for the month of September 1896 in response to the depressed prices lingering after the panic of 1893. This was two years after the death of Abram Gaar in 1894; John Milton Gaar died in 1900.

The Gaar plant was one of the largest agricultural implement factories in the United States. In 1898, Gaar may have sold the most threshing equipment of any company in the country, but the J. I. Case Threshing Machine Company soon surpassed Gaar's sales. In 1906, the Gaar firm introduced the Big Forty, a massive rear-mounted steamer with tandem compound cylinders. In 1910, the firm built initial models of a TigerPull 40–70-horsepower oil-powered tractor.

This Gaar-Scott is pulling a house using a chain and cable arrangement.

On December 9, 1911, Gaar, Scott & Company was transferred to M. Rumely, which had also taken over Advance. Dr. Edward A. Rumely planned to assemble an implement empire to compete with such companies as International Harvester. In 1912, the Gaar firm began to concentrate on producing rear-mounted plowing engines. Then, on January 19, 1915, the M. Rumely Company and Rumely Products went into receivership. The Gaar firm had built its last threshing machines in 1914. Even though advertisements for engines persisted until 1918, the grand old company had come to an untimely end. A surprising number of mid-nineteenth-century Gaar portable engines exist in preservation and perhaps attest to their durability.

Note the straw piled high on the Gaar-Scott water wagon behind this Gaar-Scott engine.

The Werner brothers of Marshall, Minnesota, were the proud owners of this return-flue steam traction engine.

The water tank on this elegant Gaar-Scott engine proclaims that the steamer was built "specially for George Kirschbaum." Courtesy Batesville (Indiana) Historical Society

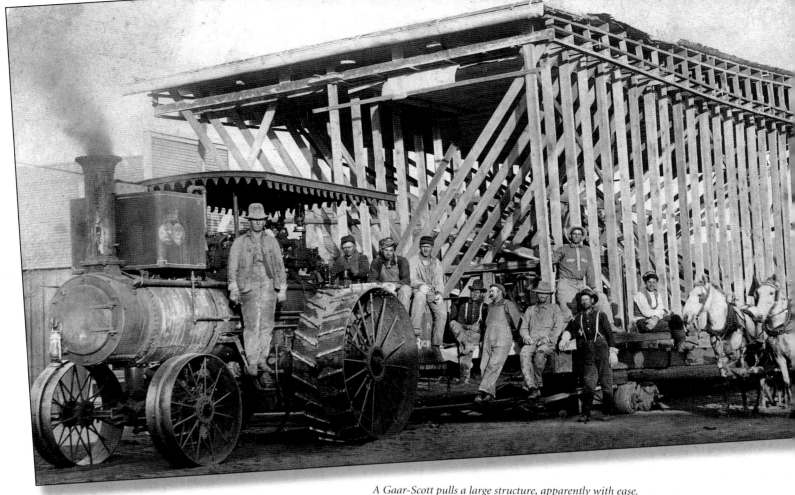

A Gaar-Scott pulls a large structure, apparently with ease.

This Gaar-Scott is ready to haul a big load from Floete Lumber Company of Dallas, South Dakota, to Qually's Drug Store.

Pinehurst is advertising purebred Holstein-Friesian dairy cattle in this photo of a Gaar-Scott. Note the barrel of pitchforks on the water wagon.

Here is an extremely rare photo of a Landis Peerless steam traction engine before the Geiser Manufacturing Company purchased the F. F. and A. B. Landis Company. Courtesy William U. Waters, Jr., from the Mark H. Landis estate

Geiser Manufacturing Company

The Geiser Manufacturing Company's history is woven into that of the Frick Company, as well as the work of the Landis brothers, which were all ultimately based in Waynesboro, Pennsylvania. Peter Geiser was born in Smithsburg, Maryland, in 1826. When he came of age, he concentrated his efforts on designing a thresher that would separate the grain from the stalk and also from the chaff. He ultimately patented such a thresher in 1852. Geiser began selling his machines from his shop near Smithsburg, and Jones & Miller of Hagerstown were selling Geiser threshers by 1855. Around 1858, at least half a dozen companies were licensed to offer Geiser machines, and many more had joined the throng by the eve of the Civil War. To relocate his factory in 1866, Peter Geiser purchased land in Waynesboro that included two and a half acres sold by George Frick, who was erecting new brick buildings across the street. In 1867, Geiser, Price & Company established "the train," which was an assembly line for producing threshers.

While Peter Geiser's star was rising, other stars of the eventual Geiser constellation were forming. Franklin Frick Landis was born in 1845. Franklin's brother Abraham B. was born in 1854. Franklin Landis completed mechanical training at Mount Joy, worked as a toolmaker for the Norris Locomotive Works in Lancaster, built patent models, and eventually opened a machine shop. In 1870, he took brother Ezra into his enterprise. In 1872, Franklin and Ezra sold their business to John Best & Company, where Franklin became a manager. Abraham Landis, who had

An unusual head-on view of an early Geiser shows every patent date recorded for posterity in the smokebox door. Courtesy William U. Waters, Jr., from the Mark H. Landis estate

This is an early Geiser Peerless traction engine. Notice this engine has a handwheel reverse mechanism. Courtesy William U. Waters, Jr.

This is what a Geiser with a handwheel reverse mechanism looks like from the other side while plowing. A hand windlass lifts the plow. Courtesy William U. Waters, Jr.

Firm

This old Geiser is a surrogate source of steam.

The man in front takes pride in the Geiser engine and the Hagerstown Empire threshing machine.

been apprenticed to his brothers' business, continued to work for Best. In the nation's centennial year, Franklin and Abraham founded F. F. and A. B. Landis to manufacture portable agricultural steam engines in Lancaster. Their engines were produced under the Peerless name. In 1878, their failure to please one of their most important customers almost brought an end to their firm. They were forced to temporarily assign their business to Francis Hershey, a brother-in-law, who paid their debt. William U. Waters, Jr., has found that during this time, Franklin designed a horse-steered traction engine. The company was back in full swing by 1879 and Franklin and Abraham sold their engine plant to the Geiser Manufacturing Company. Geiser added the brothers to the payroll, thereby launching great careers for both. Franklin designed the Peerless steam engines, which began to roll from the factory in 1880, as well as numerous improvements in Geiser threshers. Abraham supervised the machine shop. The Frick firm, also located in Waynesboro, had relinquished the building of threshers to Geiser, but as Geiser's Peerless engines began to compete with Frick's steamers, Frick retaliated by resuming production of threshing machines.

As reported by George B. Coffman, Franklin Landis and a crew drove a Geiser

This Geiser stands before a shop of yesteryear.

Here is a typical silhouette of a Geiser Peerless engine.

The family gathers to have its picture taken with a roofed Geiser steam engine in a sawmill. The girl makes sure her doll is included in the photograph.

traction engine pulling a thesher, water wagon, and maintenance vehicles toward Cincinnati, Ohio, from Waynesboro for the 1881 Cincinnati Industrial Exposition. Franklin encountered a steep descent into McConnellsburg, so he felled a hefty chestnut tree and dragged it behind the train to act as a braking mechanism. At Zanesville, Franklin decided to make the rest of the journey by railroad. While the engine was climbing heavy planks to board a flatcar, one of the timbers broke. The steamer suddenly leaned toward one side, the smokestack toppled off, and the engineer jumped for his life. There was no lasting damage to either the engine or the engineer, and the crew managed to load the engine safely. Franklin credited the wooden spokes of the drive wheels with absorbing the shock of the abrupt tilt, and he continued to favor wooden spokes long after the incident.

Note the fancy striping on the boiler support. The belt guide consists of two rollers on this Geiser Peerless steam engine.

The crew of this Geiser steam engine uses mules.

A Geiser engine that is helping build a bridge uses "That Good Oil," as the side of the can proclaims.

The father and brother stare at the one child that dashed off just as the shutter was opened.

The crank disc cover is lifted on this Geiser, serial number 11838.

Franklin Landis added a highly touted steam-lift plow to the Geiser implement line in 1884. In 1889, Franklin and Abraham formed Landis Brothers, a machine-tool firm specializing in grinding machines. Geiser also manufactured steamrollers.

The Emerson-Brantingham Implement Company of Rockford, Illinois, bought the Geiser firm, as well as the Reeves Company, in 1912, so as to compete with International Harvester and similar diversified lines. Peter Geiser had died in 1901. In 1928, Mark H. Landis, Franklin's son, and former Geiser interests bought the Geiser Manufacturing Company from Emerson-Brantingham, but the Great Depression loomed. The firm slowly declined and went into receivership.

This Geiser Peerless steamer hauls lumber beside a railway.

A shy girl poses before a pair of Geiser engines and a Minneapolis thresher.

Owner Peter Bly is on this Greencastle engine, and his father is on the thresher. The picture was taken in Strasburg, Virginia, around 1900. The engine still has a tailrod water pump, which was gone by 1962 when William U. Waters, Jr., acquired the steamer. Courtesy William U. Waters, Jr.

The man near the driver wheel of a Greencastle traction engine is Jeff Hooper. The scene was near Taylorsville, Maryland, and the photo was taken around 1885. Courtesy William U. Waters, Jr.

Greencastle, Built by Crowell Manufacturing Company

The Crowell Manufacturing Company of Greencastle, Pennsylvania, was located approximately eight miles from Waynesboro, where Frick and Geiser engines were built, as William U. Waters, Jr., has reported. Henry B. Larzelere served as a machinist and designer and may have been a partner in the business. Larzelere was born in Willow Grove, Pennsylvania, and moved to Greencastle in 1882. Around 1887, he moved to Muncy, Pennsylvania, and started the Muncy Traction Engine Company. The Muncy engine and the Greencastle engine were twins. The firm was better known for a successful grain drill but did produce 13 threshers, 12 of which were returned to the factory because of faults. The 13th was destroyed in a barn fire and was paid for with insurance. Waters spoke with old-timers who remembered having heard of Greencastle engines and surmises that around a dozen steam engines were manufactured. Crowell also advertised sawmills and portable engines. Crowell passed into receivership in the late 1890s. Around 1901, Geiser purchased the factory to build gasoline engines. Larzelere spent the remaining years of his career with Farquhar in York, Pennsylvania, selling and installing sawmills. Larzelere held various patents, including one in 1884 for a device built into the kingpost and designed to level the boiler by raising or lowering the front

of the engine. One of three Greencastle engines shipped to Woodstock, Virginia, is the only Greencastle in existence. Waters restored this engine and exhibited it at shows. As the water level in a Greencastle was intended to be higher than the boiler, the steamdome had to be extra large to trap enough steam to power the engine. The traction wheels were mounted on rubber in the hubs, and the kingpost was mounted on a coil spring.

Groton Manufacturing Company

Around 1847, Daniel Spencer began building threshers in Spring Brook, New York. He moved his shop to Groton, where William Perrigo joined as a business partner. In 1849, brothers Charles (born in 1817) and Lyman Perrigo established a foundry business. They produced horse powers for William's threshing machines. Oliver Avery, Jr., served his apprenticeship with Charles and Lyman Perrigo and became a partner. Ellery Colby purchased an interest in Charles and Lyman's firm. In 1877, the thresher works and the iron works merged to form Charles Perrigo & Company. In that same year, Perrigo incorporated the Groton Iron Bridge Company to manufacture iron bridges; Colby and Avery held offices in the new organization. A decade later, a reorganization produced

This Conger, the descendant of earlier Groton steamers, is pulling a thresher.

The Conger steam traction engine popped off while waiting for the photographer to snap the picture of this road-grading scene. Courtesy Robert T. Rhode

the Groton Bridge and Manufacturing Company, with Colby serving as the first president and Avery as treasurer. Frank Conger was vice president. The combined Perrigo firms manufactured bridges, steam engines, threshers, and farming implements.

In the late 1890s, the Perrigo agricultural engines were called Groton engines. In 1900, the Groton bridge building firm was absorbed into the American Bridge Company, and the Groton works continued for only one more year before it shut down. The traction engine portion of the business became the Groton Manufacturing Company. In 1902, the Groton Bridge Company sprang back to life. In 1920, Groton sold out permanently to the American Bridge Company.

Judge Raymond L. Drake, Derek Rayner, and Dr. Robert T. Rhode have uncovered much of the history related to William Churchill Oastler. In 1899, Oastler, long an importer and distributor of British Aveling & Porter products in New York, began to market Oastler steamrollers assembled by the Cooke Locomotive Company of Paterson, New Jersey. This machine conformed so closely to British designs that historians suspect parts may have been shipped from England to the United States. Not long after the Oastler prototypes had appeared at the Cooke Locomotive Works, Oastler came into control of the Monarch steamroller business at Groton, New York. The Monarch model of roller was nearly identical to the Oastler until around 1901. That year, Oastler introduced a new design of Monarch roller called the "King of the Road" that lasted throughout the firm's production. In late 1901, the Groton Manufacturing Company was renamed the Conger Manufacturing Company.

British citizen Edward T. Wright became superintendent of the Groton steamroller firm in 1903, as his descendants Virginia D'Antonio and Tom Wright have learned. Edward had served his apprenticeship in the shops of the Aveling & Porter Company and understood standard road roller design. Edward's father, Thomas, joined him to work part-time as a draftsman, and two of Edward's younger brothers also found employment with the firm. In August 1903, the business was named the American Road Roller Company but was also known as the Wright Roller Company. In September 1903, the Monarch Road Roller Company evolved from the American Road Roller or Wright Roller firm. By June 1905, American Road Roller was in receivership, but the Monarch enterprise continued.

In 1914, the Monarch Road Roller Company was absorbed by the Good Roads Machinery Company, which called its manufacturing branch the American Road Machinery Company. Groton served as the company's manufacturing center, and the American Road Machinery Company corporate headquarters were located at Kennett Square, Pennsylvania, to be near New Jersey, with that state's powerful movement for good roads. The words "Good Roads" were cast into the valve chest cover on Monarch tandem rollers. The Monarch name was retained on the firm's rollers until the Groton plant closed in 1925.

With its tarpaulin rolled up along the perimeter of the canopy, this Groton road locomotive is ready for work.

This engine is the product of the Groton Bridge and Manufacturing Company.

Harrison Machine Works

Thomas Kirshman, who went by the nickname "Uncle Tom," worked for Harrison Machine Works of Belleville, Illinois, and his likeness was immortalized in a caricature drawn by an artist employed by Harrison. The Indiana Manufacturing Company acquired the caricature when it bought Uncle Tom's patent for a windstacker from Harrison. Uncle Tom had invented the idea of having the straw go through the fan, and Harrison had been producing so-called "Uncle Tom's stackers." The Indiana Manufacturing Company purchased several additional patents so as to have a monopoly on the best form of windstacker. The Indiana Manufacturing Company did not build windstackers but licensed other manufacturers to equip their threshing machines with them. The purchase agreement with Harrison permitted the Belleville works to waive the Indiana Company's customary licensing fee. Uncle Tom died in 1905, but his image peers out from within a circular transfer attached to thousands of windstackers across North America.

John Cox and Cyrus Roberts began building groundhog threshers in Belleville in 1848, and in 1855 Theophilus Harrison bought an interest in the firm. William C. Buchanan became a partner in Harrison and Company two years later. In 1874, probably in response to the panic of 1873, Cyrus Thompson, Hugh W. Harrison, and Lee Harrison became connected to the business of the Harrison Machine Works, which incorporated in 1878. The principal stockholders were Theophilus Harrison, Hugh W. Harrison, Buchanan, and Thompson.

Phineas Taylor Barnum (better known as P. T.) attempted to purchase an immensely popular elephant from the London Zoological Society in 1881. Based on an African word for elephant, Jumbo was the name chosen for the pachyderm. The zoo surprisingly accepted Barnum's offer, and Barnum fanned the flames of anticipation as Americans awaited Jumbo's arrival. Souvenirs depicting Jumbo sprang up like peanuts. Thousands turned out to meet Jumbo's ship in New York on April 9, 1882. While buying and transporting Jumbo cost Barnum a fortune, he recouped his expenses in the first 10 days of exhibiting the elephant. Jumbo rode in a private railway car from city to city and was easily the most famous animal in the world. In 1885 in St. Thomas, Ontario, a locomotive struck and killed Jumbo. His likeness lived on, cast into the circular valve chest cover of early Harrison engines, which were named after the celebrated mammal.

The Harrison Machine Works built the boilers for the firm's Jumbo engines. The smokeboxes were strapped to the boilers and could easily be removed. Jumbos boasted a two-speed device. Larry G. Creed uncovered the facts that Harrison built its first steam engine in 1874 and that the firm's first traction engine appeared in 1881. The latter steamer's drive consisted of a chain and sprocket gear. A gear drive was introduced in 1885.

Creed has reported that Harrison engine sales were robust from 1898 until 1916, when sales began to decline. As Joe Park and Joe Graziana have suggested, a depressed farm economy in 1926 threatened the firm. Despite a grim financial forecast (or perhaps in response to it), the company purchased four acres on East Main Street in 1927 and built a new plant, which opened the following year. Only a handful of steamers were sold from 1928 through 1937—a far cry from an early 1900s catalog proclaiming

Here is an example of threshing from the "beehive" stacks in the field. Note the smokestack running through the steamdome. This was done in an effort to produce a drier steam.

Note the image of Jumbo the elephant cast into the steamchest cover and the fancy bracket supporting the front water tank of this Harrison Jumbo steam engine.

that there were 250 working Harrison threshing rigs in St. Clair County, Illinois, alone.

A catalog from the early 1900s predicted, "Statistics show that the percentage of gas tractors sold yearly is many times that of steam tractors, but so far gas power has not, and probably will not, replace steam power for many purposes. For threshing, sawing, and general traction work where water and fuel are plentiful, steam is the most satisfactory and economical power." History failed to support Harrison's sunny forecast.

An article in the July and August 1962 issue of *The Iron-Men Album Magazine*, which was quite possibly the first to be devoted entirely to restoration, focused on salvaging an 1882 10-horsepower Harrison (serial number 714) from Howell Island near St. Louis, Missouri. That venerable machine featured a steamdome surrounding the smokestack.

This old Harrison has fenders on the driver wheels.

Heilman Machine Works

In 1982, Mary Rose Heilman Johnson published a limited edition of the memoirs of her grandfather, the Evansville, Indiana, industrialist William Heilman.[1] Steam-engine enthusiasts recognize Heilman as the manufacturer of Heilman agricultural engines. Only a few examples exist in preservation, with perhaps no more than two Heilman steamers remaining in Indiana. At the time of this writing, Al New of Pendleton owns a 16-horsepower Heilman built in 1910, and Bernie Eisert of Buffalo has the Heilman that once belonged to Frank Miller of LaCrosse. Despite the rarity of such engines today, the man for whom they were named contributed prominently to the early history of steam power on American farms. Heilman's memoir was written while on a vacation trip to Germany in 1887 and records his daring business decisions set against the backdrop of significant national events, including the Civil War. Heilman's reminiscences contrast sharply with those of A. B. Farquhar. Where the latter is flamboyant, as one might expect of a mogul, Heilman is understated. They represent extremes in nineteenth-century business profiles.

On October 11, 1824, William Heilman was born in Albig Rheinhessen, Germany. His father, Valentine Heilman, was a farmer and died in 1826, when William was a child. Mrs. Heilman later married Peter Weintz. William and his stepfather, mother, two brothers, and three sisters emigrated from Germany to the United States in 1843. William was 19 years old. The family landed at New Orleans and spent a short time in St. Louis. The Heilmans and Peter Weintz settled on a 120-acre farm in Posey County, Indiana, 10 miles from Evansville on the New Harmony Road. William learned how to speak and write the English language on his own and never took a lesson.

Peter died in 1846, and William's mother inherited the farm. Soon after Peter's death, Christian Kratz married Heilman's sister Mary. Christian had been working in Louisville as a stove molder. He recommended that the farm be sold and a foundry started in Evansville. William favored the idea. In August 1847, William's mother sold the farm to Martin Mann for $2,800. In a public sale, certain personal property brought $900. Each of the three brothers received $500, each of the three sisters received $300, and their mother kept the extra money.

Christian had saved $300, and with Mary's $300 and William's $500, Christian and William entered into a partnership to build a foundry and machine shop in Evansville, then a city with a population of 4,000. William considered Evansville's location at the terminus of the Wabash and Erie Canal to be an advantage. Evansville also boasted a branch of the State Bank of Indiana, which was incorporated in 1836. On September 10, 1847, William and Christian bought a lot for $400, paying $100 down and spreading the remainder over three years.

The partners hewed timber on what William called "old man Kratz's farm" in German Township.[2] German friends hauled the lumber at no charge. Christian and William put up a log frame foundry and molding shop. They built stoves and hollowware with power supplied by two blind horses. "Certainly a slow way," commented Heilman. The partners soon employed six men.

In April 1848, they started a retail and wholesale stove store with a tinshop on Main Street. They made their own stove trimmings and tinware. With remarkable timing and more than their share of good luck, William and Christian watched as their business sharply increased. As chance would have it, a large wave of German immigrants in the spring of 1848 brought a sudden demand for stoves. Heilman recalled, "They were sold as fast as we could remove the molding sand. In fact, we did not have the time to put the black finish on them."[3]

On June 28, 1848, William married Mary Jenner. She was born in Erdmannhausen Obermat Marback Wurtemberg, Germany, on February 24, 1830. Heilman wrote, "We were not born rich, but both of us were blessed with healthy constitutions and a determined will to make life a success of comfort and happiness."[4] They rented rooms for $3 a month upstairs in a frame house between Main and Locust on First Street, but they resided there only one month.

On July 6, 1848, tragedy struck. William's brother Michael, who at 22 was two years younger then William, was kicked by one of the company's horses and died on July 9. Heilman's diary refers to Michael as "my only brother," and it is not clear whether William means that another brother preceded Michael in death or that his other brother was the son of Peter Weintz.

In any case, it was only four days after Michael's death that William bought the south quarter of a lot fronting on Pine Street at an administrator sale. The lot had a small frame house (No. 343), and William and Mary soon moved in and lived there for eight years. The structure was relocated "a half dozen times from one place to another about our yards and shops, but we always stayed in it," Heilman said.[5]

William's future success depended on a timely, generous loan. "I could never forget when I walked up and down the streets of Evansville in the early years of my business to obtain a bank loan for $650. I met Willard Carpenter and asked him if he would endorse my note. He said, 'Certainly I will endorse it for a working man like you.' And I got the money for a barge of coke."[6]

Early in the spring of 1850, William and Christian erected a 50x75-foot brick finishing shop in the hope of one day manufacturing steam engines and mill machinery. They borrowed money from a bank to pay for lathes and other tools on credit. They hired patternmakers to design a line of upright sawmills, which were "very much in demand at that time."[7]

William described the effort it took to provide power for their new shop: "We built the engine ourselves and bought a tubular upright boiler from a German patentee named William Miller." The boiler measured 50 inches in diameter and stood 8 feet tall. It had 16 flues, each 5 inches in diameter, "hanging down into the furnace." Heilman commented, "It made steam pretty easy as long as it was clean, but when the flues became clogged, the devil was up. The burned flues would explode and put out the fire." Such delays were "ruinous."[8]

Other factory owners in what was then the West used boilers without tubes, and Heilman said that half a dozen woodchoppers were needed to keep such boilers fired. "Most of the millers and manufacturers that used them broke up," Heilman commented. Before long, William and Christian replaced their vertical boiler with a two-flue boiler "and got along a little better."

The water supply, however, left plenty to be desired: "We used the water from an ordinary well dug with curbing all the way down about 65 feet deep sand, and a good part of it quicksand, walled with brick about 5 feet wide. We had to pack the pumps four and five times daily with new leather valves. They pumped up sand so much so that it undermined the buildings, and we went to the expense of about $3,000 and laid pipes to the canal. In a short time the canal was neglected and was not kept up, and all this expense was a loss." The partners dug another well outside the buildings, but the trouble recurred. When drive wells were invented, they had no more difficulty with the water supply.

Heilman and Kratz built many sawmills. Olmsteads and Van Duzon on Pigeon Creek sawed 2,500 feet of poplar lumber a day with one of them. Such productivity was considered extraordinary back then.

The year 1850 proved extremely profitable. The following year, Christian and William added a two-chute hand corn sheller to their product list. "We sold many in St. Louis and along the Ohio and Mississippi Rivers," Heilman wrote. The partners hired more employees, bought more land, and borrowed more money. William remarked, "We could have done . . . a much larger business if we had been able to put more money into it."[9] Christian and William saved rent by building a one-story frame house for the Kratzes and William's mother.

In 1851, the partners bought land on Main Street near Second and put up a three-story brick store building to accommodate their booming stove trade. In February 1852, Heilman journeyed to Lowell, Massachusetts, and bought a large lathe and planer, as well as numerous smaller tools. He and Christian added a 50x75-foot expansion to the finishing shop, doubling its size, and a third story over the entire building. They also established a boiler yard where they began to manufacture their own boilers, "a business heretofore unknown in Evansville."[10] Heilman reflected, "Our business brought money to Evansville" that had been going to Cincinnati and Pittsburgh, "and our banks and citizens began to feel the favorable effects."[11]

A fact of special interest to steam aficionados is that in 1854, Heilman and Kratz's City Foundry and Machine Works built the firm's first portable steam engine. At about the same time, Heilman did $25,000 worth of work for a rich man, R. A. Alexander, a Scotsman who founded a blast-furnace and iron-making business in Muhlenberg County, Kentucky. Heilman lamented, "It was a great loss to our section of country not finding iron ore in large enough deposits to make it pay him to work the mines. . . . Had he been successful, it would have been of immense value to Evansville."[12]

Kratz and Heilman realized vast profits in 1855. The cost of pig iron rose during the same year. Heilman always said that the value of pig iron was a sure economic indicator—a trustworthy predictor of the financial future—and he kept a close eye on the rise and fall of pig iron prices and based many of his business decisions on what he saw.

The Indiana legislature chartered a new state bank in 1855. Heilman and Kratz's company paid Democratic politicians $14,000 for the charter to create the Evansville branch. When it began doing business on January 1, 1856, William became a director of the new bank. Heilman commented, "My ability to handle our finances undoubtedly had qualified me to be selected as a director in the bank of the state of Indiana. I worked seriously for the interests of that bank. I brought them many good customers and depositors and linked my fortune with that bank and its successors."[13] Meanwhile, Heilman built a two-story brick house for his family on the corner of Pine and First Street in 1856. Financially, Heilman and Kratz were enjoying "very brisk times." As Heilman summarized, "The money was pushed from one hand into the other. Everybody had money."[14]

William and Christian built large engines and boilers for a cotton mill in Alabama owned by the president of the Memphis & Charleston Rail Road. Through the contacts of an Evansville resident who had been born and raised in Paris, Tennessee, Heilman and Kratz developed Southern business connections. Kratz and Heilman attracted skilled mechanics from Cincinnati, Madison, and Louisville. At one point, a group from Madison built a competing foundry and machine shop in Evansville, but the venture failed.

It was a time of inflated currency. The free banking system permitted "sharpers," as Heilman called them, to establish banks at any crossroads and in any small town, particularly in the Northern states. Currency from such banks flooded into villages and cities, including Evansville. "It made business very lively while it lasted," Heilman wrote.[15] The antidote was swift and painful: the panic of 1857. All at once, business centers north of the Mason–Dixon line filled with carpetbaggers trying to redeem wads of paper money. Banks failed and commerce came to a standstill. Meanwhile, companies in the South "were affected very little by the Wildcat Bank System of the Northern states," Heilman said. William and Christian quickly arranged a lively trade with Southern businessmen; the Evansville firm turned out steamboat machinery and millwork destined for Southern cities. Heilman and Kratz survived the rough economic weather: "We experienced close times during the panic but got along fairly well. . . . We had some limited accommodations at the banks which helped us through the storm."[16]

The machinery department had grown into the leading branch of the Heilman and Kratz firm by 1858. In the early spring of 1859, Christian and William erected a three-story shop on First Street and quit making stoves and tinware. The partners decided to begin building threshing machines modeled on the Pitts patent, a design invented by brothers Hiram A. and John A. Pitts of Winthrop, Maine. After moving into the new shop, Heilman and Kratz rented their retail store on Main Street, and sold it a year later. Meanwhile, they brought out their first threshing machine in 1859.

The year of 1860 "began with great political excitement," Heilman wrote.

> "The Democratic Party had for the last twenty years been controlled by the pro-slavery wing of their party. The anti-slavery and abolition party in the North had educated the free laboring masses against abominable slavery. They were especially successful in winning over the laboring masses since the pro-slavery Democratic wing insisted on carrying slavery into Kansas and Nebraska, two of our territories forming new states. At their national convention, the Democrats split and could not agree on a platform. The consequence was that the Northern and conservative wing of the Democratic Party met in convention at Baltimore and nominated Stephen A. Douglass.

The pro-slavery wing met at Charleston, South Carolina, and nominated Jeff Davis. The great conservative masses of the North had formed a new party called the Republican Party. They met in national convention and nominated Abraham Lincoln of Illinois. The old Whig Party, which continued to hold on, met and proposed to save the country by nominating John Bell of Tennessee. . . . The great Republican Party had its best speakers in the field and presented a solid front and carried almost solidly the laboring vote of the North. They formed large Wide Awake Clubs all over the country, uniformed with oil-cloth capes and caps. These clubs worked zealously for the ticket. When the fall elections came, all the Northern states but a few cast their votes for the rail splitter Abraham Lincoln, and he was elected President of the United States. . . . When the different state elections of the Northern states came along, they elected Republican state officers in many of the states such as had not been done for twenty-five years and more. These elections indicated . . . that the Northern people were aroused at the outrage of making our Northern territories slave states. They would not submit to it, and the people so decided by an unmistakable vote. . . . After the election of Mr. Lincoln, the Southern states began to talk about war and secession; matters began to look very blue, and a war between the North and South looked . . . inevitable. . . . Everything was done by the well-meaning statesmen to avoid a war, but it seemed like an impossibility. . . . James Buchanan, when president, declared there was no power in the Constitution of the United States to prevent the Southern states from seceding."[17]

Perhaps Heilman's strong support of Lincoln stemmed from the fact that, between the years 1816 (when Indiana became a state) and 1830, the Lincoln family had lived on Little Pigeon Creek at a point only 30 miles northeast of Evansville. William may have perceived a commonality with others who, like the Lincolns, tamed the wilderness in southern Indiana.

Heilman recalled that during Lincoln's election, business came to a virtual halt. All employees of Heilman and Kratz's company voted a straight Republican ticket. In 1860, an unusually good wheat crop in the United States, especially in Wisconsin and Minnesota, helped boost the Evansville partners' business at a critical crossroads in American history. "We sold all the threshing machines we had on hand and could make until very late in the season to the northwestern states. It helped us very much to keep our men employed during the election excitement. Most of the other establishments had little to do." During the first months of 1861, money quit changing hands. Southerners often refused to pay Northern creditors. Many of Heilman and Kratz's Southern accounts were never paid.

"At last the fourth of March came," Heilman said, "and Mr. Lincoln was sworn in as President of the United States."[18] As Heilman put it, "A new day began to dawn." After soldiers were called to volunteer, business began to improve. The government issued notes and greenbacks to pay for the army's needs. Money became more plentiful and caused business to pick up "as soon as the people saw and felt that we had a government that was trying to sustain and protect itself." The moneyed interests "had confidence in Mr. Lincoln"; therefore, the government could borrow at low rates.[19]

Heilman said, "I contributed my services to the war as much as I could. I employed so many people by doing work for the government that I could not leave my business and join the army. I made many recruits and furnished them means and assisted them in whatever they needed and in whatever their families needed."[20]

In 1861, the harvest was bountiful, people in the North felt hopeful, labor was in demand, wages were advancing, foreign export was strong, and farmers paid for the Heilman and Kratz threshing machines they had purchased. William and Christian had money once again by the fall and winter of 1861. "New saw and grist mills were needed everywhere to supply the army," Heilman recalled.[21]

In the territories conquered by Union troops, Southerners built distilleries. "In the two years from the beginning of the war we sold more distillery machinery and copper stills than we did in the ten years before the war," Heilman wrote. During this time, Heilman and Kratz received mostly cash on delivery.

The year 1862 also proved a prosperous one for Northern businesses. "We worked our full force and had all we could do," Heilman remembered. Congress, meanwhile, imposed taxes, including a 5 percent income tax on manufactured goods and 3 percent tax on repairs. Heilman noticed that the price of pig iron was going up. He also discovered that many bankers, especially those of German descent, were investing in government bonds. William paid off several debts and followed suit by putting his spare money in bonds.

"This year," Heilman said, referring to 1863, "started in with terrible cold weather, and there was a very hard-fought battle at Murfreesboro, Tennessee."[22] In September,

"the terrible battle of Lookout Mountain or Chickamauga was fought. It proved to be a standoff battle with very heavy losses on both sides. By this time it was evident that something was wrong in carrying on this war. It could be plainly seen that God the Almighty was not with it. A terror struck the nation."[23]

Heilman credited Lincoln's Emancipation Proclamation with reversing the momentum and inspiring more terror in the South than was felt in the North. The South "began to falter," Heilman claimed. "From this time on the fate of the rebellion was obvious."

Business continued to be strong in 1864. William and Christian erected a new 75x100-foot brick foundry molding shop that could cast anything, "up into the tons."[24] Unfortunately, a dispute erupted among the workers at Heilman and Kratz's factory. "We had a little trouble with our help but soon settled the matter by giving them an increase in wages." One wonders if the unrest among the employees might have led to a disagreement between William and Christian, but whatever the cause, on September 20, 1864, Christian told William that he wanted out of the partnership. An audit revealed that the company held $250,000 in assets and was carrying $50,000 in liabilities, which was down from the $105,000 in liabilities at the start of the Civil War. Once Christian verified that he was not backing out of the partnership to gain exclusive ownership of the business, William wanted a day to decide what he would do. The next day, William consented "to take the business."[25]

Christian received outside real estate and city property worth $30,000 in government bonds, as well as $35,000 in cash. Heilman also provided notes payable over five years. Each note was for $8,000 at 6 percent interest and totaled $40,000. The grand total of Kratz's share was $105,000.

For the first time in 17 years, William ran the business his own way. Heilman found that he could pay his $40,000 in notes in only 18 months, rather than 5 years. Heilman accepted the company stock at an assessed value higher than he considered reasonable, but business was good. He sold the stock at the high prevailing prices of the day. In the meantime, the Civil War came to an end. As Heilman phrased it, "the life was beaten out of the rebellion."[26]

Heilman briefly described the shocking event that ended a chapter in American history: "On April 14, 1865, Wilkes Booth shot and killed President Abe Lincoln in the theatre in Washington, D.C. The country was horror-stricken at this outrage. But the life of the nation did not depend on a single man, and there was nothing to gain as far as the rebels were concerned." At the end of the war, the government disbursed a great deal of money to stimulate business.

In 1865, Heilman began to invest in the gas company and he bought real estate. Christian Kratz started a small foundry and machine shop, but it was unprofitable and failed. In 1866, Heilman's inventory showed he had earned $100,000 in a year and a half. He was worth $200,000. William built a new threshing machine shop, a new blacksmith shop, a new steam boiler yard, and a large addition to the finishing shop. The work was completed by December. He sold his older three-story buildings to a firm wanting to establish a cotton-weaving mill. William was to become the principal owner of the new factory. The deal included machinery and shafting for $40,000. Heilman bought old equipment in Cannelton, Indiana, for $10,000, and enhanced it with a few new machines.

Early in the spring of 1867, the cotton mill began to make yarns and brown sheeting, but its capacity was too small to earn a profit. William rearranged the shops at his new factory to increase production. His firm was doing a lively business in distillery and copper work, as well as sheet-iron work. The company was simultaneously "building a large number of portable engines of all sizes."[27] In general, Heilman manufactured agricultural implements timed to be sold in the appropriate seasons and produced other machines and items throughout the year, thereby keeping business steady.

Heilman said, "The business was now as large as I cared about having it, and I decided I had enough invested." For $12,500, William bought the largest lots on the highest ground in the city (306x425 feet) to establish a magnificent residence. He had considered building his home on Pigeon Creek but chose the city location for the conveniences of gas, water, and good schools. Heilman commented that he had made the mistake of putting over $6,000 into remodeling his old house, "which soon proved to be inadequate for my family."[28] He visited elegant homes in other cities to develop a clear picture of what he wanted in a new mansion. Heilman apparently shared Andrew Carnegie's view: "It is well, nay, essential for the progress of the race, that the houses of some should be homes for all that is highest and best in literature and the arts, and for all the refinements of civilization, rather than that none should be so."[29]

The architects built his palatial Italian Renaissance home in 1868, and he and his family moved in on November 15, 1869.[30] The new house cost more than $50,000, according to Heilman's memoirs, but other sources put the cost several thousand dollars higher. William justified the expense by saying, "It was a great deal to pay for a residence, but there is nothing like a good healthy home." Nine of his children were living. One had died at five months; another, at three years of age. The new residence had plenty of space for Heilman's large family; the second story alone held 13 rooms.

Among the mansion's appointments were two kitchens, one a story above the other; a billiard room beside a refreshment room; Italian marble mantels; stained glass entry doors protected by storm doors when necessary; a skylight of leaded stained glass above a two-story grand staircase; 14-foot ceilings on the first floor with 12-foot windows; two-tone doors composed of ash, chestnut, and black walnut; a glass conservatory filled with exotic flowers and ferns; fresco work on the walls and ceilings of all the principal rooms; two bathrooms on the second floor and one on the first; a sitting room decorated with blue velvet furniture and silver ornamentation; a drawing room done in pale green and salmon tones; pastel and gold Brussels carpets; Dresden and Meissen figurines; Bristol vases; Staffordshire urns; five complete sets of French and English china; Austrian white satin damask banquet tablecloths; and numerous paintings. Heilman had hired the A. B. Closson Company of Cincinnati to furnish the entire house, from the artwork, through the furniture, to the crystal. The majestic results had been shipped to Evansville in crates carried by steamboats. Visitors' carriages entered a circular drive that afforded a splendid view of the mansion before arriving at the entryway. From the observatory on the roof, guests admired the grounds, including two fountains in front of the home and one in back, a large gazebo, and a carriage house with eight rooms to house the help. Heilman's conveyances included a carriage with white harness. The mansion required 1,000 feet of gas pipe and 2,500 feet of water pipe. Seven cisterns surrounded the house for fire protection. Attention was paid to every detail. For example, cedar strips were inserted into the baseboards to keep moths out of the carpets. A boiler and steam engine provided heat to the home.

William and his wife bought interests in the Evansville Land Association, the Street Railway Company, the Evansville National Bank, the gas company, and the cotton mill. At the time when Heilman was building his mansion, the "critical time had now come." Prudent businessmen husbanded their means. "I was well invested and had a large income," Heilman said, "and business was good."[31] Values declined, and those who were overly invested "were getting pinched pretty hard. . . . Merchants who were not careful buyers lost fortunes because of high prices they paid," Heilman wrote.[32]

Heilman's firm sold a great deal of machinery in the South, especially in Texas. *The Evansville Journal* for 1869 carried advertisements for Heilman's cotton and tobacco presses. "Profits were still very large on sawmills and portable engines," Heilman said.[33] A salesman named Captain

This dual-chain-driven Heilman is rumored to be the first Heilman traction engine ever produced.

Jones drummed up Southern business.

Beginning in 1852, Heilman had served several terms on the city council and was elected to the Indiana legislature on the Republican ticket in 1870. The Republican Party swept Vanderburgh County that year to bring about "a complete change of our delegation in the legislature."[34]

By this time Heilman was a corpulent man and had long enjoyed cigars. "After I was married in 1848, I began to smoke and became an inveterate smoker. I was encouraged to smoke cigars by John Gilman, whose house I bought on Main Street. I let him stay in the house to close out his hat store. He smoked all the time and averaged about twenty-four cigars a day. It killed him before his time." Heilman averaged 16 cigars—the best Havana and imported varieties—per day for the 23 years that he smoked. William smoked so much that he could not see and suffered terrible headaches "so that I could not go to sleep at night unless I used a wet towel to steady my nerves."[35] In the first days of April 1871, he had dental work, which he had neglected "under the pressure of business." The dentist filled the hole where the cigars had always fit. "After my tooth had been filled, I put a cigar in my mouth and it did not fit any more. I could not possibly smoke. I threw it away. I lighted a second one shortly thereafter but there was no go; it did not fit anymore." Heilman never smoked again. He remarked, "There are ever so many people in this world who cannot control themselves." Heilman was not one of them.

In 1872, Heilman was nominated for the U. S. Congress. Despite the fact that his district was Democratic and the press viciously attacked him, he lost by only 112 votes.

In 1873, the cotton mill stockholders decided to erect a larger mill with increased production and profit. The new facility was to produce 25,000 yards of cotton sheeting per day. The stockholders bought 10 acres of land where they could have access to gas and water but would not have to pay city taxes. Over 4 million bricks were baked on Heilman ground, and the building eventually cost $100,000.

"In September 1873, Jay Cooke and Company, who had been for many years the financial agents of the U.S. government, failed. They had undertaken to build the Northern Pacific Railroad and got swamped with it; the load was too heavy, and it took too much money," Heilman added. "After Jay Cooke . . . had failed, it looked pretty scary to build a new mill."[36] Congress passed a law for specie resumption that would take effect five years later; this act eased the minds of people in business. Heilman responded by buying more stock in the cotton mill. An expanding Canadian market for the goods from his engine and thresher factory made William less vulnerable to American economic woes.

In 1875, William went east to buy cotton mill machines from the Lowell Machine Shop. The new cotton mill began operations in early November of that year. The money came from a $90,000 loan from the Evansville National Bank. Stock shares were valued at $250,000. Charles E. Robert's *Evansville: Her Commerce and Manufactures*, published in 1874, reported that the Heilman plant extended from First to Second Street along Pine Street and had three fronts three stories high. A Heilman 40-horsepower stationary engine with a 20-inch stroke and a 12-inch bore supplied the power for the factory. Robert stated that the firm employed between 175 and 200 men and that it sold 500 portable steam engines.

Upon the death of the president of the Evansville Gas Light Company, William was elected to fill the vacancy. He bought the majority of the stock and established a board of directors. On October 15, 1876, the cotton mill was enlarged and new bonds were issued through the Evansville National Bank. "This let us out of the woods completely, and we had the money to pay all our debts and carry on the business to its fullest capacity," Heilman remembered. "To make a success of this big enterprise, undertaken in this most critical time," Heilman continued, "was a great satisfaction to me."[37] He built tenements to house the workers at the mill.

The centennial year of 1876 also marked Heilman's election to the Indiana state senate. Heilman gave President Rutherford B. Hayes and Secretary of the Treasury John Sherman much of the credit for materially improving business conditions in the United States during 1877. In that year, Heilman entered into partnership with Major Albert C. Rosencranz, the husband of Heilman's daughter Mary, in the Heilman-Urie Plow Company. The name changed to the Heilman Plow Company in 1879.[38] Rosencranz stayed with the firm for many years. For some reason, Heilman's memoirs did not specifically mention the plow works.

The Paris Exposition was held in 1878, and Heilman took the opportunity to tour the fair and also visit several European countries. He wanted to go to his homeland, which he had not seen for 35 years. While he was in Liverpool, he received a telegram announcing that the Republican Party had again nominated him for the U. S. Congress. Heilman accepted the nomination and continued on his travels through England, France, Switzerland, and Germany. Upon his return to Evansville, he campaigned hard and won the election.

Heilman's first session in the Congress of the United States "lasted about ninety days as we had many fellows in this Congress that were windbags and liked to hear themselves talk." On the positive side, "Gold and silver that had been hidden when the war began started to surface again," said Heilman.[39] By 1880, "We had, with the coin that had been locked up for so many years, from 300 to 400 million more money in circulation."[40] Of course, pig iron prices advanced again.

The Democrats added Pike County to Heilman's district in an attempt to defeat Heilman in the next election, but he won anyway. Heilman served a total of four years in Congress.

In 1881, Heilman made the mistake of joining a railroad investment plan that consolidated a local railway with the Louisville, New Albany, and St. Louis Railroad. "This was one of the most foolish trades we ever made," Heilman commented. "Our property was worth double [the amount received through the consolidation]. I could never see for the life of me why we did it, excepting to get a railroad to Louisville."[41]

"Some of the richest men in Boston" helped to finance the consolidated railway. They put a second mortgage on the road but still had too little money to meet the construction costs. The group went bankrupt. The stock that

Heilman and others had in the company was declared worthless. David J. Mackey, a stockholder in the cotton mill, gave up a successful dry goods business to step in as president of the railroad. Through careful management, he financially rescued the line.

Heilman owned 2,000 shares in the railroad. In 1881, he sold 1,000 shares at $65 a share, which was believed to be a good price at the time. In 1882, the value increased to $85 per share. Heilman reflected, "A man can't always strike the highest prices."[42]

In 1882, Heilman sold all of the threshing machines and portable engines his firm had manufactured for the year. He had a strong interest in the Heilman Roller Flour Mills. He built a large hominy mill, which became a success. The cotton mill made a strong profit, and another $125,000 was pumped into improvements in the factory to boost daily production to 35,000 yards of sheeting. This action stretched the stockholders as they paid out all the mill's money, which left no working capital. Money was borrowed and the interest ate into the profits.

In 1884, "[t]he stars began to shine much brighter," as Heilman put it.[43] Heilman sold some of his gas and electric stock and bought an additional 3,200 shares worth $160,000 in the Evansville and Terre Haute Railroad, giving him 5,200 shares in all at a value of $260,000. He retained 2,000 shares in the gas and electric company, good for $100,000. He incorporated the foundry and machine shop and received $200,000 in notes at 6 percent interest for portions of stock he sold to others. Heilman assigned to his son William Alexander 200 shares; thus he was relieved "from all care and attention as far as the foundry business was concerned."[44] The business was now in the hands of a corporation. Heilman continued to be the majority stockholder in the company.

After the inauguration of Grover Cleveland in 1885, "values declined very materially, especially farmers' products," Heilman recalled. Wheat and corn prices dipped low. The cotton mill earned very little in 1885 and 1886. Heilman's railroad stock, though, climbed in worth to $300,000. In 1886, he sold 1,300 shares for a profit of $52,000. "Matters were now moving in the right direction," Heilman remarked.[45] Heilman and others bought portions of railways and assembled an improved Evansville & Indianapolis Railroad, "one of the best coal roads in this state," according to Heilman.

In 1886, Heilman and others acquired the Peoria, Decatur & Evansville Railroad. They invested $1,359,000 in it. At the annual election, the railroad was turned over to the friends of the Evansville & Terre Haute (E&TH) Railroad by making six of the nine directors E&TH men. "We increased the earnings of the road considerably and earned the confidence of the stockholders," Heilman recalled. Seeing stock values of the E&TH Railroad increase, Heilman sold all of his except a thousand shares and put the profit into the Peoria, Decatur & Evansville line.

Heilman's foundry was yielding an annual 22 percent investment profit. His flour and hominy mills "did well, although grain was cheap and work had to be done at lower prices."[46] The hominy mill ran around the clock and daily produced 1,200 to 1,400 barrels. The cotton mill profits went up in 1887. Heilman increased his life insurance to $95,000. He explained, "I think it is the duty of every man at the head of a family to carry as much insurance as his means will allow."

In May 1887, Heilman, his wife, and two of their children visited Europe. On June 28, 1887, the Heilmans celebrated their 39th wedding anniversary. Seven of their children were already married and were "all well to do." William felt free of what he called "business annoyances" while he was overseas. Heilman enjoyed Dresden, the mineral baths in Baden Baden, and the sites around Berlin. Of the latter city, Heilman remarked, "I could content myself to stay here for the balance of my life, provided my wife would. She has the say so about it."[47] When Heilman visited his boyhood home of Albig, he was presented the four specimens of his handwriting that were kept in 1837 and 1838. Students customarily entered specimen writings in a small blank book each month of March. "I am always overcome with the most pleasant sensations when I visit the home of my childhood," Heilman said, "where I received the foundation and education that guided me all my life. To my teacher . . . I owe . . . great respect and my gratitude. He was a noble man, and he made every effort to bring out all the good qualities and talent of each scholar."[48]

While in Germany, Heilman learned that the cotton mill had suddenly made a 28.5 percent profit. On May 23, 1888, the Heilmans returned to the United States after an absence of approximately 11 months. William wrote of the welcome they received: "At home we found everything in the best order and all our children waiting for us. The weather was very fine, and our grounds and house never looked better. All were pleased to meet again, as we had a merry reunion flavored with nature's glorious beauty surrounding us on all sides. Everything was in full bloom on our grounds. All of us were happy."[49]

Republican leaders had often talked of having Heilman run for governor or the U. S. Senate, but William felt that he had already occupied enough political positions. He intended to enjoy his life to the fullest. For him, that meant concentrating on business. The excellent crops of

1888 brought some profit, but Congress bogged down on the issue of free trade. Heilman declared no dividend on the foundry and machine shop that year; however, the cotton mill made 20 percent, and Heilman could declare a 5 percent dividend, the second since July.

Mackey and Heilman greatly expanded their railroad interests in 1889. They formed the Mackey Heilman Syndicate and raised $1,717,487. They paid the Boston stockholders $1,605,487. William commented that his railways "should generate a great deal of money."[50] He negotiated to buy a railroad in Benton Harbor, Michigan, and connect it to an Evansville line at Rushville, Indiana. He said, "These are large undertakings, and we hope to complete them successfully. I am sure that we will realize great benefits from controlling so many miles of railroads to Evansville." That statement was the last one he wrote in his memoirs.

Heilman began to experience an ache deep within him. Heilman was a methodical man and customarily went to bed at eight and arose at four in the morning, but now he could find no comfort in lying on a bed and took naps sitting in a chair. William traveled to the Hotel Del Coronado in California for his health. When he returned to Evansville, he passed away at 6:10 a.m. on September 22, 1890. The cause of death was pancreatic cancer. Mary Heilman died on January 1, 1904.

A survey of the many obituaries published after Heilman's death indicates that, over his lifetime, he lost over a quarter of a million dollars in security debts, trying to help struggling firms to earn a profit. Some companies survived as a result of Heilman's intervention and aid. Many writers noted his confidence and his philanthropy. He was on the board that created the Evansville City Library. He helped start a reformed Lutheran church, but he contributed money to all churches.

Heilman said, "Success must be earned. That was my motto for all I have undertaken."[51] Reflecting on his life, Heilman commented, "Nothing saved me but self-reliance and confidence in my ability to accomplish and bring to success what any other man could. My healthy constitution assisted me; failure never entered my mind."[52] William Heilman's memoirs may serve as a testimony to the power of positive thinking, an echo of the proverb, "Confidence in success is almost success." Heilman possibly was a Gilded Age entrepreneur who, in some ways resembling the heroes of Horatio Alger stories, arose from obscurity to a position of prominence and a lifestyle of opulence—all by trusting in himself. A careful reading of his memoirs, however, reveals that Heilman's achievements grew from his keen understanding of business, his shrewd knowledge of when to change, and his unusually good fortune.

Holt Manufacturing Company

Benjamin Holt (1849–1920) and his brother Charles formed the Stockton Wheel Company in 1883. Three years later, Benjamin Holt produced a combined harvester, or "combine." Holt was testing a steam traction engine by 1890. Holt's firm became incorporated as the Holt Manufacturing Company in 1892.

Holt was convinced that self-laying (or "endless") tracks would help keep a heavy steam-powered engine from miring in the moist peat around Holt's home in Stockton, California. Holt's first successful Caterpillar, the name Holt coined for his machine, crawled into history on November 24, 1904.

In 1908, Holt began switching to gasoline-powered tractors. In 1909, Holt bought out the Colean Manufacturing Company of Peoria, Illinois. Colean built agricultural traction engines. By the end of 1913, the British firm of Richard Hornsby & Sons Ltd. became convinced that a track-laying tractor was

A Holt steam engine with serial number 37 is involved in clean-up operations after the devastating San Francisco earthquake of 1906.

impractical. Hornsby sold Chief Engineer David Roberts' track patents to the Holt Manufacturing Company in 1914. According to F. Hal Higgins, Holt was the first to make the endless track truly practical. Track-laying vehicles played an important role in World War I.

Five years after Benjamin Holt's death, Holt Manufacturing Company merged with its longtime rival, the C. L. Best Tractor Company, to form the Caterpillar Tractor Company, located in Peoria. As Caterpillar is a name known around the world, many websites feature Holt's enterprising contributions to the history of track-laying vehicles.

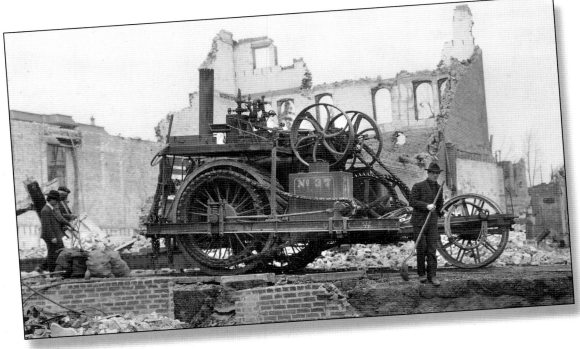

This model of Holt has a silhouette somewhat different from other Holt steamers.

On October 11, 1907, this Holt pulled a combined harvester-thresher owned by Edward Nash.

A big Holt is plowing a big field.

Old Holt serial number 49 is shown with a large load of California lumber while its crew takes a breather.

Huber Manufacturing Company

Edward Huber was born in Dover, Indiana, in 1837. As Alan C. King reported, when Huber was 15 years old, he was apprenticed to the blacksmith who made the hardware for the farm wagons that Huber's father manufactured. Huber felt that he had mastered the art of making wagon hardware after only three weeks. His father purchased a blacksmith shop for Huber to enter into business.

Huber patented a hay rake in 1863, and in 1865, he married Elizabeth Hammerle. Amilia Huber, Edward's sister, had married John K. Hammerle, Elizabeth's brother, who had an interest in a planing mill in Marion, Ohio. Hammerle persuaded Huber to move to Marion. Huber rented shop space within the planing mill building of the Kanable brothers to manufacture his hay rakes made from local hickory and ash lumber. In 1866, Huber served as superintendent of the new firm of Kowalke, Hammerle, Monday, and Huber, which acquired the planing mill from the Kanables. Huber and Lewis Gunn formed a partnership in the mill business in 1870.

By adding the machine shop (formerly a grain elevator) of Holmes & Seffner to the Huber and Gunn holdings, the Huber Manufacturing Company was established in 1874 and was incorporated in January 1875. The firm manufactured hay rakes and road scrapers. Huber patented a return-flue boiler wherein the hot gases from the fire passed from one end of the boiler to the other and back again. The firm began production of steam engines and threshers. Huber and Fred Stroble designed the threshers. The firm eventually built threshers for wheat, oats, barley, beans, peas, and rice. Huber also produced plows.

In 1874, the Huber shops provided the manpower and the financial support to erect Henry Barnhart's first steam shovel, the first such machine built in Marion. When the Marion Steam Shovel Company was assembled, Huber served as its president while Barnhart served as its manager and superintendent.

The firm experienced a rapid expansion and moved to a more spacious location in 1889. In 1898, Huber bought a gasoline-powered tractor patent held by Van Duzen of Cincinnati and produced 30 prototype units. Huber soon became a leader in the gasoline tractor industry.

According to James N. Boblenz, Edward and Elizabeth Huber took a three-month tour of Europe in 1900, including a visit to the Paris Exposition. They encountered rough seas on the return trip. Elizabeth prayed that if the ship were

This little old Huber might best be described as "cute as a bug."

This Huber sports a half canopy and is bedecked with alluring pictures of women on the bunker and on the thresher.

Women with unusual turbans pose with an early Huber traction engine.

spared, she would donate bells to St. Mary Church in Marion. While most residents call them, "St. Mary's bells," Huber descendants call them, "Elizabeth's bells." Edward Huber died in 1904.

By 1907, the daily capacity of the plant was two to four engines and six to eight threshers. Huber manufactured its first steamrollers in 1908. Soon, the company was producing a line of road construction machines, including scrapers. The Huber firm was supplying several models of gasoline tractors by 1910. During World War I, Huber introduced the names Light Four and Super Four—names that remained with Huber tractors for more than 30 years.

With a jack holding the engine in place, this engineer has raised the smokestack and is spinning the crankshaft on this small Huber.

William Howard owned this Huber threshing outfit, which was photographed on September 7, 1909. Note the jugs lined up in front.

This Huber is advertising the 1912 Plainview fair.

In 1938, the Huber firm brought out the Model B tractor, and Huber introduced the Harvest King combine in 1940. During World War II, Huber concentrated its efforts on producing road-building machines for overseas airfields. After the war, Huber continued to devote most of the firm's resources to serving the compaction industry.

Huber eventually dropped its agricultural products. A-T-O Construction Equipment acquired Huber and closed the plant. The Huber Museum on the Marion County Fairgrounds commemorates the firm's achievements.

A coffee break with fresh doughnuts brings everyone into the social circle around the Huber steamer. It was a common scene but was rarely photographed.

This is the unmistakable profile of a Huber.

The engineer of this Huber hauling engine has amassed three cylinder oil cans so as not to run out while pulling the train of cars.

D. June & Company

David June was born in Ithaca, New York, in 1824. In 1833, the June family relocated to Sandusky, Ohio. Young June became a machinist, and he apprenticed with a mechanical engineering company when he was 17. June was the brother-in-law of Charles Waterous, and the two briefly worked together on a railway project. The Cuyahoga Iron Works of Cleveland employed June in 1842. During the next several years, June amassed considerable engineering experience with various steamships.

This chain-driven D. June steam engine offers a silhouette unlike those of other engine makes.

In 1853, June established the firm of June & Curtis to build engines and boilers in the former plow shop of F. I. Norton in Fremont, Ohio. Within six months, Curtis had withdrawn, and Daniel L. June, David's brother, had replaced him. June & June lasted until 1856, when Lyman Gilpin bought Daniel's interest in the firm. Gilpin had relinquished his role in the company by 1859. June repaired several steamship engines in the 1850s. Throughout the Civil War, Curtis was again a partner in the firm but left in 1869. O. S. French joined the company, which began to operate under the name of D. June & Company. The factory was located at the foot of Garrison Street in Fremont, Ohio.

Beginning in 1877, D. June & Company built a vertical-boilered engine known as the Champion. June gave the Champion patent rights for Canada to Waterous, who began production in 1877. Waterous' firm built only 9 engines that first year, but the company manufactured 210 engines by 1880. Waterous eventually produced some 2,500 Champions. Waterous began mounting the Champion engine on a horizontal return-flue boiler in 1890.

A typical advertisement for the D. June Champion announced, "The new fire-proof traction farm engine manufactured by D. June & Co., Fremont, Ohio. Over 1,000 are now in use, and can be run with perfect safety in cotton-gin house or barn."

D. June later added a horizontal-boilered engine called simply the D. June Traction Engine. The first steamer LeRoy Blaker owned was a D. June engine with a horizontal boiler. Blaker helped found the National Threshers Association, host of the longest continuously operating steam show in the United States. Blaker said that in 1907, Wood Brothers bought out D. June and from the start, Wood Brothers engines retained D. June's curved-spoke flywheel, grouter design, and star trademark cast in the ssmokebox door.

This wood-lagged D. June steamer is engaged in barn threshing in Arthur Township, Ontario. Photo by J. S. Byers, Rochester, New York, 1890; Courtesy Robert T. Rhode

Keck-Gonnerman Company

In 1873, brothers John C. Woody and Winfield T. Woody began a foundry business in Mount Vernon, Indiana. Winfield died in 1877, and John Keck bought Winfield's interest in the firm. Illness forced John C. Woody's retirement in 1880, and John Onk of Louisville, Kentucky, purchased Woody's interest in the foundry. Keck & Onk planned to manufacture hollowware, but when Onk returned to Louisville, William Gonnerman became a partner in the Keck-Gonnerman Company. The firm started manufacturing engines, threshers, and sawmills in 1884. In 1885, Louis H. Keck, John's brother, joined the company, which was incorporated in 1901. As president,

This Keck-Gonnerman threshing rig has stopped to pose momentarily en route to the next farm.

A side-geared Keck-Gonnerman with serial number 714 poses in a barnyard.

Keck-Gonnerman also built rear-geared steamers.

Keck-Gonnerman

A Keck-Gonnerman steam
tractor rests as a young
woman uses her pet dog to
impress the crowd.

This is a brand-spanking-new, double-cylinder Keck-Gonnerman! According to the Warren County, Indiana, Historical Society, this photograph was taken
in Williamsport, Indiana.

This 1912 photograph, taken in Elberfeld, Indiana, shows George Menke's 18-horsepower, double rear-geared Keck-Gonnerman taking on water. George was a longtime Keck-Gonnerman employee. Courtesy Tom Hart

The crew of this Keck-Gonnerman engine, serial number 1304, stops for a photo opportunity. Note the boy entrepreneur selling Grit, a money-making venture in the early 1900s. Courtesy Tom Hart

A promotional postcard depicts this rather rare 1908 Keck-Gonnerman engine: a 20-horsepower double side-geared steamer known as the Springfield Fair Engine. Courtesy Tom Hart

John Keck focused on purchases and sales. Gonnerman, the vice president, centered his efforts on manufacturing. As secretary-treasurer, Louis H. Keck devoted himself to office management. Sons of all three men later joined the firm.

The company began to produce mining machinery in 1904, and its location in a city on the Ohio River brought Keck-Gonnerman steamboat repair business as well.

When Dr. Robert T. Rhode's mother was a girl growing up in Mount Vernon, she and her siblings played on Keck-Gonnerman steamers in the factory yard after quitting

time. She had a fondness for Keck-Gonnerman engines ever after.

In 1918, Keck-Gonnerman began to build 12–24-horsepower gasoline tractors in addition to the company's steam engines. In 1920, the firm introduced the 15–30-horsepower tractor to replace the 12–24 model. Keck-Gonnerman bean and pea threshers found a ready market, particularly in the areas where "cowpeas," or black-eyed peas, were grown.

Keck-Gonnerman discontinued its tractors in 1942 and distributed Allis-Chalmers farm equipment for the duration of the decade.

Here is an exceptionally rare photograph of a steamer built by Rinehart, Ballard & Company. Oliver S. Kelly founded his industrial empire on his purchase of the old Rinehart firm.

O. S. Kelly Company

Studying the life of Oliver S. Kelly affords insights into the fact that industrialists of the nineteenth century diversified their businesses in extraordinarily creative ways. Kelly kept positioning himself on the proverbial cutting edge of new developments in a wide array of industries. Many present-day firms descend from his genius.

Oliver Smith Kelly struck it rich. He had worked as a carpenter, but the lure of gold proved too strong to resist. He left his home in Springfield, Ohio, looped through Nicaragua, and arrived in the California gold fields. He spent the better part of 1852 through 1856 mining "placers," deposits of gravel containing small particles of ore that could be washed out. Luck smiled on Kelly. The man who returned to Springfield was wealthy.[1] Oliver had ample capital to risk in establishing a series of industrial enterprises. The Kelly name would come to be associated with steam engines, threshing machines, road rollers, pianos, trucks, and tires. Like the Carnegie, Vanderbilt, and Rockefeller stories, the

account of Kelly's life invites readers back to an era when it was possible to become rich through good fortune and to stay rich through inventiveness and hard work.

Born in 1824, Oliver was the grandson of James Kelly, an Irish immigrant who first settled in Virginia. James felt the despair at Valley Forge and the exhilaration at Yorktown while serving under General George Washington. Hazarding the privations of a trek through the Cumberland Gap and across the rugged highlands of Kentucky, this patriot of the Revolution and his dozen children arrived in Springfield in 1808.[2] To look then at the hamlet situated on the wooded knolls of the Mad River would have given James Kelly no glimpse of the sprawling city of factories that Springfield would become, with his own grandson significantly contributing to that future growth.

John Kelly was born in 1789. He fought in the War of 1812 and then returned to farming in Clark County, Ohio. His untimely death in 1825 left one-year-old Oliver

This Springfield engine heads toward its next set with a C. Aultman American threshing machine.

Note the wooden spokes in the front wheels of this product of O. S. Kelly's factory in Springfield, Ohio.

without a father. Other members of the large Kelly family, which Oliver later called "the Kelly neighborhood," helped raise the infant.[3]

Oliver's earliest recollections were of the log house on the farm that his father carved from

Here is a clear side view of a Springfield steamer.

the wilderness four miles south of town.[4] Oliver's grandfather lived a half mile to the north. Most of James' seven surviving sons and four daughters resided in the vicinity.[5] Patches of cleared land floated like islands amid forests of oak and black walnut, mammoth sycamores sheltered the river, and every boy and girl quickly learned to handle a gun to supplement the larder with wild game. Oliver's aunt was a crack shot. "She could bring down a deer or anything else that crossed her path, any day," Oliver recalled. He also remembered the self-sufficiency of pioneer families: "We raised the flax and wool from which our mother spun our clothes; we raised the cattle and killed the beeves, from which we got the hides that we took to the tanner, who tanned them on shares, and in the fall a shoemaker would come to the house and stay several weeks, making shoes for all the family."

As a lad, Oliver enjoyed the responsibility of riding the horse to Springfield to run errands for his family. A

This Springfield steam engine is probably involved in barn threshing.

corduroy bridge, made by stringing together rough-hewn logs, crossed the marshes in the center of the village. Years later, Oliver recalled that, "As you rode along on it, the swamp would shake fifty feet on each side of the bridge, and if your horse got off, he would mire down in it in a short time, so that you could hardly get him out."[6] In 1830, the town of 500 inhabitants boasted two woolen mills, a flour mill established by Simon Kenton, a market house, and a distillery. When he was 10, Oliver and his family moved into the Adam Baker mill in the Mad River Valley.

In the mid-1830s and early 1840s, Oliver was fascinated with the bustling energy of Springfield. He admired the fire department with its "double-deckers," on which the men stood to operate the pumps. Brigades of volunteers brought water to the double-deckers in more than 100

leather buckets. The building of the new National Road also captured young Oliver's attention. During the political convention of 1840, the parade for "Old Tippecanoe"—General William Henry Harrison—came from Columbus along the new road. Oliver remembered the campaign tableau that included "log cabins with coons clambering over them. The poles of toll houses had to be removed to allow the procession to pass."[7]

In those early years, schooner wagons took six to eight weeks to bring dry goods from Baltimore. Most cattle were driven to Pittsburgh, and hogs went to Cincinnati. Eggs were two and half cents a dozen.[8] At age 14, Oliver decided to leave the farming and milling operation and seek his fortune in Springfield. After completing his apprenticeship as a carpenter in 1845, Oliver did his first professional work as a contractor helping to build an over-shot water wheel for James Leffel, the inventor of the turbine wheel. "It was a great day for Springfield when James Wiggins came into town with the first locomotive," said Oliver. The Little Miami Railroad opened in 1845, and was an event that marked vast change.

With a pioneering spirit and a hope worthy of his grandfather, Oliver dared to depart for California in 1852. He left behind a wife and children. Oliver returned from his journey to the American West with thousands of dollars in gold. He bought a wholesale grocery business with a small portion of his earnings.[9]

Oliver relinquished the grocery in 1857 and joined the farm-implement firm of William Whitely and Jerome Fassler. The name soon changed to Whitely, Fassler & Kelly.

This Springfield steam engine is on the road and pauses for a photograph.

This old O. S. Kelly steamer predates Wright's influence on Kelly engines and resembles Oliver Kelly's first Springfield engines. Courtesy Robert T. Rhode

The works built a well-received line of reapers and mowers. A full-color poster that advertised this company hangs in the museum of the Clark County [Ohio] Historical Society and shows the firm's spacious buildings and convenient railroad spur tracks. Oliver developed into a leader ready to adjust to new conditions by shrewdly detecting subtle fluctuations in business before competitors were aware that change was in the wind. Satisfied with the progress of Whitely, Fassler & Kelly, Oliver stayed with this manufacturing company until 1881.

When his sons were coming of age, Kelly felt the time was ripe to focus his energies in a new direction. Prior to 1882, he had served as president of the Rinehart, Ballard & Company Threshing Machine Works. In 1882, he invested part of his wealth in this company, which sold threshers licensed through John Pitts, one of the famous Pitts twins from Buffalo, New York. With Oliver as president and Oliver W., his son, as superintendent, the firm reorganized as the Springfield Engine and Thresher Company. Oliver permitted hay rake manufacturer J. H. Thomas & Sons of Springfield to put a Thomas nameplate on Springfield steamers that Thomas sold. Profits flowing into Oliver's firm increased and the business expanded. In 1889 or 1890, the name changed to the O. S. Kelly Company.[10] The firm had a capital stock of $350,000.[11]

Around the time when Oliver's lucrative firm bore his name, he became enamored with British steam engines. Edward T. Wright was a British citizen who had served his apprenticeship with Aveling & Porter, a well-known British firm that produced steamrollers. He then immigrated to Harrisburg to begin working as a draftsman for the Harrisburg Car Company. Wright's descendants Virginia

D'Antonio and Tom Wright found that between 1890 and 1891, the extended Wright family moved to Springfield. Wright began to replace the Springfield engines with a new style of Kelly engine that was closely modeled on British concepts. The valve was located above the cylinder encased in a large steam jacket, the shafts were fit on thick horn-plates, and a manstand with a box entered from the engine's left side were only a few of the British innovations to appear in Kelly manufacturing. The company even tried to promote cable plowing, which was a British strategy of positioning the engine beside the field, equipping it with a winding drum, playing out cable to the plow, and retracting the cable to pull the plow across the field. The most efficient cable plowing involved placing two steam engines on opposite sides of the field and drawing the plow back and forth between them. The large acreages in the United States, however, precluded the practice of cable plowing. For perhaps the only time in his career, Oliver had failed to identify a profitable trend.

Oliver was, nonetheless, "an industrialist of a visionary nature."[12] He recognized that his company's sales would increase if threshing equipment were manufactured in "America's heartland where it received the greatest use." Consequently, Oliver authorized opening an O. S. Kelly plant in Iowa City, Iowa. This factory built threshing machines, feed mills, and (eventually) gasoline engines. The words "O. S. Kelly Mfg. Co., Iowa City, Iowa," were cast into the fancy top-hinged smokeboxes of steam engines sold through the Iowa City office.

Oliver was wise in selecting his staff and appointed James H. Maggard general manager of Kelly's western branch. What Julia Child was to French cooking, Maggard was to agricultural steam power. Steam-engine aficionados prize their copies of Maggard's popular book, *Rough and Tumble Engineering*. The Rough and Tumble Engineers, a Kinzer, Pennsylvania, organization named after Maggard's book, hosts one of the oldest and most widely publicized annual summertime exhibits of antique machinery in North America. *Rough and Tumble Engineering*, later renamed *The Traction Engine: Its Use and Abuse*, underwent numerous editions in Maggard's day and is still available in paperback. Maggard made several revisions in the text, such as deleting his earlier advice to dump a hatful of potatoes in a boiler to prevent scale. In his last editions, he included his proverbial two-cents' worth of suggestions on gas and gasoline engines.

The book's phenomenal success originated in Maggard's inimitable writing style. For instance, Maggard begins a chapter entitled "What to Do and What Not to Do" by stating, "In order to get the learner started, it is reasonable to suppose that the engine he is to run is in good running order. It would not be fair to put the green boy on to an old dilapidated, wornout engine, for he might have to learn too fast in order to get the engine to running in good shape. He might have to learn so fast that he would get the big head, or have no head at all, by the time he got through with it. And I don't know but that a boy without a head is about as good as an engineer with a big head. We will, therefore, suppose that his engine is in good running order."[13]

Readers of Maggard's book feel he is speaking directly to them and telling them what's what: "I am well aware that among young engineers the impression prevails that a valve is a wonderful piece of mechanism, liable to kick out of place and play smash generally. Now, let me tell you right here that a valve (I mean the ordinary slide valve, such as is used on traction and portable engines) is one of the simplest parts of an engine, and you are not to lose any sleep about it, so please be patient until I am ready to introduce you to this part of your work. You have a perfect right to know what is wrong with the engine."[14] With an odd combination of solid information, acerbic wit, and verbal grandstanding, Maggard's chapters decoy readers into learning how to safely and efficiently run steam engines.

As a branch manager for Kelly, Maggard wrote promotional literature too. Issues of *The American Thresherman* and *The Threshermen's Review* from the early 1900s feature Kelly ads with unmistakable Maggard wording. Maggard had a modern and spacious factory to oversee, according to historian Irving B. Weber, who published multiple volumes of Iowa City history.[15] Weber knew this firsthand because as a lad, he had picked cherries for Ella M. McKee

Maggard, Maggard's wife. Weber was well acquainted with Maggard and knew Iowa City as only a paperboy could. The main Kelly building, located at 1301 Sheridan, measured 60 feet by 300 feet and consisted of two stories, 148 windows, double doors, and an addition on the back for a service room.[16] The Rock Island Railroad ran a siding to the company, and by 1909, a streetcar gave workers easy transit between the downtown and the factory.

Weber related the anecdote that when the Kelly factory was under construction, the foreman on the site ordered a

This new O. S. Kelly steam traction engine bears serial number 2058. Courtesy Robert T. Rhode

boy standing nearby to bring the man a left-handed monkey wrench. The youth hopped to it and asked workers where he could find such a tool. Of course, the joke was on the youngster. Maggard came by his sense of humor honestly. Maybe citizens of Iowa City imbibed wit with their water.

Just missing Independence Day to be born on July 5, 1854, Maggard was in his mid-40s when he began working for Kelly. In 1888, he built an elegant Gothic house on the south side of fashionable and exclusive Woodlawn, near the end of Iowa Avenue.[17] Weber lived one block west of Maggard's house. Maggard's daughter, Ione, was born in 1885 and married Ralph Puckett, who was in the auto parts business. Around 1918, Maggard built a bungalow in the orchard beside his house for Ione and Ralph. Gerald and Sandra Eskin purchased Maggard's mansion in 1972. They began to renovate and found 10 pounds of paper used as insulation behind the kitchen cupboard. The bundle included Maggard's letters and Kelly machinery

A newly minted O. S. Kelly steamer is shown at the factory in Springfield, Ohio. Courtesy Robert T. Rhode.

catalogs. The Eskins donated these materials to the Iowa Historical Society.[18]

The road beside the Kelly company was renamed Maggard Street and the thoroughfare's name has outlasted the factory.[19] In 1910, the O. S. Kelly Western Manufacturing Company, as it was then called, ceased operations. Unexpected low sales were blamed for the plant's demise.[20] A sweet corn cannery took over the building, which was subsequently razed.

Maggard, who served as a director for the Iowa City Street Car Company, the first interurban line in the city, died in 1924 and was buried in Oakland Cemetery. His passing coincided with the gradual end of the age when leaders were civic-minded, witty idiosyncrasy was desirable, and industrialists stood alongside the workers on the factory floor. As surely as the gazebos, band concerts, ice cream socials, and stiff boaters of braided straw—and the prosperous, secure, polite, and happy society they signified—vanished, Maggard and his beloved steam engines passed beyond the wall of oblivion.

In Maggard's heyday, the Kelly enterprise headquartered in Springfield teemed with innovations to serve an expanding country. According to the 1880 census, Clark County, Ohio, had a population of 41,947, and 20,729 of these inhabitants lived in Springfield. It was a far cry from the population of 500 back in Oliver's boyhood. Springfield was fast becoming a city of factories within the state that held the highest number of steam engine manufacturers in the U.S. The Kelly works occupied 10 acres and was located on the line of the CCC and St. L Railroad.[21] The largest buildings stood three stories tall, and the factory employed between 250 and 300 skilled employees. In his unpublished "History of the O. S. Kelly Company," located in the Clark County, Ohio, Historical Society collection, Austin Moon states that Gus Campeau, who had worked

for the Cincinnati Railway, was the yard foreman at the Kelly plant. He had a crew of Macedonians, who were immigrants from Yugoslavia. The main foundry, erected in 1899, paralleled the old boiler shop, which was built around 1880. Mark Livingston was the foundry foreman until 1906. To haul the trams loaded with iron and coke up the steep incline to the cupola building, lines of men shouldered cables as thick as their arms. The boiler shop rang with the blows of hammers striking rivets. Molten iron flowed into molds. Sparks showered from grinders, and mechanics shaped red-hot metal into the traction engines that drove the agricultural industry.

Most Kelly engines had two traction speeds, came in the popular sizes of 12, 15, and 18 horsepower, and carried a working pressure of up to 125 psi. Two countershafts completed the rear gearing. Kelly offered open-faced driver wheels similar to those made by the Birdsall Company of Auburn, New York. Kelly engines weighed between 10,750 and 15,500 pounds, according to a Kelly advertising sheet entitled "Manufactured and Sold by the O. S. Kelly Company." One writer called Kelly's manufactures "a class of machinery of incomparable excellence. It may be said that, as an evidence of the favor in which the company's products are held, they are in demand in all parts of the civilized world, and the demand is annually increasing in volume."[22]

From 1898 until approximately 1905, Kelly experimented with a triple-cylinder, cross-compound, cable-plowing engine. All three cylinders could receive steam from the boiler to produce a so-called simple engine for bursts of power, or the two outside cylinders could take exhaust steam from the middle cylinder to form, in effect, a single low-pressure cylinder.[23] A lever changed the engine from a simple to a presumably more efficient compound by routing the exhaust to the outside cylinders' steam-chests. The connecting rods attached to the crankshaft at 120-degree intervals. The engine had no flywheel—the weight of the reciprocating parts was sufficient for smooth revolutions—and used a radial valve gear. Made from 7/16-inch steel plate, the boiler barrel measured 43 inches in diameter with a double-riveted seam. The boiler had 360 square feet of heating area and carried a pressure of 180 psi. The engine could develop 120 horsepower. Its massive plate wheels (8 feet in diameter, face 2 1/2 feet, each weighing almost three tons) used three driving pins, not a differential gear. The cable drum held up to 1,350 feet of 1-inch hawser.

The *Scientific American* for July 29, 1899, featured a photograph of this remarkable engine on page 68. The accompanying article, entitled "A Huge Over-land Traction

Engine," states that such engines were shipped to Cuba. They could haul up to 112 tons each (not counting the weight of the engine and wagons) and were sold to remote plantations and mines far from railroads.

The Kelly triple-cylinder engine must have been one of the first—if not the only traction engine—to be so equipped. The fact that Kelly attempted to design such a behemoth attests to Oliver's willingness to explore unknown territory. At the turn of the century, Oliver sensed that his company's future would benefit from diversification. "Beginning in 1898, piano plates (an integral part of a piano's sound system) were manufactured at the Springfield works. The O. S. Kelly Company began to phase out its agricultural equipment production and to manufacture piano plates in earnest."[24] For years, the harp frames used in Steinway pianos came from the Kelly factory in Springfield.

By 1892, Kelly was producing steamrollers designed by Edward T. Wright. The Kelly-Springfield Road Roller Company, an outgrowth of the O. S. Kelly Company founded in 1902, later merged with the Buffalo Steam Roller Company, a division of the Buffalo Pitts Company, to form the Buffalo-Springfield Company. Buffalo-Springfield became the undisputed giant of the American steamroller industry.

In 1888, Oliver's son Edwin, who was born in 1857, served as president of the Springfield Coal & Ice Company. In 1894, he joined his brother, Oliver W., who was born in 1851, and inventor Arthur W. Grant in founding the Rubber Tire Wheel Company, forerunner of the Kelly-Springfield Tire Company. Edwin organized the Kelly Springfield Truck Company in 1910. He stayed with that firm only two years but remained with the O. S. Kelly Company until 1921.[25] Edwin served as president or otherwise led half a dozen firms, including the Home Lighting, Heating, and Power Company and the Kelly-Springfield Printing Company. For a long time, Edwin was a newspaper publisher.

In 1899, Edwin purchased Whitehall, the 1,100-acre estate situated just north of Yellow Springs, Ohio. There, he raised blue-ribbon shorthorn cattle, national-championship Duroc Jersey hogs, and new hybrids of flowers, including dahlias and peonies.[26] Edwin circled the globe twice and was a frequent visitor to Europe. He collected valuable furniture, curios,

and art during his travels. Whitehall attracted visitors from around the world. Like his father, Edwin possessed a "carefully planned, deliberate manner" that gave him the Midas touch.[27] From 1912 until his death in 1935 at age 78, Edwin was virtually retired. The magnitude of his estate eclipsed his father's gold rush fortune.

Oliver S. Kelly died in 1904. During the 80 years of his lifetime, he contributed to the growth of Springfield, Iowa City, and the nation. In 1891, Oliver's Springfield firm drew this praise: "The officers of this company are native Ohioans, and belong to that class of energetic, enterprising, public-spirited young business men in whose hands the continued development of this community rests. They are widely honored and esteemed for their inventive genius, their many accomplishments as manufacturers, and their thorough reliability in business affairs. Paying close attention to the improvement of their machinery and wares, rather than to the amount of sales or monetary returns, and endowed with a laudable ambition to excel, they have reached a preeminence in their industry of which they have every reason to be proud."[28] If the historical records that were collected for this article from California, Great Britain, Iowa, Kentucky, and Ohio tell the truth about Oliver, the above-quoted tribute to an industrial pioneer and his company is richly deserved. Oliver's example presents an opportunity for sobering reflection on the differences between his era and our own and for respecting the values of yesteryear.

The British-looking bunker on this O. S. Kelly engine bears the hallmark of Edward T. Wright, Kelly's trusted design engineer from England. Courtesy Robert T. Rhode

Kitten Machine Shop

Florenz J. Kitten, Sr., was born in Prussian Germany, according to his descendant, Jerry Kitten. In 1850, Florenz's family moved near Ferdinand, Indiana. His father, Henry, farmed and made wooden shoes for the mostly German community. Kitten became a carpenter at age 19. In 1868, he married Katherina Ligers. When he built his home, he included a machine shop on the second floor to manufacture threshers. The firm eventually built sawmills. Florenz and Katherina's son, Joseph F., was born in 1870. In 1882, Kitten began to produce traction engines, three of which were built by 1885. He patented his idiosyncratically designed steam engine in 1889 and erected a two-story factory adjacent to his home.

Florenz retired in 1906, and Joseph replaced his father as head of the Kitten Machine Shop. In 1908, the name changed to the Ferdinand Foundry and Machine Works.

As Kathy Tretter has reported, Joseph died in 1918, and his wife, Elizabeth, and her father, Tony Buschkoetter, ran the company. Elizabeth and Joseph W. Bickwermert purchased the firm. When Bickwermert became the exclusive owner in 1935, the firm's name changed to the Ferdinand Machine Company. Bickwermert sold the business in 1945. In 1952, the firm was incorporated as the DuBois County Machine Company. The shop became the property of the Ferdinand Development Corporation in 1959.

Painter Ben Weaver's brightly colored floral motifs decorated Kitten engines. The last Kitten engine was completed in 1940. Its debut marked the end of the regular production of agricultural steam engines in the United States.

A typical place for a Kitten is in a sawmill surrounded by loads of lumber.

With their short boilers, Kitten engines were well designed for the hills of southern Indiana. Perhaps the hills themselves are responsible for the fact that so many vibrant stories circulate about the Kitten firm. One such story asserts that the Kitten shop retained a boy to keep the pails of ale filled throughout the workday.

William Lamb said that while he was attending an early steam show, a man walked up to a Kitten engine and exclaimed, "I never thought I'd see that engine again! That was the day I thought my dad would be fired." Lamb asked the onlooker to explain. "My father worked for Kitten. See that steamdome?" The man pointed. "He accidentally put it on backwards and had to file down the rivets to fit the engine to the boiler." At the time of this writing, that Kitten engine still exists and is in the collection of Francis Lindauer.

A most unusual Kitten steam engine has a two-pass boiler, with the smokestack located in the center of the engine.

Here is a great close-up photograph of a Kitten steam engine.

A Lane & Bodley steam engine is shown in a sawmill. Note the eagle casting. No historical photograph of one of Lane & Bodley's traction engines has come to light.

Lane & Bodley Company

Philander P. Lane's father brought his family from Connecticut to a farm in northeastern Ohio's Portage County. Philander learned the machinist trade and moved to Cincinnati, Ohio, where, in 1850, he opened a machine shop, reports Sandra Seidman. Joseph T. "J. T." Bodley became a partner in Lane's firm in 1852. Bodley had just completed his apprenticeship with well-known Cincinnati industrialist Miles Greenwood. Lane devoted himself to purchases and sales, and Bodley focused on manufacturing.

In 1852, Lane & Bodley moved to a location that, at the time of this writing, is the practice field for the Cincinnati Bengals football team. At first, Lane & Bodley shared shop space with another manufacturing company, Reynolds and Kite. Lane & Bodley acquired Reynolds and Kite in 1858.

Lane helped found the Ohio Mechanics Institute, and he served as colonel in the Eleventh Ohio Volunteer Infantry during the Civil War. In winter quarters at Point Pleasant, West Virginia, in 1861 and 1862, Lane was accompanied by his seven-year-old son. Sophia Lane attempted to bring her children to her husband's location in the West Virginia mountains during the winter of 1863 but was ordered back because of the threat of bushwackers. Business conditions improved after the war, but Bodley scarcely had time to enjoy the renewed prosperity. He died in 1868.

Alexander Latta and Abel Shawk built the first successful steam-powered fire engine in 1852. In 1863, Latta licensed Lane & Bodley to produce the engines. The Lane & Bodley firm sold the rights to Ahrens, who founded the C. Ahrens Manufacturing Company in 1869.

In the centennial year of 1876, the firm of Lane & Bodley incorporated. On January 1, 1878, the Lane & Bodley Company began the monthly publication of an oversized folio magazine called *The Cincinnati Artisan*.

This unusual journal was filled with news and articles about science and technology and devoted most of the front page of each issue to extolling the virtues of Lane & Bodley engines and sawmills.

Over the course of the company's history, the firm produced agricultural steam engines; Corliss-type automatic cut-off engines; woodworking machines; circular sawmills; hydraulic, steam, and cable elevators; flooring machines; sash molding machines; surfacers; and equipment for mining silver and gold. The Lane & Bodley Company eventually dropped its woodworking lines to concentrate on steam engines and sawmills. To replace the fusible plug, the owner of a Lane & Bodley farm engine had to detach a plate on top of the steamdome, crawl inside the boiler, remove the old plug, and hammer in a new one to form a steam-tight joint.

Henry Marcus Lane, Philander's son born in 1854, was the superintendent of the 1881 Cincinnati Exposition machinery division. Philander P. Lane died in 1899. At this writing, the Vorhis Funeral Home occupies Philander Lane's fine Victorian house. Henry assumed the presidency of the company. Henry was educated at the Massachusetts Institute of Technology and designed inclines for several of Cincinnati's hills. The company relocated after a fire in 1901. Records imply that the Lane & Bodley firm remained in business until approximately 1920. In 1929, Henry Lane lost his life in a fire at the Cleveland Clinic, where he had gone to receive treatment.

Lang & Button

The predecessor to Lang & Button was Lang & Reynolds, which by 1878 was manufacturing a 10-horsepower,

This rarest of rare photographs has captured a Lang & Reynolds, predecessor to Lang & Button, pulling a Wood, Taber & Morse steamer.

Only a few manufacturers, such as Lang & Button, turned the governor horizontally. Note the shape of the spokes in the driver wheel and the customary toolbox.

With a relatively small water tank in front, this Lang & Button is dual-belted in the sawmill installation.

This Leader engine is truly an old one.

horse-steered, wooden-wheeled traction engine with no steamdome. The steam pipe ran part of the way up the inside of the smokestack to dry the steam before it reached the cylinder, which was adjacent to the stack. According to one engineer, such an arrangement made going downhill difficult because water from the boiler filled the pipe and ran into the cylinder. Later engines had steel wheels and steamdomes. John B. Lang and James Reynolds founded their company in 1868 in Ithaca, New York. The "Button" in the firm's name refers to Ernest D. Button, Lang's son-in-law, who replaced Reynolds when Reynolds died on Halloween, 1891. Lang & Button built sawmills, plows, and cultivators. The firm ceased to produce steamers in 1921.

Marion Manufacturing Company

Warren Gamaliel Harding, 29th President of the United States, also presided over the Marion Manufacturing Company, which was established in 1886 and built the Leader steam engine. As a publisher, Harding had made a success of the Marion, Ohio, newspaper. By taking a moderate position on most issues, he had been elected to a series of political offices, including the U. S. Senate. Harding won the presidency by a landslide and served as Commander in Chief from 1921 through 1923. He restricted the number of immigrants allowed into the country, imposed the highest tariffs in history, reduced the federal income tax, and decreased the national debt. Unfortunately, scandals plagued his administration, not the least of which was the infamous Teapot Dome scandal. Harding undertook a national speaking tour to reassure the public and win

This old Leader is engaged in stack threshing. Note the fly nets on the horses.

back support. In San Francisco, he came down with the flu and died of a blood clot. Back at the White House, his wife burned all his correspondence. Her doing so stirred speculation that she poisoned her husband to preserve her good name. Maybe Harding would have been better off subduing his political ambitions. Perhaps the presidency of the Marion Manufacturing Company was as high an office as he should have sought.

According to rumor, a squabble at the nearby Huber Manufacturing Company caused disaffected Huber employees to found the Marion firm. Marion shipped Leader engines west to the Cascaden-Vaughan Company, successors to the Waterloo Threshing Machine Company of Waterloo, Iowa. As Cascaden-Vaughan advertisements did not name the engine, a few readers of historic company literature have mistakenly assumed that Cascaden-Vaughan manufactured its own steam engines. In 1907, the Clinton Thresher Company in Ontario reached an agreement with Marion to build Leader steamers in Canada, but the

Clinton factory burned to the ground and dashed Marion's hopes. Late in its existence, the Marion firm also produced a 10-ton steamroller. Toward the end of the company's history, the firm became known as the Ohio Tractor Company, and all three names—Marion, Leader, and Ohio—appeared on company stationery. The Leader trademark featured a lion surrounded by this slogan: "As I am to the animal kingdom so is 'Leader' threshing machinery in comparison with others."

For more on Marion Manufacturing, see the entry on the George White & Sons Company.

Graced by two dogs, this Leader with an extended smokestack is powering a sawmill.

The engineer in this photograph is intent on the work at hand. He is running his Leader engine with the requisite concentration and care.

This Leader steamer is helping build a barn.

As only a handful of McLaughlin steamers were built, this view is a rare one. Courtesy Ed McLaughlin

McLaughlin Manufacturing Company

Dennis W. McLaughlin was born in Ireland in 1858, as Ed McLaughlin (grandson of Dennis) has found and Richard Backus has reported. Documents suggest that McLaughlin began manufacturing equipment in a shop in San Francisco, moved to San Leandro after the 1906 earthquake, and moved again to Emeryville, which is adjacent to Berkeley. McLaughlin eventually established a shop in Berkeley, California. McLaughlin worked for Daniel Best of San Leandro during an unspecified time. McLaughlin was engaged in manufacturing steam engines and freight wagons by 1903. According to Paul Reno, Best sued McLaughlin for infringing upon Best's patented front wheel steering apparatus, but McLaughlin proved that his design was significantly different. McLaughlin engines were built for heavy haulage and were intended for the mining and logging industries. McLaughlin's Golden Gate Gas Tractor Company was incorporated in 1914. He died in 1934.

A McLaughlin is pulling a 12-ton transformer.
Courtesy Ed McLaughlin

A McLaughlin steam engine is hauling a heavy load.
Courtesy Ed McLaughlin

Minneapolis Threshing Machine Company

In 1887, James F. MacDonald transferred his thresher manufacturing business from Fond du Lac, Wisconsin, to Minneapolis, Minnesota. The West Minneapolis Land Company was founded in the same year to erect housing for the factory workers. Early catalogs of the company instructed patrons to address telegrams to Minneapolis and mail to the Hopkins post office. Harley H. Hopkins was the postmaster. He donated the land for the building of the town's depot, and the station was named "Hopkins." In 1893, the village of West Minneapolis was incorporated. The name of the town surrounding the factory was changed from West Minneapolis to Hopkins in 1928 to honor

continued on page 150

A Minneapolis engine is mated to a Frick Landis Eclipse threshing machine.

This return-flue Minneapolis is designed to burn straw, which was more abundant in western territories and provinces than was needed to provide for livestock.

Here is a Minneapolis sporting a half canopy.

This is a full Minneapolis outfit, complete with a return-flue steamer.

A man is oiling a mule in this picture of a Minneapolis.

A tandem-cylinder, return-flue Minneapolis is running in cool weather.

A third engine tows two Minneapolis engines.

This all-Minneapolis rig includes a twin-feeder threshing machine.

The engineer in this sawmill operation has balanced the oil can on the exhaust pipe to keep the oil warm.

The men in white shirts and derby hats are probably demonstrating the Minneapolis equipment at a fair.

Note the repair to the driver wheel of this Minneapolis. Many jokes from the steam era centered on how few tools were necessary to keep a steamer running.

An acetylene lamp and a homemade cab grace this Minneapolis steam engine.

This photograph of a Minneapolis is reminiscent of the joke that a wrench, baling wire, and a hammer were all an engineer needed to repair a steamer.

continued from page 145

the community's first postmaster, but the name change was also a tacit acknowledgment that for many years, people had been calling the town, "Hopkins."

The Minneapolis Threshing Machine Company began producing steam engines as early as 1889. Around 1910, the firm's advertisers boasted excellent castings and gearing. A worker on the night shift explained that after the employees had tossed discarded well pumps and Deering mower wheels into the vat of melted iron, they threw in scrapped Model T motors until the mixture came up to test.

In addition to threshing equipment, products of the factory included corn shellers, force pumps, and plows. Minneapolis briefly built a steamer with two smokestacks, one for each of two cylinders.

Minneapolis also held a half interest in the American-Abell Engine & Thresher Company.

In 1911, the Minneapolis Threshing Machine Company perceived the need to develop oil- and gasoline-powered

With a Geiser in the background, this Minneapolis on a railcar is so new that the only smudges on it are fingerprints

Nichols & Shepard Company

In 1848, John Nichols, a blacksmith and millwright, walked from Detroit to Battle Creek in search of a suitable location for his line of work. He then brought his family there. According to Charles O. Olsen, Nichols originally entered into business with Charles H. Shepard, who invited his younger brother, David, to relocate in Battle Creek from upstate New York. In 1849, David participated in the gold rush but found nothing. He returned to Battle Creek and bought out his brother's interest in the Nichols company in 1851. The mechanically-minded David Shepard helped Nichols establish a successful foundry. In 1858, Nichols and Shepard built a vibrating thresher, which they greatly improved in 1861. Toward the end of the Civil War, Henry H. Taylor, a Chicago agent for C. Aultman & Company and for Nichols and Shepard, bought a third share in Nichols and Shepard's firm. Nichols and Shepard eventually bought stock in a new company formed by Cornelius Aultman and Henry H. Taylor in Mansfield, Ohio, where vibrator threshers were built under license to Nichols and Shepard. Aultman, Nichols, and Shepard collaborated in hunting and fishing as readily as they collaborated in manufacturing agricultural implements.

tractors and hired Walter I. McVicker to design a tractor; accordingly, the Minneapolis 35–70-horsepower model was born. The firm went on to produce a small tractor, the 15–30-horsepower model. Minneapolis eventually built a full line of tractors.

Incorporated in 1929, the Minneapolis-Moline Power Implement Company arose from the merger of the Minneapolis Threshing Machine Company, the Moline Implement Company (founded in 1870), and the Minneapolis Steel and Machinery Company (founded in 1902 and makers of the Twin City tractors since 1910). The large bore and large stroke that characterized Minneapolis Threshing Machine Company tractors were retained in the machines built by Minneapolis-Moline.

Energetic Irishman Elon A. Marsh kept the shops of John Nichols and David Shepard lively, to say the least. In 1880, Marsh, who based his work on an old English patent that he had seen, developed and patented the fixed cut-off valve gear named for him. Nichols and Shepard had just begun to produce traction engines and welcomed

The man beneath the Nicholas-Shepard rig could not stop for the photographer and had to keep repairing the machine, perhaps with tools from the makeshift toolbox on the front.

Everyone has stopped long enough to have the picture taken in this sawmill scene with an old Nichols & Shepard steam engine.

This old Nichols & Shepard steamer with its extension flywheel is busy making stumps.

Note the star on the crank disc of this Nichols & Shepard steam tractor.

Muddy and wet, this engine is doing what it was designed to do: working in the belt.

the Marsh gear. After detecting holes in the wording of the Marsh patent, Nichols and Shepard took out a reissue of the patent in the name of Andrew Hoag in 1881. When Marsh demanded royalties for his gear, Nichols and Shepard refused to pay. The resulting lawsuit spun out of control. The U.S. Congress appointed a special commission to investigate Marsh's claims.

Nichols and Shepard argued that Marsh was working for them when he designed the gear and had no right to patent the invention. After listening to depositions for more than three hours, commission members announced a noon recess, but Marsh jumped to his feet and shouted that right was on his side and that he could prove it within the next 10 minutes. Moved by Marsh's vigorous testimony, commission members awarded him the decision. A higher court later reversed the verdict and gave Nichols and Shepard the right to use the Marsh gear but not to license it to other companies. The Hoag reissue was effectively made null and void, as the court acknowledged Marsh as the first inventor. Early in the protracted

A boy holds the lines to what must surely be a well-behaved team in this photograph of a Nichols & Shepard.

Two new Nichols & Shepard steam engines stand in front of the hardware store.

The mammoth straw stack signifies that the side-mounted, double-cylinder Nichols & Shepard has performed plenty of work.

Don't be fooled! The Avery bunker has been added to what is otherwise a Nichols & Shepard engine.

court battles over the Marsh gear, Marsh and well-known mechanical engineer Minard LaFever left Nichols and Shepard's shops and worked for the Upton firm in Battle Creek. LaFever designed the Upton engine, which was the forerunner of the Port Huron steamer, and the Advance engine, both of which employed Marsh's gear. Marsh went on to design the Marsh steam pump.

Nichols and Shepard referred to the Marsh gear as their pinion reverse. Nichols and Shepard began using a link motion in 1885, but various Nichols and Shepard engines

The whole family is out with Dad on the threshing rig.

Three men are pictured beside their steamer.

Could this man be practicing barrel tossing next to this Nichols & Shepard engine?

were equipped with the Marsh gear through 1890. In 1886, the firm was reincorporated as the Nichols & Shepard Company. In that same year, mechanical engineer Eli Flagg improved the firm's vibrator thresher. In 1891, Nichols died and his son, Edwin C., assumed the presidency. In 1904, Shepard died. Nichols & Shepard built large gasoline tractors but did not seize the opportunity to manufacture small tractors when the large ones became less popular. During the last 15 years of the firm's history, Nichols & Shepard's Red River Special threshers were in high demand. Nichols & Shepard began to distribute Allis-Chalmers and eventually Lauson tractors. In

1929, the Oliver Farm Equipment Company bought out Nichols & Shepard. In the same year as the stock market crash, Minneapolis-Moline was formed from the merging of three companies, and the United Tractor & Equipment Corporation was founded.

On moving day in Hartford, Wisconsin, the Nichols & Shepard steamer and the Rumely OilPull are taking the straight route through the middle of town.

Northwest Thresher Company

Dwight M. Sabin was born in Illinois in 1843, as reported by Jerry Brosious. The Sabin family moved to the ancestral home of the Sabins in Connecticut in 1856. Dwight Sabin spent a year in the prestigious Phillips Academy in Andover, Massachusetts, before serving in the Union army in 1862. He was in the commissary department at Gettysburg. He went to St. Paul, Minnesota, for health reasons in 1867. When he was there, he took an interest in the C. N. Nelson Lumber Company and formed Seymour, Sabin & Company with George M. Seymour, a cooper, or barrel maker. According to Donald Empson, Seymour was born in New York in 1829. Seymour already had erected buildings at the Minnesota State Prison in

A horse-steered Stillwater engine and a Minnesota Chief threshing machine are pictured.

This is a Stillwater with a chain drive.

This chain-driven engine from the Northwest factory has a large, square water tank.

Stillwater, east of St. Paul. By 1870, Seymour and Sabin employed inmate labor to augment the workforce needed to put up several new buildings on the prison grounds. In 1874, Sabin and Seymour began to manufacture agricultural implements with prisoners providing much of the work. Another industry within the prison produced binder twine, which was made from hemp fiber. Twine was very much in demand during the threshing era.

The Younger brothers, who were associated with Frank and Jesse James, were imprisoned in Stillwater in 1876. Cole Younger made sieves, Jim Younger made belts, and Bob Younger made straw elevators for Seymour, Sabin & Company. Bob died of tuberculosis in 1889, and Cole and Jim remained behind bars until being paroled in 1901.

Seymour gradually had less to do with the business, which began to dwindle after various influential people, disenchanted with Sabin and Seymour for benefiting from

This chain-driven Giant is popping off. Prisoners were involved in the production of Northwest machines.

This chain-driven product of the Northwest factory meets its deadlines because the engineer has placed an alarm clock atop the dome.

the cheap labor of prisoners, had changed the contracts between the company and the prison. In 1881, the city stepped in to give the struggling firm a loan of $100,000 (financed by bonds) in exchange for the promise to build 100 houses in Stillwater and to contract to build an additional 100 houses with other companies. As early as 1878, Seymour, Sabin & Company was evolving into the Northwestern Manufacturing and Car Company, which was incorporated in 1882 for $3 million of capital stock, mostly in the hands of eastern investors. The firm had been building the Minnesota Giant, a return-flue steam engine with chain drive and wooden wheels. By 1881, the Stillwater was in production; it had both a firebox and a return-flue boiler. At least one source suggests there were earlier versions of the Stillwater that used wooden wheels and a chain drive.

Northwest made the Stillwater, the Minnesota Giant, the Giant, and the New Giant. This return-flue engine has a chain drive.

A New Giant and a Northwest threshing machine are pictured.

A smoke-blower is belted to the flywheel in this picture of a Northwest engine beside a Huber.

The belt resting on the crankshaft is ready to be removed so this Northwest engine can continue to the next threshing set. Note the distinctive grouter pattern on the driver wheels.

Sabin was elected to a term in the U. S. Senate in 1883, and he served as president of the Republican National Committee. February 6 of that year was proclaimed "Sabin's Day" in Stillwater, and threshers and engines lined Main Street. A traction engine pulled a double sleigh bearing Sabin and other dignitaries in a colorful parade.

By 1884, the firm employed 1,600 workers, 300 of them inmates. The company exercised nearly complete

While a Monarch water wagon serves this Northwest steamer, another water wagon is heading toward the horizon to refill.

control over the prison population and even chose the officers and guards. The factory produced 16 freight cars, 7 threshers, and 4 steam engines per day. Each month, 6 passenger coaches were completed.

The Northwestern Manufacturing and Car Company suddenly, and rather surprisingly, went bankrupt. In May 1884, the business was placed in the hands of a receiver, who began to discontinue building railroad cars. At Sabin's urging, the Minnesota Thrasher [sic] Company bought Northwestern. The firm was reorganized as the Minnesota Thresher Manufacturing Company. The factory continued to produce the Minnesota Giant and the Stillwater. In 1894, perhaps in response to the panic of 1893, the factory moved outside the prison walls, but work at the plant drastically decreased and then ceased altogether at one point. Meanwhile, the old Minnesota Thresher building within the prison was razed because it had long been infested with bedbugs.

The firm entered into receivership for the second time in 1900. As Bill Vossler has found, the Northwest Thresher Company emerged from the Minnesota Thresher Manufacturing Company in 1901. The Minnesota Giant had evolved into the Giant, which subsequently evolved into the New Giant. The firm also produced top-mounted, straight-flue farm engines. Sabin was never elected to a second term in the Senate and died in relative obscurity in 1902. With new leadership, Northwest more than doubled its capacity in 1903.

The April 1906 issue of *The American Thresherman* carried a story announcing Northwest's newly designed cross-compound cylinder for a special plowing engine. When the throttle was pulled, live steam entered both cylinders through an intercepting valve, which closed after steam from the high-pressure cylinder began to enter the low-pressure cylinder. Northwest's interest in a special plowing engine coincided with that of Buffalo Pitts. The latter firm had been building cross-compound traction engines since 1901, but Buffalo Pitts introduced its cross-compound special plowing engine in 1906. Even though the special engines of Northwest and Buffalo Pitts used different valve gears, both engines resembled one another so remarkably that one might think each firm had spied on the other throughout the pre-production period.

In 1910, Northwest acquired A. O. Espe's Universal tractor and marketed it the following year. In 1912, Dr. Edward Rumely bought the Northwest Thresher Company. He desired the Universal tractor and the up-to-date factory in Stillwater. Rumely renamed the Universal the GasPull. When the M. Rumely Company became insolvent in 1915, Northwest met an untimely end.

With the Northwest factory in the background, this new 1907 double-cylinder engine bears test number 323.

This is probably one of the largest Northwest Thresher engines. Notice the two women decked out in their best attire.

Port Huron Engine and Thresher Company

The Upton Manufacturing Company was the forerunner of the Port Huron Company. Upton was located in Battle Creek, Michigan. William Brown, a blacksmith, founded the Upton firm, states Charles O. Olsen. When Minard "Old Judge" LaFever and Elon A. Marsh left Nichols & Shepard because the firm denied Marsh royalties for his patented valve gear, LaFever and Marsh became chief engineers at Upton. LaFever designed the Upton steam engine, which was first sold in 1882. The city of Port Huron recruited the Upton firm to relocate to its city, and Brown became plant manager at the new facility in 1884. LaFever and Marsh remained in Battle Creek and worked for Case & Willard, the precursor to the Advance Thresher Company. In 1890, Upton was renamed the Port Huron Engine and Thresher Company.

The Port Huron Rusher thresher and the Port Huron traction engine appeared in 1891. A few of the first Longfellows—engines with boiler tubes 9 feet long—were introduced in 1907. By 1908, Longfellows had proven themselves and became so popular that today a short-boilered Port Huron is less common.

As Dr. Robert T. Rhode and Judge Raymond L. Drake have discovered, by the late 1800s, Charles Longenecker was designing steamrollers for Pennsylvania's Harrisburg Car Company, builders of railway cars. Prior to 1890, Longenecker worked for Julian Scholl & Company, an agency in New York that distributed Iroquois rollers and subsequently began selling O. S. Kelly rollers that were manufactured in Springfield, Ohio. Scholl became the New York City distributor for Russell steamrollers around 1895.

A Port Huron traction engine with the old style of smokebox door drives magisterially down the main street of town.

Humor could occasionally be found in the old photographs, such as this shot of a man serving beer in front of a Port Huron engine. Notice the man chugging away on the right.

In the early 1890s, steamroller manufacturers reached various agreements about sales territories. Among the firms entering into these collaborative arrangements were O. S. Kelly, the Buffalo Pitts Company, and Harrisburg Car. Buffalo Pitts and O. S. Kelly developed such an amicable working relationship that they merged within a quarter of a century.

The Russell Company hired Longenecker to design a steamroller under the Russell trademark around 1895. The Weston Engine Company of Painted Post, New York, began in 1896, and Longenecker became the firm's vice president. Weston built stationary engines and was a forerunner of Ingersoll Rand.

O. S. Kelly and Buffalo Pitts jointly acquired the Russell steamroller division by 1901. In 1902 and 1903, Longenecker served as agent for Buffalo Pitts rollers in

Everyone looks as proud as the proverbial peacock while stopping to pose on this Port Huron steam traction engine.

On every piece of equipment in this picture, signs are posted that these items were "Sold by the Collen Bros. of Hudson, Michigan."

A single plow is being pulled by a Port Huron engine. Note the driver wheels with the distinctive grouter pattern that was part of the casting.

A familiar scene around the turn of the last century was a complete steam outfit on a country road headed to its next job. This time it is a Port Huron steamer!

Another cabbed Port Huron steam traction engine is getting ready to hit the road during the fall harvest days.

A compound Port Huron steam tractor is blazing its own trail.

New England and southern New York. Longenecker began designing and manufacturing the larger models of Scholl's Universal roller in 1904. Longenecker abruptly left Scholl in 1905 to organize his own company.

Between November 1905 and the early months of 1906, Edward T. Wright and Longenecker designed the New York steamroller and an innovative scarifier. Wright and Longenecker had met when Wright immigrated to Harrisburg to begin working as a draftsman for Harrisburg Car. Wright had served his apprenticeship in the shops of the Aveling & Porter Company and was well versed in standard road roller design. Wright had moved to Springfield, Ohio, to create steamrollers for O. S. Kelly. In 1903, Wright contributed the American roller for the American Road Roller Company.

The Port Huron Company in Michigan bought Longenecker's New York roller and scarifier business in 1910. The new roller bore little resemblance to the Port Huron steamroller depicted in the annual catalog for 1908, for the original Port Huron roller was modeled on the firm's agricultural traction engine.

Port Huron built sawmills, hay presses, wagons, and corn shellers in addition to threshers and steam engines. A Port Huron advertisement from 1911 depicted horseshoes, wrenches, and steel forks that had been threshed by a Port Huron Rusher threshing machine without damaging the equipment.

George F. Connor (1857–1924) was born in Minnesota, lived in the Dakota Territory, worked for the J. I. Case Threshing Machine Company, and transferred to the Port Huron firm in 1897. Connor designed Port Huron's unique cast drive wheels that were thought to be self-cleaning. He left the company in 1914. Connor wrote a 174-page book entitled *Science of Threshing*.

In 1915, Port Huron developed a gasoline tractor, which was anything but a success. Only a few were built. Port Huron entered into receivership in 1920. The company continued to produce threshers until 1925, and by 1928, Port Huron was no more.

Jacob Price

Jacob Price of San Leandro, California, patented a traction engine in May 1887. He then built a steamroller designed on his patent and demonstrated it in San Jose, California, in October of the same year. The roller failed to perform well, and the *San Jose Mercury* did not mince words in condemning its poor performance. Making the excuse that the roller had not been sufficiently tested before being shipped to San Jose, the undaunted Price turned to the J. I. Case Threshing Machine Company in Racine, Wisconsin, in 1889 and asked it to build a field locomotive, or steam plow, based on his latest designs. In 1890, he received a patent for his engine and entered the Case-built steamer in the plowing contest at the California State Fair. The judges narrowly chose Daniel Best's engine over Price's. Ironically, the works that Best occupied had been sold to him by Price. Case made several engines for Price, but in 1893, Price signed over his patents to Case to settle his debts. Case and the related company known as the J. I. Case Plow Works issued a special catalog in 1894 to promote sales of the engine. By 1897, Case and the Plow Works had ceased production of the Price machine.

Reeves

In 1869, Marshall Truman Reeves, at the age of 18, founded the Hoosier Boy Cultivator Company, which manufactured plows in Rush County, Indiana. Marshall's father, William Reeves, was a native Ohioan and a farmer in Center Township. Around 1874, Marshall established a firm known as Reeves & Company in Columbus, Indiana. The firm was incorporated in 1888, the same year that Marshall T. Reeves and younger brothers Milton O. and Girnie L. established the Reeves Pulley Company. M. O. Reeves invented the Reeves variable-speed transmission, and the company eventually built hit-and-miss engines and automobiles.

continued on page 170

The Reeves in this sawmill scene carries the old style of smokestack.

Here is an unexpected photograph of a Jacob Price engine, built for Price by the J. I. Case Threshing Machine Company. Courtesy John Davidson

T. W. Crauford, the owner of this Reeves engine and thresher, advertises himself as a "Thrasherman"!

Note the homemade carrier for cans behind the smokestack of this Reeves steam traction engine that is matched with a Minneapolis threshing machine.

Reeves

The Reeves logo cast into an otherwise flat steamchest cover indicates that this engine is equipped with a plain sliding D valve.

This Reeves has a smokestack different from the styles customarily associated with this make of steam engine.

Where plowing vast fields required maximum efficiency, a Reeves engine, such as this one, took on water while on the move.

A splendidly attired woman graces this Reeves scene.

On the canopy of this Reeves is this advertisement: "E. F. Salzmann's Threshing Outfit, Giarantee [sic] Satisfaction to Everybody."

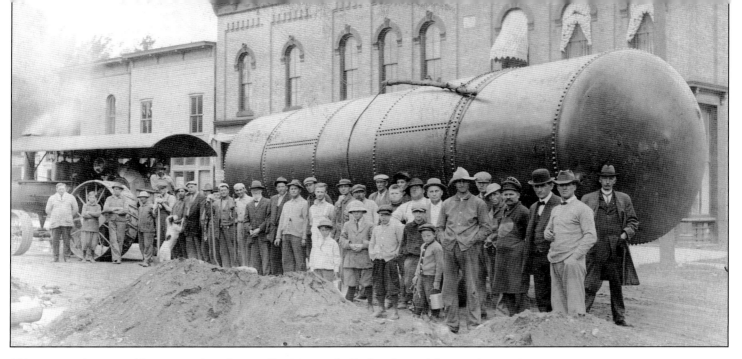

This Reeves engine poses with representatives of W. L. Dillon Waterworks, Engineering, and Construction.

The engineer of this old Reeves engine intended to keep cool. Note the fan strapped beneath the canopy. Courtesy Robert T. Rhode

This Reeves boasts a water tank behind the smokestack. The crosshatched pattern cast into the steamchest cover means the engine has a balanced valve. Covers with the Reeves logo have plain sliding D valves.

continued from page 164

In 1895, Ritchie & Dyer of Hamilton, Ohio, sold its road-engine manufactory and relevant patents to the Reeves Company of Columbus, Indiana. Reeves had built threshing machines for more than a dozen years and needed steam

engines to accompany the threshers. By acquiring Ritchie & Dyer's patterns, the Reeves firm secured rear-mounted, double-cylinder engines, which formed the foundation on which Reeves built a prosperous business.

To compete with burgeoning firms such as International Harvester, Emerson-Brantingham of Rockford, Illinois, bought out Reeves, as well as Geiser, in 1912. Reeves closed in 1925.

Albert Clay, son of Reeves' brilliant mechanical engineer, Harry Clay, designed the Hetherington & Berner steamroller of Indianapolis, according to Lyle Hoffmaster, an authority on Reeves who had conversations with Reeves factory personnel. At the time of this writing, Cummins, Inc., occupies the location of the Reeves plant.

This Reeves is moving a house without working up a sweat.

A Reeves is shown pulling a scraper.

The tender of this Reeves has been rotated sideways to plow. An Avery water wagon stands in the background

A historical Reeves photograph of Harry C. Clay, head mechanical engineer at Reeves, shows him driving the very first 40–140-horsepower Reeves engine, serial number 5143. Courtesy Gary Yeager, from the Haston L. St. Clair estate

Owens, Lane & Dyer Company, Ritchie & Dyer, and Other Engines Manufactured in Hamilton, Ohio

Farm steam engine factories proliferated in the Midwest during America's agricultural expansion, notably in towns with ready access to canals and later, to railroads. Hamilton, Ohio, typified such villages. Situated on the Miami and Erie Canal, Hamilton attracted artisans and craftsmen who built machines in a climate of considerable inventiveness. The town hosted three men who became innovators in

John C. Hooven, with his hat held near his chest, poses before his business in Hamilton, Ohio. A Hooven thresher and steamer peek out from the doors. Courtesy George C. Cummins Collection, Lane Public Library, Hamilton, Ohio

Here is an exceedingly rare look at an Owens, Lane & Dyer steamer. The front of the engine is blurry in the original photograph. Courtesy Milford (Ohio) Promont House Museum

the manufacture of steam engines for agricultural use and who demonstrated various forms of civic responsibility in helping Hamilton thrive: Job E. Owens, John C. Hooven, and William Dyer. The study of Hamilton's steam and boiler shops and the leaders who created them affords insight into how towns became industrial centers.

Reflecting on conditions in the late teens, Hamilton's *The Republican-News* reported, "The smoke from hundreds of factories, mills, and machine shops indicates clearly that a considerable business is being transacted here; the thousands of men who daily find employment in the hundreds of industries attest to the city's will power as an industrial center. . . . [T]he products of its shops . . . will be in demand as long as the industrial world revolves on its axis."[1] In actuality, Hamilton had been a hub of technological activity since the 1850s. When *The Republican-News* commented on Hamilton's importance, steam engines, threshing machines, and other agricultural implements had been steadily issuing from Hamilton's foundries for more than two generations.

Job E. Owens

Job E. Owens provided the opening chapter of Hamilton's agricultural steam history. Owens was born in Morganshire, Wales, in 1819.[2] He arrived in newly settled Columbus, Ohio, in 1824; moved to Hamilton in 1845; and founded the firm of Owens, Ebert & Dyer in that year. He established his works on the southeast corner of Fourth and Heaton Streets, immediately west of the canal fed by the

Miami River. It was a fortunate choice of locations because the Cincinnati, Hamilton & Dayton Railroad was later built near the canal, which passed along the west side of his shops, and the Pennsylvania Railroad eventually erected a trestle along the canal. Owens' new foundry "made nearly everything in metal," with iron and coal shipped down the Ohio River from Pittsburgh and up the Miami and Erie Canal to Hamilton. Living during the early years of American industrialism, Owens typified factory owners who worked alongside their employees and took an active part in the life of the town.

In the mid-1840s, a depression had concluded and a decade of prosperity began. In February 1846, Owens won the contract to create the iron portions of a new jail. The factory built "iron castings, moldings, and iron stoves. . . . By 1853, they were producing steam engines and paper-making machinery. In the 1860s and 1870s, they became known for their steam threshers and other farm machinery." Ebert died in 1854.[3] The name of Lane was added to the firm around the same time. By the start of the Civil War, the firm's agricultural products and mill gearing were being marketed under the tradename Eclipse, not to be confused with products of the Frick Company of Waynesboro, Pennsylvania, which used the Eclipse trademark for portable engines by 1874, according to a Frick catalog.

On early models of portable and skid engines designed by the Eclipse Machine Works of Hamilton, Ohio, the steamdome resembled a teakettle on a constricted pedestal. The cylinder clung to the side of the boiler beside the firebox, and the crankshaft ran across the smokebox end. Although the Eclipse engines were popular, Owens, Lane, Dyer & Co. anticipated the development of a traction engine. The firm experimented with a chain drive in 1873;[4] however, about the time the name changed to Owens, Lane & Dyer Machine Company in 1874, the manufacturer brought out a radically redesigned traction engine with gear drive, a tilted cylinder near the smokebox end, and the piston and connecting rod on an incline toward a large-diameter flywheel. Billed as a "traction or road engine," this new machine and its chain-driven predecessor gave Hamilton a mark of distinction. Job E. Owens received a gold medal for the first traction engine built west of Pittsburgh.[5] Owens probably did not deserve the honor. Newark, Ohio's iron works was manufacturing traction engines as early as 1858. Midwesterners were apparently unaware that several firms in California had invented successful traction engines before that. (See Jack Alexander's *Steam Power on California Roads and Farms.*)

A public gradually adjusting to the idea of steam-powered farming, sawmilling, and general manufacturing welcomed the firm's stationary, skid, portable, and traction engines: "Thousands of these engines were sold all over the world, and the owners grew gray in the service."[6] Engines and other equipment were sold from the headquarters at Hamilton and from the Owens, Lane & Dyer Machinery Depot located at 717 North Second Street, on the corner of Morgan in St. Louis, Missouri. The manufacturer distributed special handbills proclaiming the success of the "Road or Field Locomotive," which was the engine that won the Grand Gold Medal presented by the Ohio State Board of Agriculture at the Ohio State Fair in 1874 as the first traction engine west of Pittsburgh. One of these handbills reprinted the September 11, 1874, *Cleveland Herald's* account of the engine's tests:

"The third event was the trial of a traction engine, or steam road wagon more properly speaking. . . . Through the woods we went, turning out to the right and left to avoid trees, and backed up to a huge threshing machine, which was coupled on, and away we went again.

"The little engine responded nobly, as we passed over the rough ground until we reached the road. Seemingly the crowd had abandoned everything else. They covered the hill side and filled the grand stand until it was one dense mass of humanity. Closely following the wagon came a regiment of boys and men, each eager to see the novel sight. Then a piece of wet ground was crossed, the drivers sink deep into the yielding soil, but without any effort the engine regains the firm ground, and then we go down a steep declivity, and out into the ring, past the judges' stand. The thresher is then detached, and the wagon is put through some very fancy movements, in fact going through all the motions that a span of horses are required to do. The committee on machinery are then taken aboard and we pass out of the ring up an abrupt little hill nearly at an angle of forty-five degrees, and up the avenue to the president's headquarters. . . . Every one was highly pleased with the exhibition, and many prophesied that a new era had arrived in the application of steam to agricultural purposes, for the engine can be used as a stationary as well as a traction engine."[7]

The engine came in two sizes, 10 and 12 horsepower, both suitable for "moving and operating threshing machines, and for hauling loads of any kind, within the power of the engine." The company admitted that, "[W]e have not yet . . . tested them in plowing, but we have no question (from our knowledge of the construction of others) that in every respect they will perform in such work equal, if not superior, to any that have as yet been tried for use in this country." One engine "threshed 25,326 bushels of grain in 48 days, including time lost by wet weather." Another "threshed 25,796 bushels of grain in 49 days, that also including several days lost by wet weather." Belted to an Owens, Lane & Dyer traction engine, the California Chief, as the company's separator was named, could thresh 3,814 bushels in 5 1/2 days, while moving and setting the machines eight times. [8]

Despite the success of the firm, a resolution appeared as early as 1873 and sounded an ominous note: "Owing to the large aggregate amount of unsettled accounts unpaid or partially unpaid notes, at times accumulating upon our books, and due to us from our customers, the board of directors on the 9th day of May 1873, adopted the following resolution. . . . 'Resolved, that no past due notes or accounts will be carried by this company and that the privilege of renewal and extension of time, will be allowed only, when promptly made and with satisfactory security." In 1876, two years after the stunning achievements of the firm's road and field locomotive, the Owens, Lane & Dyer Machinery Company applied for a receiver so as to continue business. Elbridge G. Dyer's suicide precipitated the firm's financial woes.[9] According to the written request, dated August 31, 1876, "fully two-sevenths of the entire indebtedness of the company is due to the former firm of

Owens, Lane, Dyer & Co., all of whom are stockholders under the new organization of the Owens, Lane & Dyer Machine Company." Clark Lane, one of the original partners, was appointed as the receiver.[10] He had been working in Elkhart, Indiana, with his son but returned to Hamilton to accept his responsibilities. The late 1870s witnessed an economic slump, which was harder on some farmers than on others, with currency deflation and record numbers of farm foreclosures.[11] Not even a leader with Lane's reputation for sound financial planning could rescue the Owens, Lane & Dyer Machine Company, which went out of business in 1879.[12] Public-minded Lane donated to Hamilton the city's library in 1866, which has perpetuated the Lane name.

John C. Hooven

The second chapter of Hamilton's history of agricultural steam power began with John C. Hooven, whose parents were born in Pennsylvania. At the time he was born on September 29, 1843, the family lived in Montgomery County, Ohio.[13] His father worked as a farmer and cooper. After his family moved to Franklin, Ohio, in 1849, Hooven attended the common school there. Hooven's father began a hardware business in Xenia during 1864. Hooven & Sons soon moved to Hamilton and specialized in agricultural implements. Young Hooven was a member of Company B of the 146th Regiment of the Ohio Volunteer Infantry of 100-day servicemen. Hooven's father retired in 1876, but the sons retained the shop's name. In November 1878, Hooven's brother, E. P., retired and the firm's name was changed to that of the only original partner still involved in the business—John C. Hooven. The firm had manufactured threshers and engines since 1876.[14] His machines were called Monarch, a tradename bearing no connection to the Monarch road rollers produced in Groton, New York. Hooven built his boilers in one shop, the engines were built in another shop, and his thresher parts were built in several other shops.[15, 16] Although "[i]n three years he had sold seventy-five of these engines and sixty-five of the threshers," Hooven sold the implement business (but not the patents and patterns for engines and threshers) in September 1879 to Clark & Stanhope. Hooven sensed that change was in the wind.

The once-great Owens, Lane & Dyer Company had dissolved in 1879. Hooven, "as bright a commercial man as one will meet in many a day," hoped to capitalize on that fact. Accordingly, the firm of Hooven, Owens, Rentschler & Company was founded with a capital stock of $250,000,[17] and the group took over the Owens, Lane & Dyer facilities in 1880.[18] The manufacturer eventually

This is a rare look at a Ritchie & Dyer steamer with a buzz saw on the side. When Reeves wanted an engine, Reeves purchased the patterns from Ritchie & Dyer. Courtesy Ron Harris

expanded from Lowell Street on the south to Vine Street on the north.[19]

As president, Hooven contributed his Monarch portable engine, Monarch traction engines, and Monarch thresher to the firm. By January 1882, the factory had made "one hundred of the Monarch [portable] engines, fifty traction engines, and one hundred and fifty threshers."[20] The former Owens, Lane & Dyer products—the Eclipse line—were also built and sold. The manufacturer thus became known as the Monarch and Eclipse Machine Works.[21] Stationary, skid, portable, and traction engines, threshers, and sawmills crowded the shipping docks of the new company.

Owens retired from the firm in 1882, although his son Joe became a stockholder.[22] Retaining the Owens name, the reorganized business became known as the Hooven, Owens & Rentschler Company. The factory concentrated its efforts on designing and building "high-class stationary engines of the Corliss style."[23] The first of these engines appeared in 1883.[24] It boasted "a cylinder eighteen inches in diameter and forty-two inch stroke . . . and produced results as to

economy of fuel and close regulation of speed which were up to the highest standard."[25] By 1892, 750 "of these magnificent engines" had been constructed and varied from 35 to 2,000 horsepower. In 1901, the manufacturer's name changed to the Hooven, Owens, Rentschler Company, and "[t]he present shop with its very high bays was completed" in 1902.[26] Hooven, Owens, Rentschler stationary engines powered several machinery exhibits at the 1904 St. Louis World's Fair.[27]

The future held vast promise for Hooven, Owens, Rentschler. In 1928, the well-known Niles Tool Works merged with the company to form General Machinery Corporation.[28] Hooven's 1880 plan to acquire the firm of Owens, Lane & Dyer thereby contributed to the birth of an industrial giant.

In the late nineteenth century, Rentschler attained considerable prominence and gained a "standing in business and social circles" that was "of the highest order."[29] His home graces Hamilton's historic district. At the time of this writing, descendants of Hooven and Rentschler continue their ancestors' tradition of taking active roles in community improvement.

William Dyer and William Ritchie

The third chapter of Hamilton's agricultural steam heritage began with William Dyer, who had entered into a new manufacturing agreement by 1881. With William Ritchie as senior partner, the firm of Ritchie and Dyer had begun operation.[30]

Ritchie was born in Cincinnati, Ohio, on May 26, 1839.[31] He was educated in the public schools and at age 14 apprenticed as a machinist in Hamilton. By the mid-1850s, he was with Owens, Lane, Dyer & Company and became the superintendent of the works—a position he occupied until Owens, Lane & Dyer ceased operations in 1879. Ritchie's tenure with the firm sustained a significant interruption.

In 1861, Ritchie "responded to the President's call for three-year troops."[32] He enlisted in the 50th Ohio Volunteer Infantry but was transferred to the 69th "and served over three years at the front."[33] Shortly after the battle of Murfreesboro, "he was transferred to the engineers' corps of the Cumberland Army, and was there enabled to turn his

This Robert Bell steam engine is built under a licensing agreement with the Port Huron Company. The windstacker is a Decker produced by MacDonald.

mechanical knowledge to good account." Such engineers were known as "sappers and miners." They were exposed to the most "dangerous positions" in advance of the troops and were often "under fire while the main army was sleeping." Their work demanded endurance, "hence only strong, able-bodied men with fearless hearts were selected." They felled trees to protect crossings or bridges, hefted heavy planks to strengthen bridges, and strung pontoon boats across unfordable streams. Ritchie faced harrowing circumstances more than once:

"He was in Atlanta at the time the city was burned and was ordered by General Sherman to return to Chattanooga to conduct a pontoon train to Atlanta. Returning with the train as far as Big Shanty, he was stopped by pickets who reported that Rebel General French was between his train and Big Shanty. They retired to Moon Station, where they lay until about one o'clock at night, when scouts reported French's advance within half an hour's march of the station. The train was then backed to Altoona Pass, where there was a fort garrisoned by twelve hundred soldiers, while there was a million and a half of rations there awaiting shipment to Sherman's army at Atlanta. About twenty minutes after his arrival at Altoona he received a dispatch from General Corse, at Rome, Georgia, to unload the train and hasten to Rome for troops. This was done and the train returned with General Corse and about twelve hundred soldiers to reinforce the garrison at the fort. They arrived about five o'clock the next morning and immediately after unloading, the pickets were driven in by the advance of French's army. Here was fought one of the bloodiest little battles of the Civil War. Out of twenty-six hundred men engaged, twelve hundred fifty were killed and wounded in the fort; but they held possession, thus saving to the government a million and a half of rations, and enabling Sherman to make his memorable march to the sea."[34]

After Ritchie was mustered out at Savannah, Georgia, in 1865, he returned to his former post with Owens, Lane, Dyer & Company, only to see the firm dwindle by 1879 and be purchased by Hooven, Owens, Rentschler & Company

in 1880. Ritchie served as chief of the fire department from his election in 1879 through 1880. He joined Dyer in 1881. They established their factory on the south side of Vine Street between Fourth and Lowell Streets.[35]

The partners began business with "only about two thousand dollars . . . and the new concern had a hard time in getting along."[36] The shops made new patterns for sawmills, steam traction engines, ice-cutting implements, and small machinery.[37] Despite lack of capital, the young firm succeeded, largely through the drive and business acumen of the partners. In 1882, Dyer retired and left Ritchie in full command: "Mr. Ritchie pushed the business and everything turned out splendidly. Selling agencies were established in all prominent cities north and south and west and the line of products was increased to include traction engines from 10 to 40 horsepower, and various sizes of sawmills, varying in capacity from 3,000 to 70,000 feet of lumber per day."[38]

Approximately 50 traction engines and 300 sawmills were sold annually. The manufacturer employed between 40 and 50 mechanics.[39]

The Butler County Historical Society and Museum has Ritchie & Dyer Company stationery, dated 1884, that bears the subtitle "Owens, Lane and Dyer Machine Co." By that year, the Hooven, Owens & Rentschler Company had begun to concentrate exclusively on the building of Corliss

double-cylinder engines—the foundation on which Reeves built a prosperous business.

According to city directories, Ritchie entirely closed out the Ritchie & Dyer Company around 1892 to concentrate his efforts in the Advance Manufacturing Company. Benjamin Harrison, the 23rd President of the United States, appointed Ritchie a federal commissioner to the World's Columbian Exposition in Chicago.[44] Ritchie chaired the committee on machinery and planned "the marvelous exhibit in Machinery Hall." Ritchie served on Hamilton's board of education, where he championed "manual training and domestic science courses." He also served on the board of the Lane Free library.[45] Ritchie passed away in 1905, but his name is perpetuated in the Ritchie Auditorium, part of the Butler County Historical Society and Museum facilities.

Hamilton, Ohio, contributed as many as three significant chapters to the history of agricultural steam power. The city's industrial story spans the pioneer era, through the age when Civil War veterans walked the factory floors, to the zenith of steam-engine production, and beyond. When *The Republican-News* surveyed Hamilton's industrial might, the paper accurately reported, "If a city is to be judged by its products, and there seems to be no more certain method of judging a city, then greater Hamilton may well boast of its unexcelled reputation as a manufacturing city."[46] For historians, Hamilton occupies a prominent place on the map of America's agricultural and industrial legacy.

Robert Bell Engine and Thresher Company

Robert Bell first built sawmills and farm implements while running a repair shop in Hensall, Ontario. He and carpenter John Finlayson designed and poured patterns for a side-crank engine, which they mounted on a boiler Bell had purchased in London, Ontario. The Bell-Finlayson portable engine threshed in the 1899 season. The success of the steamer prompted orders, and Bell moved to a small foundry in Seaforth, Ontario. His business soon came to be known as the Robert Bell Engine and Thresher Company. As traction engines were in demand, Bell obtained a license to build Port Huron engines in Canada. He constructed his first traction engine in 1901. Bell also manufactured portable engines along Port Huron lines. Even though Robert Bell steamers were essentially Port Hurons, various features made Robert Bells distinctive. For example, Robert Bell rear-mounted engines boasted a heavy channel-iron frame running from the front axle to the sides of the firebox. Port Huron's customary cast driver wheels were not always present on Robert Bells. Bell built his last new engine in 1928, although rebuilds and repairs continued for a few more years.

engines and had relinquished rights to the Owens, Lane & Dyer business. Ritchie & Dyer then traded on the reputation of the old firm's name and kept Owens, Lane & Dyer equipment in repair.

Ritchie possessed "the sterling qualities of energy, intelligence, economy and personal push."[40] Ritchie was an excellent mechanic and never better satisfied than when "examining and studying the constituent elements of some complicated piece of machinery."[41] He "accumulated a handsome competence through industry and wise management, and . . . reached the point on life's journey where he need not be further annoyed by the perplexities of business life."

Ritchie, with a capital stock of $50,000, created a new firm in 1887.[42] The Advance Manufacturing Company, not to be mistaken for the Advance Thresher Company of Battle Creek, Michigan, built gas and gasoline internal-combustion engines that Ritchie designed. The works were located on the northwest corner of North B Street and Wayne Streets. In the process of establishing his new shops in 1895, Ritchie sold his road-engine manufactory and relevant patents to the Reeves Company of Columbus, Indiana.[43] Reeves had built threshing machines for more than a dozen years and needed steam engines to accompany the threshers. By acquiring Ritchie & Dyer's patterns, Reeves secured rear-mounted,

This Robinson attained approximately 8 horsepower and resembles

A Robinson engine is shown here performing some drilling.

Robinson & Company

Francis W. Robinson was born in Baltimore in 1810, two years before his family moved to Philadelphia, Michele Bottorff and William A. Stahl report. One of Robinson's ancestors was Sir William Robinson, who journeyed to America with William Penn. Robinson migrated with a sister and an uncle to Darke County, Ohio, in 1829. From there, he moved on to Richmond, Indiana. In 1842, he organized the Robinson Machine Works, which was powered by a horse. Robinson began to manufacture portable engines and Pitts threshers in 1860. The works was incorporated in 1872. In 1877, the firm was reorganized and became Robinson & Company; it was incorporated under that name in 1889. Bascom B. Clarke, editor of *American Thresherman* and the subject of Charles E. Whelan's biography *Bascom Clarke* (1913), sold the very first engine for Francis W. Robinson.

Steam aficionados often mistake Robinson engines for Gaar-Scott engines in historic photographs. Robinson engines had a wooden band encircling the inner rim of the flywheel, and clutch shoes pressed against that band. F. W. Robinson invented this clutch mechanism and called it La Grippe. Robinson manufactured sawmills and hay balers in addition to engines and threshers.

Robinson died in 1897. Henry E. Robinson, his son, assumed the presidency of the firm. Henry died in 1909. Samuel E. Swayne, Francis' son-in-law, then became the president.

Robinson steam engine production ended in 1920. On St. Patrick's Day in 1999, a fire destroyed the factory. At the time of this writing, the Porter family near Rushville, Indiana, has a complete Robinson rig consisting of a steam engine, thresher, and water wagon.

Note the grouter pattern on the drive wheel of this Robinson, which is pulling a heavy load.

The spectacle of a steam engine affords an occasion for everyone to pose.

M. Rumely Company

For many students of Rumely history, Dr. Edward Rumely's failed efforts to found an empire overshadow his grandfather's achievements, and articles about the Rumelys customarily devote more words to Edward than to his grandfather Meinrad. Perhaps such a practice is only fitting, as Dr. Rumely brought an untimely end to several proud companies, including his grandfather's.

Meinrad Rumely was born in 1828. As Scott L. Thompson has found, Meinrad envisioned a military career in the Prussian army. During inspection one day, Meinrad was standing out of line and his officer slapped Meinrad with

Crum and Western owned this Rumely in a photograph dated August 29, 1892.

Beginning in the late 1800s, bicycle clubs became a craze. Bicycles thus turn up in photographs of steamers, such as this Rumely with an Avery Yellow Fellow thresher.

This is an old Rumely with a long belt to keep the engine far enough away from the thresher that no sparks will set the straw stack on fire.

a pistol. Meinrad was knocked unconscious and spent three days in the hospital. The tearful officer begged Meinrad to forgive him, as he was facing a court martial, but Meinrad refused. Meinrad was given a pass to recuperate at his parents' home. The family later helped Meinrad join brothers Jacob and John, who were already in Ohio.

Meinrad arrived in America in 1848, but without his trunk, which was stolen during his journey. After landing he saved money by working in a machine shop. He then journeyed to Canton, Ohio, where he joined Jacob in making wooden pumps. In 1850, Meinrad moved to Massillon, where John was a patternmaker for the Russell brothers. Meinrad built horse sweeps for Russell, and then went on to set up threshers for the Moffet Company of Wapakoneta, Ohio. In 1851, Meinrad moved to Chicago, where he worked in a machine shop and helped build a steam fire engine. He eventually made his way to La Porte, Indiana, where he purchased a blacksmith shop. John and Meinrad formed the M & J Rumely Company in 1853. The brothers produced flour mills, machinery for harvesting ice, and sorghum presses. Meinrad developed a thresher in 1854, and M & J Rumely expanded in 1862. By the late 1860s, the firm was building stationary engines, and in the early 1870s, the Rumelys began production of portable farm engines. Meinrad bought his brother's interest in the company in 1882, and the firm was incorporated as the M. Rumely Company in 1887. Meinrad groomed his sons, William and Joseph, to take over his firm. After his death in 1904, mechanically-minded William became the next president of the company, and business-minded Joseph served as a director.

Joseph's son was Edward, who attended Notre Dame University and spent a year at Oxford University in England. Edward matriculated to Heidelberg University in Germany, and then enrolled in Freiberg University, also in Germany, where he graduated *magna cum laude* as an M.D. Dr. Rumely returned to La Porte three years after Meinrad's death. Dr. Rumely incrementally assumed control of the business, focusing on the production of plowing engines. Dr. Rumely persuaded John Alstyne Secor and William Higgins, Secor's nephew, to design a kerosene tractor. The first production model appeared in 1910, and the renowned OilPull was born. Its sales were felt throughout the world.

In late 1911, Dr. Edward Rumely took over the Advance Thresher Company, and Rumely grabbed American-Abell in early 1912. Dr. Rumely's plan was to form a machine empire to compete with and to eclipse International Harvester. On December 9, 1911, Gaar, Scott & Company was transferred to M. Rumely. In 1912, Dr. Edward Rumely bought the Northwest Thresher Company. He wanted the

This Rumely steamer has a side water tank tucked behind the driver wheel. Note the front axle arrangement of this vintage Rumely traction engine.

Would it be overkill for a multiple-ton steam engine to pull one wood-handled plow? The engineer may think so.

Kids in knickers join in a boxing match in front of this Rumely steamer.

firm's modern factory in Stillwater and the Universal tractor, which Dr. Rumely renamed the GasPull. Dr. Rumely established Rumely Products, a company devoted exclusively to sales of the various implements manufactured by the various firms now under the Rumely wing.

The panic of 1907 had persisted into 1908, and business remained wary and sluggish through 1912. By 1914, Dr. Rumely was watching his empire's ledgers plummet. On January 19, 1915, the M. Rumely Company and Rumely Products both went into receivership. The Rumely takeover of Advance at the end of 1911 had signaled the denouement of American-Abell. The Gaar firm had built

its last threshing machines in 1914. Even though advertisements for Gaar-Scott engines persisted until 1918, the grand company had reached a premature end. Northwest had met its demise in 1915.

Meinrad Rumely's son, William N., apprenticed in his father's machine shop in 1872 and in the late 1870s took a course in drafting and design at the Stevens Institute in Hoboken, New Jersey. He had received an educational foundation in private school and college. By 1882, the year thought to be the inception of traction engine production, William was superintending his father's works and also contributing designs. He became vice president in 1887

Don't be misled! A New Giant tank has been added to the back of this Rumely steamer.

A Rumely steam tractor with extension rims is plowing with a 10-bottom plow.

The especially heavy driver wheels feature prominently on this Rumely engine.

A Rumely with extension rims is pulling an eight-bottom plow.

This is a massive-looking Rumely!

and was president in 1904. As Dr. Edward Rumely's empire crumbled, William sought a way out. When 1913 began, William resigned and launched the Illinois Thresher Company. As Scott L. Thompson has shown, William found a solid investment in buildings once owned by the Marsh Harvester Company, Elwood Wagon Company, and F. C. Patton Company in Sycamore, Illinois. P. Bradley McIntyre, a Rumely branch manager in Billings, Montana, became William's secretary and treasurer. G. E. Dutton became vice president, and W. C. Roby became superintendent of threshers and hullers. Within the year, William had a thresher that easily converted to a clover huller—a thresher much like the Rumely Ideal threshing machine. Full production of the new thresher began in 1914. William also produced steam traction engines in both 20- and 25-horsepower models. About 63 steamers were built during the firm's all too brief tenure. In 1917, William reorganized his firm as the Rumely-Robbins Company and, calling himself the dean of American threshing machine manufacturers, took out ads for combination

thresher-hullers. Despite his efforts to succeed, bankruptcy ended William's hopes for a company to rival his father's.

Meanwhile, the receiver of Rumely's empire, Finley P. Mount, decisively governed the reorganization, which kept OilPull tractor manufacturing in La Porte, Indiana, and steam-powered thresher production in Battle Creek. The Advance-Rumely Company was launched on September 7, 1915. For a short time, Mount continued the building of Advance engines and related machines in Battle Creek, even after the Advance-Rumely firm entered the market.

Dr. Rumely took control of the *New York Evening Mail* newspaper. Until the sinking of the *Lusitania*, Dr. Rumely's columns supported Germany, but when America entered World War I, his paper championed America's cause. Despite his patriotism, Dr. Rumely was convicted on circumstantial evidence of accepting German funds to finance the *Evening Mail* and was sentenced to prison. He was released after a month. In 1925, President Calvin Coolidge granted him a full pardon and an apology.

This impressively large Rumely is preparing to move this auditorium. The photograph states that the scene is American Falls, Idaho.

This Russell is powering a thresher with a webstacker. The trademark of the Russell firm was a Holstein bull named "The Boss."

This old Russell engine is involved in a logging operation.

A Russell takes the lead, while a C. Aultman and a Robinson assist in moving a house.

Russell Company

In 1842, brothers Charles M. Russell, Nahum S. Russell, and Clement Russell entered into partnership in the C. M. Russell & Company to erect houses, construct furniture, and sell stoves. Four years earlier, Nahum and Charles had collaborated in contracting. In the 1830s, they made "knockouts," groundhog threshers that knocked the grain loose from the stalk. By the mid-1840s, they were producing a Pitts-type thresher that included several innovations by Charles Russell. In 1845, the firm built a steam engine to power the factory. The Russell brothers also manufactured plows, mowers, and reapers. In 1853, Charles joined Joseph Davenport and Marshall Wellman in building railroad cars. C. M. Russell died in 1860. In 1864, three more brothers—Joseph K., Thomas H., and George L.—began working

Russell's unique tandem-compound cylinders have a separation between them.

This fairly old Russell stands poised to work.

The engineer of this Russell engine sports a hat with an extremely broad brim. Such hats were fairly common in the early years of steam threshing.

This photograph depicts the typical silhouette of Russell engines manufactured during the company's heyday.

A Russell panoramic view portrays derrick threshing. A derrick lifted the headed wheat onto a table so that the grain could be gathered for threshing.

Note the long smokebox of this tandem-compound Russell, which has stopped, with a road grader, in front of the home of a doctor.

for the company, and the firm name changed to Russell and Company. Allen Russell, yet another brother, became a partner in the firm in 1871. The Russell Company was incorporated in 1878.

Russell engines were using a link-motion during the year the company was incorporated. The Marsh gear was employed in 1882, and the link-motion was phased out by the following year. In 1883, the Russell Company welcomed a double-ported valve and a friction clutch designed by C. M. Giddings with help from the mechanical engineers of the Russell firm. Russell began using the Giddings reverse mechanism the following year.

Around 1895, the Russell Company hired Charles Longenecker to design a steamroller. The Longenecker Russell steam-powered road roller was one of at least three

continued on page 190

This is a charming photograph of a Russell on the road. These Russells had cast smokeboxes.

Only one Russell engine is required to pull this great big building.

This tandem-compound Russell is running a Cyclone thresher.

This is an eye-popping picture of a 150-horsepower Russell road locomotive, with the driver on his perch before the flywheel.

Perhaps the man with the shovel is pretending to play a banjo in this photograph of a stone-crushing operation with a Russell traction engine and a Farquhar portable steamer.

continued from page 186
distinct types of Russell rollers. One type was modeled on the agricultural traction engine that Charles M. Giddings produced beginning in 1882. Another type displayed Longenecker's design, and yet another design was an especially rugged machine with a massive kingpin housing.

By 1913, the Russell plant had expanded to cover 26 acres. Over time the firm produced sawmills, threshers, horse powers, stationary steam engines, and steam shovels.

Russell traction engines, road rollers, compound road locomotives, and steam shovels helped build the road from Massillon to Canton to Alliance. A dummy locomotive ran on a narrow-gauge rail line parallel to the road and transported the necessary construction materials. Once steamrollers had created a solid bed of gravel and sand, bricks were cemented together to form the pavement.

Russell built its last steam engine, serial number 17152, in 1924. After the company shut down, four more engines were assembled from unused parts. In 1927, an auction eliminated whatever was left of the factory.

Sawyer-Massey Company

In 1835, John Fisher moved from New York to Hamilton, Ontario, where he opened a shop. In 1836, he built what may have been the first thresher in Canada. He based his design on the Maikle thresher of Scotland. The machine was a decided improvement over the flail. Dr. Calvin McQuesten, a medical doctor who was a cousin of Fisher's, left Lockport, New York—and his profession—to become a partner in Fisher's business. L. D. Sawyer and his brothers, Payson and Samuel, who were nephews of Dr. McQuesten, joined Fisher & McQuesten in the early 1840s. Fisher served as Hamilton's mayor. He died in 1856. The business became known as L. D. Sawyer and Company, and the factory was called the Hamilton Agricultural Works. L. D. Sawyer produced reapers, threshers, and horse powers. Portable steam engines were added in the early 1860s. The firm was an agency for British-built Aveling & Porter steamrollers.

In 1892, H. A. Massey became president of L. D. Sawyer and Company, which was renamed the Sawyer & Massey

A full Sawyer-Massey outfit is on the road to the next "thrashin'" job.

Company. Walter E. Massey and Chester D. Massey also joined the firm, which erected a spacious warehouse in Regina for supplying implements to western Canada. By 1906, H. P. Coburn, a nephew of L. D. Sawyer, was serving as vice president and general manager of Sawyer & Massey.

The Goodison story is linked to Sawyer & Massey, as well as to Waterloo and Waterous. It begins in 1847 when John McCloskey was born in Ireland. In 1864, McCloskey's family emigrated to Canada and settled in Oldcastle, not too far from Windsor, Ontario. McCloskey and his oldest brothers established a carriage manufactory. Given his mechanical background, McCloskey soon was working in the MacPherson factory in Fingal, where he invented improvements in the new vibrator threshers that were gaining market share from the older apron variety of threshing machine. A firm in London, Ontario, built McCloskey's threshers with its patented improvements. David Darvil and Company soon became licensed to produce McCloskey Threshers. The Waterloo Manufacturing Company briefly built the same machine but called it the Counterbalance Thresher.

In 1887, John Goodison, who was born in Ireland in 1849, and George H. Samis sold their interest in a bankrupt firm, for which Goodison had served as general manager, to Sawyer & Massey of Hamilton, Ontario. The insolvent implement factory was in Sarnia, directly across from Port Huron, Michigan. Sawyer & Massey kept Goodison as manager. After becoming sole proprietor in 1889, he abandoned the reapers, plows, and cornshellers that the Sarnia factory had once produced and focused his firm on the building of threshers.

In 1892, the John Goodison Thresher Company brought John McCloskey to Sarnia and began production of the New McCloskey threshers. Goodison distributed Waterous steam

Belted and running, this Sawyer-Massey exemplifies the powerful design of the engine.

This Sawyer-Massey is belted to a buzz saw.

engines. In 1902, the year that McCloskey died, Goodison began building his own portable engines, and the first traction engines appeared in 1904. The Waterous Company supplied the boilers for early Goodison engines, and Sawyer & Massey built the boilers for the later steamers.

John Goodison died in 1915. His son, William Thomas Goodison, assumed the presidency of the company. William was born in Strathroy in 1876 and passed the bar in 1899. The Goodison firm began distributing Hart-Parr tractors in 1899. In 1923, the John Goodison farm hosted an international plowing match. From 1925 until 1928, William T. Goodison served in the Canadian House of Commons. The Goodison firm moved to Toronto in 1951.

Back in 1910, the Masseys had wanted to focus on the development and sale of gasoline tractors, but other interests in the firm preferred to expand the manufacture of steamers. The Masseys parted company with the business, and the reorganization produced the Sawyer-Massey Company.

Sawyer-Massey entered the gasoline tractor trade on the eve of World War I and produced shells and steam road wagon engines for Great Britain during the war. After the war, the firm concentrated on supplying the road-building industry. T. A. Russell became president in 1927 and also presided over Willys Overland of Canada. Sawyer-Massey began distributing Austin Manufacturing Company road-construction products in the 1930s. The company ceased to exist after World War II.

This photograph probably was taken at an engine trial, as suggested by the Winnipeg gas-engine cylinder oil box on the ground. Here are two Sawyer-Massey steam engines.

A Sawyer-Massey is pulling a train of wagons.

Scheidler Machine Works, John H. McNamar, and Julius J. D. McNamar

Vying with A. B. Farquhar for the title of "the most flamboyant industrialist" was Reinhard Scheidler. Recognized as a showman, Scheidler took a fierce enjoyment in competition. His ardent pursuit of profit, however, proved to be his tragic flaw.

M. W. Edgar left Barnesville, Ohio, traveled 70 miles through rough terrain, and arrived in Newark, Ohio, a happy man. But on the evening of Wednesday, April 29, 1903, he returned home with a tale of horror.

Edgar had brought his old 18-horsepower portable engine to be overhauled at Scheidler Machine Works, the factory that built it. The repairs were completed, and while his machine was wheeled from the shop to the yard, Edgar eagerly awaited the final test.

In the front office sat Henry and Oscar, sons of founder Reinhard Scheidler, and Wales C. Collins, Reinhard's son-in-law.[1] Reinhard was born in the province of Hessin in Germany in 1834 and had come to America in 1851.[2] He never lost his German accent. Reinhard spent his apprenticeship as a machinist in Mt. Savage, Maryland, but fire destroyed the factory. Afterward, he found employment first in Zanesville and then in Mount Vemon, Ohio. In 1855, he came to the city with which he would be identified forever—Newark.

On that Wednesday, Reinhard Scheidler was the picture of the successful businessman: his hair neatly parted, his long beard and mustache combed, and his apparel immaculate. He served as vice president and director of the Newark Savings Bank.[3] The newspapers credited him with seeking every advantage for his chosen city. He built the first streetcar line for Newark and was largely responsible for extending the Electric Interurban Line to nearby Granville. Reinhard rose from his chair "in robust health and buoyant spirits" and passed through a door from the office into the machine shop.[4] Stanley Miller, his grandson, was working there, learning the machinist trade. He watched Reinhard step across the shop, through the wide-open double doors, and out into the afternoon sunlight of the yard.

Scheidler was a showman and commanded attention wherever he went. Workers such as Elmer Swonger, busy at his machine on the Franklin Street side of the shop, noticed Scheidler any time he strode along the floors of his factory. They admired their boss and proved their devotion at the annual birthday party in Mr. Scheidler's honor. Every June 4, at four o'clock in the morning, Scheidler was awakened from slumber by the clangor of a brass band serenading his home.[5] Chuckling jovially, Reinhard accompanied his workers to the factory, where everyone boarded a train of wagons hooked to Scheidler's road locomotive—the one he specially designed for speed—its safety valve popping off with a rush of steam so loud that people had to shout to be heard. The merry cavalcade rolled down the Dog Leg Road. At the spot where the big tree grew in the middle of the thoroughfare, the revelers stopped for speeches, applause, and cheers. Then the train pressed on to the lake for a day spent in games and festivities, punctuated by laughter inspired by Scheidler's impromptu rhymed verse.

Scheidler was impressive, as was his factory. The main building—50 feet wide by 150 feet long—was a slate-roofed, brick and stone structure fronting First Street. On both ends of the building, painted letters two feet tall proclaimed, "Scheidler Machine Works, Portable & Stationary Engines and Sawmills, Business Established in 1861." The machine works occupied the first floor of the building. The woodworking department and paint shop were on the second floor, and lumber was stored on a mezzanine suspended toward the back.[6] No support pillars interrupted the expanse of the second floor. At the grand opening of his factory on February 16, 1882, Scheidler held a ball. He decorated the hall with three runners of cloth bunting

McNamar steamers quietly competed with engines that were much ballyhooed by the showy Reinhard Scheidler.

This Scheidler steam engine is powering a stone crusher and grader.

that looped downward from the rafters, large American flags above every window, pairs of smaller American flags in between the windows, and pine trees along the sides of the floor. A double row of gas jets "cast their refulgent, mellow light over the assemblage of bright, smiling faces."[7] One thousand five hundred invitations had been sent.

In the evening, rain fell in torrents, but throngs of well-wishers who were eager to attend Newark's social event of the century braved the elements. At any hour, 400 people danced to the music of Bauer's Orchestra from Zanesville. The employees presented Mr. Scheidler with a gold-headed cane, and the citizens gave him a sterling silver tea service. For perhaps the only time in his life, Scheidler was speechless. Not even a rhyme came to mind. All he could do was smile. In a speech commemorating Scheidler's achievements, Judge Hunter expressed the city's thanks to their esteemed citizen by saying "With abiding faith in the future of Newark, believing in himself, he laid the foundation and built these splendid works, under whose roof we are sheltered now." Scheidler replied, "My friends, I am surprised. If it ver any other time I could make you a rhyme, but I'm knocked clear out of time." The dancing continued until dawn, and all wished Mr. Scheidler long life and prosperity.

On that afternoon in 1903, Scheidler crossed the yard and entered the room housing the large Scheidler stationary engine that ran the plant. This room was attached to the main building and to a wing extending northward from the western quadrant of the main building that measured 60 feet wide and 100 feet long. The wing contained the blacksmith shop and foundry.[8] From the wing's northern end, a boiler shop paralleled the main building. Engineer Bert Viall, who was 45 years old, looked up from his work to see his chief beckoning him. "Come into the yard,"

Scheidler directed. "I vant you to keep up the steam in the engine ve are testing."[9] Viall reluctantly obeyed. As he later stated, "[T]his was the first time in ten months that I had been engineer that I was called upon to do this kind of work." Scheidler felt confident that Viall could do the job. Unswerving confidence stood as one of Scheidler's greatest strengths. Some might have called his self-assurance arrogant or brash, but his tenacity and spirit were precisely the qualities that led to his success. His mettle had been tested for over half a century in the steam business, and during that time he forged powerful convictions

By April 1854, Joseph E. Holmes, from New York's famed Crystal Palace, and J. W. Gray, from the Gordon-Mckee Company of Massachusetts, were brought into the Newark Machine Works to build engines.[10] After studying steamer design in Europe, Holmes and Gray manufactured the Joseph E. Holmes portable. When Scheidler arrived in Newark, the city was buzzing with steam talk. The rapidly expanding Newark Machine Works hired the young German as a journeyman machinist.

By the late 1850s, the company was in trouble from the effects of overcapitalizing amid a disturbed economy.[11] The Newark Machine Works went bankrupt and entered into receivership in 1860. The bank appointed Reinhard Scheidler as one of the receivers.[12]

The 26-year-old Scheidler had struck up a friendship with a fellow machinist, John H. McNamar, the 30-year-old son of another receiver. Scheidler agreed to have John manage the plant for the receivers. By 1861, the Newark Machine Works was virtually closed down.[13] In that same year, Scheidler started a small machine shop of his own on Railroad Street.[14] He repaired engines and did other iron work.

In 1864, what was left of the Newark Machine Works was sold to the Blandy Company of Zanesville.[15] Blandy

A McNamar steam engine powers a threshing rig along a road. Reinhard Scheidler and John McNamar were business partners until they had a falling out.

already manufactured steamers but began building skid and portable engines in Newark. When fire destroyed the Zanesville plant in 1866, Newark took over the production of parts and service for Zanesville Blandy machines. Meanwhile, John H. McNamar and Reinhard Scheidler had formed a partnership, the Scheidler & McNamar Company, in 1864.

The courageous new firm occupied a "humble group of shanties at the comer of Walnut and Third streets."[16] The foundry and boiler plant were on the south side of the railroad tracks, and the machine shop, erecting floor, and warehouse were on the north side.[17] Scheidler and McNamar built portable and stationary engines and circular sawmills. By 1871, the business had earned enough money to build a new works on Third Street. For the next decade, the company boomed—even during the panic of 1873.[18]

In 1879, the Blandy Company of Newark was sold to the Union Iron Works, which specialized in attachments to transform portable engines into traction engines.[19] Its leather-belt drives were unsuccessful because the belts frequently broke, which made for hair-raising rides down the Welsh Hills. The chain drives were more acceptable.

On March 29, 1881, the Scheidler & McNamar company abruptly ended.[20] Scheidler could no longer tolerate McNamar's insufferable cautiousness. Scheidler wanted freedom to experiment in engine design and utterly abandoned the 16-year partnership. He withdrew by selling his interest in the business to McNamar.[21] On the morning of April 2nd, John McNamar started the day's business alone.[22] Scheidler quickly set about planning for his new factory on First Street just south of the canal. In the competitive field of equipment manufacturing, the former friends were now bitter rivals.

Both men devoted entire pages in their catalogs to criticism of the other's engines. Scheidler flamboyantly promoted his machines and soon surpassed McNamar in engine sales, but the patient McNamar slowly and surely kept his business going.

In November 1883, Scheidler sued Jacob Tustin for buying a McNamar engine that Scheidler claimed had infringed his patent for "a bed plate and heater for portable boilers."[23] The case was brought to the U.S. Circuit Court of the Western District of Pennsylvania, in Pittsburgh. Scheidler lost. McNamar's lawyers proved to the court's satisfaction that Scheidler's "invention" was not legally patentable, as numerous other manufacturers had built exactly similar bed plates in advance of Scheidler's patent. Furthermore, the lawyers argued that McNamar's engine merely combined two patterns sold to John when Scheidler ended their partnership.

By 1885, John began releasing control of his engine works to his son, Julius J. D. McNamar, who inherited his father's traits of prudent planning and careful testing before implementing any change in a product. John passed away in 1888. His death did not end the Scheidler–McNamar enmity. Scheidler prolonged the war by attacking Julius.

Scheidler built his first traction engine in 1891. It was a horse-steered, 10-horsepower engine and was sold to Silas Preston.[24] It boasted two long levers on the platform to disengage whichever bull pinion was on the inside of the turn.[25] Unfortunately, the gears kept breaking. A differential was installed later. Still, Scheidler had bested his rival by being first. Julius did not bring out a traction engine until 1892.[26] He invented and patented its compensating mechanism, which consisted of spur gears. It never broke.

After 1890, the Union Iron Works brought in a Canadian by the name of Walker, who built two engines. At the 1893 Columbian Exposition in Chicago, noted steam authority Professor John Edson Sweet complimented the Walker engine on display.[27] That engine was top-mounted on a typical locomotive boiler. The other Walker engine combined a vertical and horizontal boiler, as early A. Gaar engines did. At the Licking County Fair, one of the Walker engines demonstrated its power by lifting a mass of pig iron.[28] It accomplished this feat by means of a chain rigged over a pulley that was bound to the limb of a tree. Scheidler would brook no such triumph by a Johnny-come-lately in the engine business.

Through friends who were strangers to the Canadian, Scheidler provoked Walker into wagering $100 that no other engine could perform the stunt. Scheidler dramatically took the bet and the contest was set for the next morning. In the meantime, he attached special mud lugs to the driver wheels of his fast road locomotive.[29] When dawn came, Scheidler had what he wanted—a huge crowd. His engine chuffed into view with its mud hooks flashing like spades. Walker and the employees of the Union Iron Works protested, but nothing in the bet had denied the use of such lugs. The multitude demanded satisfaction and the trial began. One of Scheidler's sons ran the engine. At first, the wheels slipped in the mud and a murmur of disapproval ran through the audience. Scheidler's son stopped and slowly opened the throttle. The engine crept forward. Once the drivers emerged from the soft ground, the engineer gave the road locomotive full steam. All eyes were on the massive weight lifting high into the air. Walker ran toward the Scheidler engine shouting, "Stop her! Stop her!" Taking his orders only from his father, Scheidler's son kept going. The pig iron smashed into the pulley; the limb groaned, cracked, and crashed to the ground; a hurrah went up from the gathering; and the road locomotive pulled its trophy of tree limb, pig iron, and pulley back to the Scheidler equipment exhibit. Walker was humiliated. The Union Iron Works quit business in the early 1900s.[30]

At another Licking County Fair, Scheidler challenged Julius to a speed contest around the half-mile oval track. The engineer on the special Scheidler road locomotive "waited impatiently for the rival McNamar engine."[31] It never showed up. Gleeful at his apparent victory, Scheidler took over the levers himself, and to the delight of the crowd, he ran the engine around and attained speeds up to 15 mph.[32]

Scheidler understood competition. He placed serene confidence in his machines while denigrating the equipment of rivals. Scheidler proclaimed the advantages of his patented piston valve while pointing out the flaws of McNamar's double-ported slide valve.[33] Scheidler vaunted the benefits of locating the steamchest outside the cylinder so that the crankshaft could be positioned close to the boiler. He praised his unique arrangement of valve cranks. He championed his method of shifting the intermediate gear along its bearing for traction. Meanwhile, he denounced McNamar's engines, with their Grimes reversing mechanism. McNamar rejoined by condemning Scheidler's cast-iron gearing and his pipe-spoke wheels.

On that Wednesday afternoon in April 1903, when Bert Viall accompanied his boss to the yard where Mr. Edgar's old portable was facing the boiler shop, it already had a good head of steam. Scheidler directed Viall to take over the firing of the boiler and the running of the engine. August Hess was 20 years old and was only one year younger than Scheidler had been when he first arrived in Newark.[34] Hess was the machinist whom Scheidler entrusted with the repairs to this engine, and Hess was in immediate charge of its final test. He hopped up on a temporary platform beside the engine and began to oil the bearings.

For the trial, a long, wide plank was brought beneath the flywheel and a fulcrum was built beneath it, "close to the point of contact with the wheel." James Cain, Fred Bausch, William Jennings, and Emmet Siegel were prepared to sit on the free end of the so-called "pry plank," and their combined weight forced the other end against the undersurface of the flywheel. Through this means of creating a load, the engine's power could be approximately determined. Cain and Bausch were 19 years old, Jennings was 18, and Siegel was only 16. Cain was a boilermaker apprentice, Jennings was an apprentice in the machine shop, and Bausch and Siegel were helpers.

A Scheidler steamer is belted backward to a sawmill.

The best engineers steadily kept a hot fire going with no black smoke. Perhaps the photographer asked this Scheidler engineer to create black smoke for a dramatic picture.

Machinist James Markham strolled into the yard. Seeing that the trial of Edgar's engine was about to get underway, Markham joined Scheidler and Edgar in front of the engine to watch. The safety valve was set to release steam in excess of 90 psi, but Scheidler was "anxious to show that an even greater pressure could be carried with safety and to a better advantage for the purpose of the test." As many told of the account, Scheidler shouted, "Give it more steam, Got damn it!" According to traditional accounts, he ordered Hess to stand on the safety valve.

In a later statement to the press, Hess said he screwed down the pop valve one and three-quarters turns, which set the release at 115 pounds of steam per square inch. Before long, the safety valve was shrieking with escaping steam. Viall began to run the engine, while Cain, Bausch, Jennings, and Siegel sat down on the plank. The smokestack chuffed loudly under the sudden load, but the engine did not stop. The test was presenting every promise of being a success.

According to his testimony later, Viall noticed that the steam gauge was registering a pressure of 120 psi. Steam was being generated faster than the engine could use it under load and faster than the open safety valve could release it. Perhaps the safety valve lacked the proper capacity. "I thought this was too much for the old boiler," Viall stated that evening. He went back behind the engine and threw open the firebox door. Perhaps he was intending to pull the fire from the

firebox, an action taken when it is known that a boiler has enough water but the heat must be brought down quickly, or possibly he thought that opening the firebox door would help to cool down the fire. In any event, Viall knew nothing more until he recovered consciousness.

The time was 3:55 p.m. From the sound, several men nearby thought that two freight cars had collided on the Baltimore and Ohio line close to the Scheidler works. After all, a locomotive was switching cars on the depot tracks just north of the canal. The concussion of Mr. Edgar's exploding engine was not as loud as might be imagined.

The force, though, was terrifying. A cloud of ash from the yard blew outward in all directions. The wooden elevator shaft immediately behind the engine was splintered halfway to the top, while hot ashes and cinders shot up the shaft. The blast that came through the open double doors was so powerful that in the machine shop, Elmer Swonger was knocked off his feet and thrown flat. The panes in the windows on the Franklin side of the main building shattered. Dust flew up through cracks to the second floor.

Cain, the boilermaker apprentice, suffered three cuts to his lip and several of his teeth were knocked out. He had been hurled 40 feet. Bausch's left leg was bruised. Jennings, the machinist apprentice, had been thrown 35 feet and was badly bruised. He came to rest under the cupola, the small furnace for melting metals. Siegel's head was bruised. The four had been tossed off the pry plank like rag dolls while the exploding engine flew over them.

Both of Bert Viall's feet and the left side of his head were scalded when steam rushed out at him from the open firebox door. His left leg was injured, probably from being hurled 40 feet toward First Street.

A split second before the detonation, James Markham, the machinist, noticed a small obstruction beneath the free end of the pry plank, and he bent over to remove it. The engine soared up and over Markham while he was leaning down. His left arm was scalded, but he was otherwise spared serious injury.

August Hess, with oilcan in hand, was leaning over the engine when the explosion occurred. He was carried up with it and fell 30 feet east of the engine's original location.

M. W. Edgar's face and head were cut. When the crownsheet blew down at the same instant that Viall opened the firebox door, the bulk of Edgar's engine traced an arc high into the sky and impaled itself on the heavy roof timbers in the southwest corner of the new boiler shop. In its crashing descent, the boiler tore away part of the wall. One of the guides of the engine flew over the boiler shop and the canal before clattering onto the B. & O. freight tracks. The flywheel spun crazily into the air and lodged in the eastern end of the roof of the boiler shop. Parts of the flywheel broke like glass and pelted First Street.

Once they had recovered from the shock of the explosion, workmen rushed from the buildings. Many thought that all eight of the prostrate men in various parts of the yard were dead.

Reinhard Scheidler "was lying on the ground close to where he had been standing, and as he was tenderly turned over, it was seen that he was dead, a ghastly wound on the left side of the head having been made by a flying piece of steel, the skull being crushed as with the sharp edge of an axe." His death was instantaneous and caused by a jagged edge of a casing attached to the valve-rod box "which had been wrenched away and fell whirling through the air." Ironically, Scheidler was the only fatality.

Physicians were summoned to the scene and pronounced Scheidler dead. He was carried into the machine shop and laid on a planer. A handkerchief was draped over his face. Employees stood about with bared heads and tears streaming down their cheeks. Men with blanched faces discussed the accident in whispers. The body was taken to Bowers and Bradley for embalming and then removed to Scheidler's home at 139 South Third Street. Reinhard's sons, Henry and Oscar; his son-in-law, Wales C. Collins; and his grandson, Stanley Miller, were dazed. They had seen Scheidler leave the office, enter the machine shop, and

proceed into the yard. The next moment, or so it seemed, his corpse was stretched on the planer.

Stanley's father, Senator William E. Miller, received the news by telephone. He inquired about his son's safety at once and he was given the false report that the boy was dead. He jumped into a buggy and raced for Newark. The first person to greet him was Stanley. Senator Miller was later named receiver for the company.

Marshal Vogelmeier, Deputy Sheriff Linke, Patrolman Carroll, Constable Wulfhoop, and a man named Joe Haslop guarded the premises and kept the crowds of curious people from entering the factory. To prevent photographs from being taken, workmen drew a tarpaulin over the engine protruding from the boiler shop roof. Edgar went home to Barnesville on the B.& O. No. 8 that evening.

In his lifetime, Scheidler had received several patents. He was an inventor with a flair for showmanship. His engines had plenty of power for their size. Once, an agent who had delivered a new corn shredder was skeptical about using a little Scheidler engine to run the machine. The factory expert patronizingly agreed to a test. When two loads had been shredded without difficulty, he admiringly circled the engine then told the owner, "Gentleman, I have been around engines all my life, but that little engine has fooled me completely. Your engine has all the power you will ever need for your shredder."[35] All the same, had Edgar carefully inspected the grounds sometime earlier, he might have deduced a serious weakness in Scheidler engines, "since there were always around the factory several old Scheidler boilers—every one of which was blown down in the crownsheet."[36] None, however, had been launched like a cannonball as Edgar's had been. It is a fact that continues to trigger debate about the cause of the explosion.

William T. Richards' father arrived in time to see Scheidler lying dead in the yard. Richards had asked Julius J. D. McNamar to build a 16-horsepower engine, but McNamar had refused. On that fateful April 29, Richards left the scene of horror and went to McNamar's works. He again asked Julius to consider manufacturing a 16, and this time McNamar consented.[37]

By 1920, the McNamar works operated primarily as a machine shop, although a few engines were built, including at least one special order for an 18-horsepower traction model. On October 9, 1921, Julius J. D. McNamar died. His son sold everything.[38] By the 1920s, the Scheidler factory quit business as a machine shop, and by about 1925, the last Scheidler engines were built.[39] The long rivalry had finally ended, but so had a chapter in American history, which for all its acrimony and tragedy, was nevertheless characterized by unparalleled inventiveness and dreams of success which not only could—but often did—come true.

Lavosier Spence

The chroniclers of North American steam traction engines have overlooked Lavosier Spence of Martins Ferry, Ohio. Spence was born on January 14, 1829, in a cabin on a farm that his parents rented in Mount Pleasant Township in Jefferson County, Ohio. On August 20, 1857, he married Elizabeth Dakan, a native of neighboring Belmont County. The couple had two sons. John L. was born on November 3, 1862, and died on August 3, 1895. He was married to Texa Arnett, who died in 1899 at the age of 24 and left two children, Elizabeth D. and Grover L. Spence's other son, George L., was born on November 11, 1866. George became a prosperous citizen of Martins Ferry, a city platted by Ebenezer Martin in 1835.

A book entitled *Centennial History of Belmont County* and *Representative Citizens* portrayed Lavosier as resembling "the majority of self-made men" who became a capitalist "by climbing up a hill of toil." With few educational opportunities, Spence was a laborer when still in his youth. The writer of the *Centennial History* concluded that "his struggles developed his character as well as his mental and physical being." Spence was first a carpenter and then a machinist. He began building threshing machines in Martins Ferry in 1857, the year of his marriage. Between the 1840s and the 1870s, no fewer than six agricultural implement factories stood closely together in the narrow lowland between the steep bluff to the west and the Ohio River to the east. The situation for business was ideal, with the river at First Street and the Cleveland & Pittsburgh rail line at the foot of the high cliff. Readers who have driven along Interstate 70 will remember that Martins Ferry is across from Wheeling, West Virginia.

A mechanism permits the boiler of the Lavosier Spence engine to be brought level in hilly country. This is a rare photograph! Courtesy Frank E. Goulde

Recognizing the area's advantages, Spence based his Ohio Valley Agricultural Works on lots bounded by Hickory Street, Walnut Street, and First Street. About seven miles north of Martins Ferry lay Warrenton, Ohio. On November 4, 1858, Joseph McCune of Warrenton wrote that he ran a traction engine built by the Newark Machine Works "out to the Cadiz Fair and back, a distance of 46 miles." Spence undoubtedly was aware of the Newark engine's amazing accomplishment, and its success may have influenced him to begin the manufacture of steam traction engines.

Spence built his first steam engine in 1867. Martins Ferry had 3,000 residents in 1870, when the census described Spence as a threshing machine builder. He supplied steam engines to the Belmont Furnace of Wheeling in 1872. Lavosier's son George attended the Ohio State University in 1886. *The Wheeling Daily Intelligencer* for September 14 of that year stated that L. Spence employed about 25 workers and paid about $10 per week. The *Intelligencer* mentioned that Spence also ran a general repair shop. During his sophomore year of college, George left Columbus to join his father in his engine and thresher business. George was made a partner in the L. Spence Company in 1890, and on October 12, 1892, George married Flora A. McCord. The couple had two daughters, Emma A. and Gertrude E. In the 1892–1893 directory of Belmont County, Lavosier's business was listed as L. Spence & Son, manufacturers of portable, stationary, and rolling mill and blast furnace engines.

The Spence traction engine was equipped with a device to level the boiler in hilly country. Lavosier continued to produce steam engines until 1899, when the L. Spence Company merged with the Riverside Bridge Company, which was incorporated that same year. Spence held an interest in Riverside. George presided over the Stanton Heater Company, and Lavosier served on its board of directors. Simultaneously, he was president of the People's Savings Bank and vice-president of the First National Bank of Bridgeport, Ohio. He was a member of the board of directors of both the Aetna and the Standard steel works and held interests in other manufacturing firms in Martins Ferry. Spence began to build stoves in 1873. By the following year, he had accepted partners and the firm had become known as Spence, Baggs & Company, which was a name retained by the establishment until 1900, when it incorporated as the Spence-Baggs Stove Company. George served on the firm's board of directors, and the stove business prospered. Lavosier built a handsome residence on the precipitous bluff overlooking the Ohio River. He staunchly supported the interests of Martins Ferry, felt proud of its achievements, and looked on its future with hope.

A. W. Stevens Company

In 1815, Abram W. Stevens was born in Genoa, New York. He was the son of Daniel Stevens, a knitter and weaver. The young Abram tried his hand at carpentry, boat building, and equipping a flour mill. Stevens and Joseph Mosher became partners in a thresher manufacturing business in 1842. Hiram Birdsall, later of the New Birdsall Company,

continued on page 204

This is an opportunity for readers to stand behind a Stevens engine.

Note the small size of this Stevens engine.

This crew has folded up the feeder platform on the thresher and is ready for the Stevens steamer to lead the way to the next farm.
Courtesy Focal Point

The giant intermediate gear found on such Stevens steam traction engines is of special note.

After the Stevens firm relocated from New York to Wisconsin, employees who remained in New York formed Bowen & Quick, which continued to sell Stevens engines for a time.

was briefly associated with Stevens. During his time in Genoa, Stevens manufactured such agricultural implements as plows, harrows, and corn shellers, as well as wagons, buhrstone mills, and roof brackets.

After a disastrous fire in 1878, the Stevens firm moved to Auburn. Around that same time, the factory began to produce steam engines. When LeRoy W. Stevens joined the firm in 1870, the name changed to A. W. Stevens & Son. Abram retired in 1898. The officers of the business accepted Marinette, Wisconsin's offer to purchase Stevens for the sum of $300,000 that was raised by area businesses to promote local investment. The Stevens firm, now named the A. W. Stevens Company, welcomed the opportunity to be near the mushrooming western trade and to compete more effectively with such firms as the J. I. Case Threshing Machine Company. Still, the Stevens firm kept an office in Auburn, where family members lived. Abram died in 1900.

J. B. Bartholomew of the Avery Company obtained an injunction against the Stevens Company for potential infringement of Avery's patents on an undermounted design. At the time that the injunction was served, Stevens was exhibiting one of its undermounted engines at a state fair. The Stevens firm was forced to hide the engine beneath

This Stevens steamer is equipped with a saddle tank and an extra tank above so it can pull a road grader for long stretches of time.

a canvas. According to Marcus Leonard, that event hastened the end of Stevens, which ceased to exist around 1910.

Charles B. Quick, long-time secretary of A. W. Stevens & Son, lived to celebrate his 100th birthday in 1960 and was honored by President Eisenhower. When Stevens moved from New York to Wisconsin—changing the name to A. W. Stevens Company in the process—Quick entered into a partnership named Bowen & Quick that purchased the Wide-Awake business and moved it from Waterloo to Auburn. Like Quick, Bowen and other employees of the new firm had worked for Stevens. As William U. Waters, Jr., has found, Bowen & Quick considered manufacturing its own steamers but decided instead to distribute the Stevens engines produced in Wisconsin.

A Stevens is pictured grading a road.

This is a crystal-clear factory photograph of a 20th Century.

A 20th Century steam engine is shown in the snow.

Note the especially heavy wheels of this 20th Century steamer.

20th Century Manufacturing Company

Mennonite minister Gideon D. Miller established the Improved Traction Engine Company in Somerset County in southern Pennsylvania. To capture the excitement at the beginning of a new century, and to be closer to a railroad, Rev. Miller renamed his firm the 20th Century Manufacturing Company and relocated his business to Boynton, Pennsylvania. Rev. Miller patented his undermounted engine design where the boiler's tubes extended halfway across the top of the firebox, much like John Abell's boiler.

In 1914, 20th Century acquired the Champion Thresher Company of Orville, Ohio, to provide threshers to complement Rev. Miller's engines. During World War I, anti-German sentiment led Congress to pose harsh fines for factories that failed to cooperate in the production of war materiel. Rev. Miller's faith forbade him from making armaments. In response, the government prohibited him from purchasing what he needed to build engines and threshers. The company quickly became insolvent and ended by 1918.

The crew is most likely trying to plug the thresher as a joke at the moment that the photograph is being taken. If so, the engineer of this Waterloo steamer may not find it funny.

Waterloo Manufacturing Company

Jacob Bricker was born in 1818. As a lad, he studied the blacksmith and wagon-making trades. In 1851, he opened a tool and implement shop in Waterloo, Ontario. His foundry was named Bricker & Company, and it supplied stoves and saws. Bricker cast a cannon that was fired to celebrate Waterloo's incorporation in 1857. Bricker began producing apron-type threshers and added treadmills and horse powers to his line. In 1880, Levi, Bricker's son, joined the firm, which purchased John Beam's invention of an improved thresher. The Brickers called the new machine the Champion. The Brickers started building steamers in the 1880s. Their early spark arresters were bulbous contraptions near the bottom of the smokestack and were

reminiscent of those of John Abell. Elias Weber Bingeman Snider, born in Waterloo in 1842, entered into partnership with Levi Bricker in 1884, and the plant was renamed the Waterloo Manufacturing Company. Jacob retired the following year.

Snider and Levi Bricker referred to their threshers and engines as the Lion Brand. At the turn of the century, Waterloo engines began to feature a smiling lion's head cast into the smokebox door. By 1906, Snider ended Bricker's involvement by purchasing all outstanding shares in the business.

Snider championed not only steam power but also publicly-owned hydroelectric energy, for which he is honored in Ontario history. He helped persuade the Ontario

This old Waterloo has a smokebox door characteristic of Waterloos from this time period.

This Waterloo steam engine with extension flywheel is wed to a Goodison threshing machine.

government to permit municipalities to buy power generated by Niagara Falls and chaired the Ontario Power Commission. Snider's interest in hydroelectric energy mirrored that of George Westinghouse.

When the Haggert Brothers Foundry in Brampton closed, Waterloo Manufacturing gained a considerable number of highly skilled workers. The firm added rear-mounted plowing engines to its line in 1910. Waterloo Manufacturing tried to enter the gasoline tractor field in 1911 but built only a few such machines. Waterloo followed most Canadian threshing firms and established warehouses in Winnipeg and Regina.

J. H. Sharpe owned this Waterloo that posed for a characteristic photograph of a threshing rig.

A family proudly poses beside a Waterloo engine on the road.

Men are roping this Waterloo steamer forward. By looping a rope around the flywheel, the men greatly enhance their strength and can easily pull the steam engine.

This is a complete Waterloo rig. Steam engine manufacturers such as Waterloo boasted of the medals awarded to their machines at industrial expositions.

E. W. B. Snider died in 1921. His son Cranston assumed the presidency and the general management of the business. A. Melville Snider, Cranston's son, served as plant manager. The last new traction engine was built in 1925, and Playfair and Company of Toronto bought the firm in 1972.

In 1930, H. V. McKay Company of Australia and Waterloo Manufacturing began a joint business called the Sunshine-Waterloo Company, which manufactured combines under the Waterloo name. The Great Depression ended the production of combines, and Waterloo Manufacturing withdrew from the joint venture in 1934. Waterloo began to manufacture construction equipment, as well as garden and orchard cultivators and small threshers. After World War II, Waterloo became a distributor of Minneapolis-Moline tractors and Belle City threshers.

This Waterloo steam tractor boasts a lion's head cast into the smokebox door.

The whole crew poses on this Waterous steam engine and the threshing machine.

Waterous Company

Philip C. Van Brocklin learned molding in New England before he began working at a small iron foundry in Normandale in southern Ontario in the early 1830s, as found by Mike Hand. Van Brocklin and fellow iron-worker Elijah Leonard soon started a foundry in nearby St. Thomas. When their business failed, the partners separated. In 1841, Leonard established a hollowware business in London. He was manufacturing steam engines by 1880. Meanwhile, Van Brocklin built a foundry in Brantford. His power source was a one-horse sweep in the basement. He manufactured plows, stoves, fireplace irons, and andirons.

Van Brocklin entered into several partnerships. The first, with Arunah Huntington, and the second, with F. P. Goold, were brief. The Goold partnership ended in 1848 when Van Brocklin rejected Goold's offer to buy him out. Goold began a competing foundry in Brantford. Van Brocklin next formed partnerships with Thomas Winter and Charles H. Waterous (1814–1892).

After an apprenticeship in a machine shop in Brandon, Vermont, during 1834, Waterous worked in Norwalk, Sandusky, and Cleveland, Ohio. He had also served as chief engineer on the steamer *Governor Mansy*. Waterous and Thomas Davenport became partners and set about perfecting an electric magnetic motor in New York. Samuel F. B. Morse shared shop space to develop his electric telegraph. The Davenport motor would not generate enough power. Unable to invest in further speculation, Waterous borrowed the fare to return to Sandusky. There he rented a machine shop. He married Martha June in 1839. Within two years of his marriage, his business failed. He and Julius Edgerton began manufacturing grinding mills in Painesville, Ohio. Fire destroyed the factory in 1845. Waterous and Edgerton next formed a partnership with John D. Shepard to found the Shepard Iron Works in Buffalo in 1847. The following year, Waterous arranged with Van Brocklin to take charge of the machine shop and foundry in Brantford. Waterous began producing sawmills and steam engines. Van Brocklin and Winter left the firm in 1857.

By 1864, the firm's name was C. H. Waterous and Company. The business incorporated as the Waterous Engine Works Company in 1874. During the 1860s, Waterous supplied pumping engines for the booming oil business.

David June of Fremont, Ohio, was Charles Waterous' brother-in-law. In 1877, D. June & Company began building a vertical-boilered engine, known as the Champion, to compete with C. Aultman's Canton Monitor. June immediately licensed Waterous to manufacture the Canadian version of the Champion. Waterous supplied a horse-steered, chain-drive traction engine in 1881. Fire engines were added to the line at the same time. In 1888, Waterous opened a branch in St. Paul, Minnesota. In 1890, Waterous began mounting the Champion engine on a horizontal return-flue boiler. Waterous produced the New Economic Boiler, a return-flue boiler with a water-bottom firebox, in the 1890s. Charles Waterous died in 1892.

The company expanded in 1895 and added several product lines. In the 1890s, the Waterous Company began building traction engines that used the same gearing and controls as Buffalo Pitts engines. The first of these were mounted on the New Economic Boiler. The Pitts engines were of the open-bottom, top-mounted locomotive type. Most of the firm's engines were double-cylinder models by 1904.

Buffalo Steam Roller Company gearing also figured in the construction of Waterous steamrollers. By 1905, Waterous steamrollers were selling at the rate of 30 to 35 units per year. The factory also supplied road graders and stone crushers. In 1910, the Waterous firm could not build enough steamrollers to meet demand and imported Pitts rollers from the United States. The firm began the switch to gasoline engines and built its last steam traction engine in 1911, but the company continued to produce steam-powered road rollers for several years.

A big double-cylinder Waterous with an extra water tank is shown here.

Watertown Engine Company

In 1848, cheesemaker Moses Eames decided that a small steam engine might be helpful to farmers. He approached Gilbert Bradford, a foreman at George Goulding's Machine Shop, with the concept. By 1849, Bradford had developed a model of such an engine. He put it to work powering the printing press in Major Haddock's newspaper office. During a visit to Watertown in 1850, Horace Greeley was so impressed with Bradford's engine that he described it in his newspaper, the *New York Tribune*. As commissioner to the London Crystal Palace Exhibition in 1851, Greeley praised Bradford's engine. Bradford and Charles B. Hoard opened a shop in 1851. Hoard & Bradford won a prize for a portable engine at the New York State Fair in that same year. By 1857, Hoard & Bradford employed 150 machinists, which was a high number for those times. Hoard & Bradford merged with the Watertown Engine Company in 1873.

By 1894, John S. Davis & Sons of Davenport, Iowa, were distributing Watertown traction engines. Watertown boilers had a fluted, cast-iron steamdome surmounted by a finial. The Watertown Engine Company met its demise before 1900.

The Watertown steamers feature an unusual casting topped by a finial instead of a steamdome.

The crew members of this old Watertown steamer are threshing from perfectly contoured beehive stacks of grain. Courtesy Robert T. Rhode

Westinghouse Company

George Westinghouse was born in 1846. His father, also named George, journeyed from Vermont to Ohio but decided to return to the East. He became a farmer in Central Bridge, New York, where he invented several improvements in agricultural implements. In 1856, he founded the G. Westinghouse Company in Schenectady. The eighth of ten children, his son George was raised in Central Bridge and Schenectady. The son inherited the father's inventive spirit. After serving in the Civil War for two years, the younger George patented a rotary steam engine in 1865. Westinghouse is best known for the brand of electrical appliances bearing his name. Obsessed with

This Westinghouse is powering a threshing machine that has a platform for a crew member to stand on while feeding bundles into the machine.

This Westinghouse steamer is ready to move out.

This Westinghouse is belted to a sawmill in the Westinghouse factory yard.

This is a Westinghouse in the factory yard. The gentleman sports sideburns similar to those worn by General Ambrose Burnside, for whom sideburns were named.

railway safety, he is also widely recognized for inventing the railroad air brake. Westinghouse became world famous for tapping the potential of hydroelectric power and for setting up alternating current electrical power systems. Westinghouse won the bid to harness the energy of Niagara Falls.

Westinghouse was one of the greatest inventors in history. For that reason, his development of a successful farm steam engine is often overlooked in favor of his more prominent inventions. Westinghouse threshers that were built as early as the 1860s and steamers that were manufactured as early as the 1880s remain in preservation.

Westinghouse died in 1914. The Westinghouse firm stopped building steam engines in 1916. In 1924, the Westinghouse thresher division reorganized as the Pioneer Threshing Company in Shortsville.

Perry Hayden, a Quaker miller of Tecumseh, Michigan, planted 360 kernels of wheat in 1940. After the wheat was harvested the following year, Hayden gave a tenth of the kernels to his church and planted the remainder. In 1942, he harvested a much larger amount of wheat than he had gleaned in 1941. As before, he presented a tenth of the kernels to his church and planted the rest. In 1943 and 1944, Henry Ford delivered antique threshing equipment from Greenfield village to thresh Hayden's crop. Film clips show Ford working with a Westinghouse steamer. Ford is said to have been a great admirer of Westinghouse machines, which had been used on the Ford farm.

A Westinghouse is shown at the factory

George White & Sons Company, MacPherson & Hovey Company, and Haggert Brothers

The history of George White is intermingled with that of MacPherson, and the history of MacPherson is intermingled with that of Haggert Brothers.

Daniel MacPherson was born in Scotland and immigrated to Canada with his family in 1819, when Daniel was three. In 1847, he journeyed to Lockport, New York, where he met woodworker William Glasgow and ironworker Matthias Hovey. They began a foundry called MacPherson, Glasgow and Company in Fingal, Ontario. MacPherson opened a branch named Glasgow, MacPherson and Company in Clinton. Glasgow, D. F. MacPherson (Daniel's son), and Charles Hovey (Matthias' son) ran the Clinton business. MacPherson produced an array of agricultural implements. In 1869, the firm marketed the Climax thresher, which was an apron type. When vibrator threshers began to replace apron threshers a decade later, MacPherson acquired the rights from Seymour, Sabin & Company of Stillwater, Minnesota, to manufacture that firm's Minnesota Chief threshers. John McCloskey, later associated with the John Goodison Thresher Company, worked for MacPherson when the latter business was beginning to sell vibrator threshers.

J. W. Pierce of Deloraine, Manitoba, owned this Cornell, which is threshing from the stook, or shock. Note the large headlamp.

Note the ornate striping of this George White steam tractor on a railcar.

This is a rare look at an old Cornell.

Equipped with an extension flywheel to run the buzz saw, this George White has a smart engineer who has placed a stash of thirst-quenching cream ale nearby.

A George White and a well digger are hard at work.

A George White is showing off by spinning its crank disc.

A large George White steamer stands impressively in the field.

Also born in Scotland, John Haggert served his apprenticeship in the United States. He established a foundry in Brampton, Ontario, in 1849. Two of his brothers became partners in the enterprise. In 1870, Roderick Cochrane, the Haggerts' brother-in law, joined the company to found Haggert Cochrane Agricultural Works, a branch located in St. Thomas. From 1874 to 1877, John served as Brampton's first mayor.

Born in England, George White arrived in Canada on his honeymoon in 1857. He was 20 years old and first tried his hand as a blacksmith in London, Ontario, and then farmed nearby. He eventually returned to the foundry trade and named his business the Forest City Machine

Works. He produced a portable return-flue steam engine in the 1870s. He established a distribution warehouse in Brandon, Manitoba. White was building traction engines by the 1890s.

Haggert Brothers purchased the rights to the Cornell steam engine designed by J. E. Sweet. He was a well-known inventor, mechanical engineer, and professor in the Sibley College of Mechanical Engineering at Cornell University in Ithaca, New York.

Beginning in 1876 or 1877, MacPherson sold Canton Monitor steamers built by C. Aultman in the United States. Glasgow died in 1882. MacPherson and Hovey advertised the Challenge thresher for the eastern trade and the

*George White
steam engines are
great to climb on!*

This George White steam engine with cab belonged to C. A. Wertzbaugher & Son in 1915.

Advance thresher, built in Battle Creek, Michigan, for the western trade.

Haggert Brothers ceased production in 1891. J. M. Ross and his sons, F. J. and A. H., purchased the firm and renamed it J. M. Ross, Sons & Company. The Rosses continued to produce Cornell portables and traction engines. In the early years of the new century, the company moved to St. Catharines. Gaar, Scott & Company granted Ross the rights to manufacture threshers, but soon after, the Ross firm declined.

MacPherson died in 1895. Two years later, his sons sold their business to George White & Sons of London. Hovey died in 1903. The Clinton branch of the firm, named the MacPherson & Hovey Company, sold Cornell engines. The MacPherson & Hovey firm had the rights to build Leader steam engines that resembled those produced by the Marion Manufacturing Company in Marion, Ohio. The striking similarity between the Leader portable and the Cornell portable suggests that Leaders, particularly portables, were licensed under the Sweet patents. For that matter, the Waterloo portable built by the Waterloo Manufacturing Company of Waterloo, Ontario, looked remarkably like the Leader and Cornell portables. The Leader traction engines marketed through Cascaden-Vaughan, Marion's western branch in Iowa, bore a certain resemblance to Cornell traction engines, but the similarity among these traction engines was less astonishing than that among the portables. White engines were built through 1924.

Here is an unanticipated photograph of one of J. O. Spencer's Wide-Awake steam engines.

J. O. Spencer, Son & Company

J. O. Spencer was born in Delaware County, New York, in 1834. He taught school but turned to farming and became a skilled mechanic when he was 20.

In 1855, millwright brothers William, Henry, and Lewis McFarland established a foundry in Union Springs, New York. William and Henry eventually purchased Lewis' interest in the business. The firm built horse powers and Wide-Awake threshers. Henry died in the late 1860s, and William died in 1874. The administrator of the McFarland estate ran the firm until J. O. Spencer bought the Union Springs Agricultural Works in the spring of 1875. Spencer manufactured Wide-Awake threshing machines. In 1877, Spencer began building portable steam engines, which also bore the Wide-Awake name. The following year, he constructed 10 threshers and 25 steamers. Spencer greatly increased his production of threshing machines in 1879. Otto, Spencer's son, served as machine shop foreman. In 1882, Spencer relocated to a new plant in nearby Waterloo. In its up-to-date facility, J. O. Spencer, Son & Company expanded its steam engine business.

At the turn of the century, Charles B. Quick, who was the secretary of A. W. Stevens & Son for many years, formed the partnership of Bowen & Quick to purchase the Wide-Awake business. This acquisition occurred when Stevens was moving from New York to Wisconsin. Bowen & Quick transferred the Wide-Awake firm from Waterloo to nearby Auburn. William U. Waters, Jr., has said that Bowen & Quick considered manufacturing steamers but chose instead to distribute A. W. Stevens Company engines produced in Wisconsin.

S. W. Wood Engine Company

Seth Henry Wood was born in Yonkers, New York, in 1821. Sidney Watkins Wood, Seth's brother, was born in Kingston in 1829. Their father, Israel, moved the family to a farm in Galen, New York, in 1830. Seth became a cabinetmaker, and Sidney went to work for the Seneca Lake Foundry

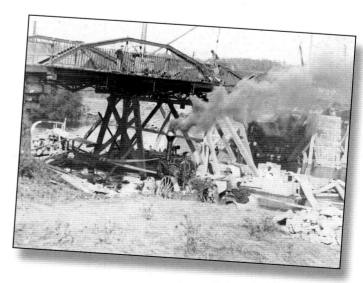

This is a rare view of an S. W. Wood engine helping build a bridge.

An S. W. Wood steam traction engine is pointed uphill.

and Engine Works. In 1866, George Chandler, Seth, and Sidney became partners in Chandler, Wood and Company, a steam engine manufactory in Clyde. When Chandler retired shortly thereafter, the name of the business became S. W. Wood and Company.

As Steve Davis has found, the factory was producing portable steam engines by 1868. Horse-steered traction engines were supplied in 1881. Engines in the following year needed no horses to guide them. S. W. Wood apparently made only steamers and no related machines, such as threshers.

When Seth died in 1886, Henry I. Wood, Sidney's son, became a partner in S. W. Wood & Son. In 1898, Sidney, Henry, and Ray Wood, Henry's brother, bought property for an expansion, and the company erected several new buildings in 1899. Sidney died in 1913. The following year, the firm incorporated as the S. W. Wood Engine Company.

Beginning in 1926, repair work and machining were the primary industries of the factory. When Ray died in 1942, Henry sold out to Burt A. Morley, whose machining business ended in 1954.

Wood Brothers Thresher Company

In 1886, brothers Robert "Bob" L. and Franz John "F. J." Wood began threshing in Spink County, South Dakota. In 1890, F. J. built a self-feeder that was so successful that he and his brother decided to begin a manufacturing business.

This Wood Brothers steam engine with serial number 497 provides the occasion for the entire crew with pitchforks to pose for a photograph.

In 1893, the brothers bought a foundry and machine shop powered by water in Rushford, Minnesota. They named their firm the Wood Bros. Steel Self-Feeder Company. Bob and F. J. were still threshing for a living in 1894. When F. J. was 86 years old, he wrote a brief reminiscence for the Old Threshers Reunion in Mt. Pleasant, Iowa. He described a harrowing experience near Pipestone, Minnesota, when a stack of barley caught fire. The men cut the drive belt and folded the feeder while Bob backed the Frick engine toward the thresher. Pulling forward, he slowly took the slack out of the chain, but the thresher would scarcely budge. As F. J. put the matter, "The fire from the stack was pouring right down upon him." Bob pulled the throttle wide open, and the engine and threshing machine careened away from the danger. The crew threshed the remaining stacks at a breakneck speed to save what they could.

The brothers went on to design a full line of threshers at the Wood Brothers factory in Des Moines, Iowa, beginning in 1899. The Wood Brothers threshing machine was called the Humming Bird. In order to acquire a steamer to complement their threshers, Bob and F. J. bought out D. June of Fremont, Ohio, in 1907. According to LeRoy Blaker, from the outset Wood Brothers engines retained D. June's curved-spoke flywheel, grouter design, and star trademark cast in the smokebox door. The Wood Brothers Thresher Company was incorporated in 1911, and the Wood Brothers factory underwent a major expansion in 1926.

According to Marcus Leonard, the Nichols & Shepard Excello thresher body and separating mechanism were copied from the Wood Brothers thresher, and Wood Brothers complained. Nichols & Shepard's settlement with Wood Brothers involved contracting Wood Brothers for Excello parts made in the Wood Brothers' modern facility. Nichols & Shepard soon discontinued the Excello.

F. J. Wood lived into the era of the first steam shows and frequently attended such events. He served as president of the Wood Brothers firm until 1945. F. J. published a memoir. He died in 1956 at the age of 92. The Wood Brothers plant was sold to Dearborn Motors and then became part of the Ford Motor Company.

Wood, Taber & Morse Steam Engine Works

Ken Morse, Mike Curtis, and Cheryl Nettleton have done much to research this early firm of Eaton, New York. Allen N. Wood and Enos Wood, Allen's uncle, erected a shop that built and repaired cotton and wool milling machinery in 1830. The business briefly relocated to Pierceville but moved back to Eaton in 1848. In 1852—only a year behind Hoard & Bradford of Watertown—Allen N. Wood began producing steam engines. In 1857, coincident with a decline in the milling trade, the firm relocated in Utica. A. N. & E. D. Wood & Company produced steam engines after taking Charles A. Mann as a business partner. Allen sold his interest early in 1859 and returned to Eaton, where he established A. N. Wood & Company. Its plant was known as Wood's Portable Steam Engine Works. Meanwhile, the Utica plant lasted 15 years. With the discovery of oil in western Pennsylvania in 1860, the firm sold many engines to pump crude from wells. The arrival of the railroad in 1868 afforded the firm ready access to customers. The company had previously relied on a local canal to ship its products.

Around 1875, Wood entered into a partnership with Walter Morse, business manager, and Loyal Clark Taber, chief engineer. Wood traveled the country and promoted his company's products. By 1876, a Wood, Taber & Morse branch office in Chicago was distributing engines. The firm was developing four-wheel-drive steamers by 1880. At a demonstration, the operator of a road grader built by a competing company plotted to stall a Wood, Taber & Morse steamer. The operator came to a hard-packed intersection and lowered the blade. The governor on the engine responded, and the Wood, Taber & Morse steam engine pulled the grading machine in two.

Both Wood and Taber died in 1892. Walter Morse retired, and the firm ceased production shortly thereafter. A Wood, Taber & Morse advertisement depicting a horse-drawn steamer has been widely reprinted and circulated for many years.

The long gear train of this Wood, Taber & Morse, owned by G. W. and S. H. Folmer, made traction possible. Courtesy the Kenton County (Kentucky) Public Library, Tim Herrmann, Librarian

Main photo: *The beginnings of the now-famous John Deere firm began with this early entry, the Waterloo Boy.*

Right: *Two different models of the Rumely OilPull tractor stand proudly in their 1900s farmyard.*

Chapter 3
Gasoline and Kerosene Tractors

An old automobile punctuates this busy threshing scene, featuring an International Harvester gas tractor made in Chicago, Illinois.

These hard-working threshermen take a photo break with their Avery gasoline tractor.

An old Holt tread-style tractor pulls a complete threshing line of equipment through the fields. The Holt firm later became the famous Caterpillar company.

One of the more unusual tractor products at the turn of the century was this single-rear-wheeled Common Sense made in Minneapolis, Minnesota.

This 1910 40–70 Buffalo Pitts gasoline tractor, made in Buffalo, New York, is shown pulling a four-bottom plow.

Pride is shown here in the faces of every man, save one, at the conclusion of an apparently successful International Harvester Mogul tractor field trial.

Two men balance on the rear fender of their Aultman & Taylor gasoline tractor while it is belted up at the turn of the century.

One man watches while the operator attempts to maximize belt efficiency on this 40–70 Gaar-Scott gasoline tractor made in Richmond, Indiana.

Gasoline and Kerosene Tractors **235**

Another example of the behemoth prairie tractors is this International Harvester 30–60 Mogul tractor, shown here with its loyal crew and thresher.

This exceedingly rare three-wheeled Hart Parr tractor, built in Charles City, Iowa, is heading through town.

This daring man has the best view in town as a Rumely OilPull tractor prepares to transport this home to another location.

Dwarfed by the rear wheels of this Pioneer tractor, built in Winona, Minnesota, the driver poses with his train of wagons.

A pair of brand-new IH Titans with IH separators on the road are labeled as the Harry Langdon outfit.

A Big 4 tractor is en route to its next job with a plow, cookhouse, water wagon, and drums of fuel in tow.

One complete outfit is being pulled down the road by a large Minneapolis Threshing Machine Company gasoline tractor.

The well-known Hart Parr "Old Reliable" is in action and breaking sod with a single plow in the early 1900s.

A Reeves 40, built in Columbus, Indiana, stands poised with its respective thresher and crew. Notice the spiked rear wheels for traction.

Gasoline and Kerosene Tractors **241**

When friends get together, a Holt, Rumely OilPull, and IH 15–30 all take turns at "bush hoggin.'"

The famous Townsend oil tractor was manufactured by the LaCrosse Tractor Company of LaCrosse, Wisconsin. It was designed to resemble a steam engine

This man is "on top of the world," sitting in the exhaust stack of a Case 20–40.

Main photo: This is a fantastic picture of the exceptionally rare Abenaque hit-and-miss engine built in Westminster Station, Vermont.

Right: A hit-and-miss engine used a barrel for its water tank. Because of their availability, old wooden barrels were commonly drafted for this duty.

Chapter 4
Gasoline Engines

This photograph was taken inside an old hit-and-miss assembly plant. Notice the buzz saw attached to the engine that is being worked on.

Five men are working hard at a makeshift sawing operation utilizing a hit-and-miss engine as its power source.

A Foos hit-and-miss engine is getting set up to do some barn threshing. Notice the apple stuck in the center man's pitchfork!

A buzz saw, powered by an early hit-and-miss engine, is making fence posts. A mother and daughter who are dressed alike observe the activity.

Another hit-and-miss and buzz saw combination, common around the turn of the century, is shown here.

A corn-shelling operation has been undertaken by a large hit-and-miss engine. If the clothing is any indication, the temperatures must be brutally cold.

This is a nice photograph of an old hit-and-miss engine sitting idle and waiting for its next assignment.

Manufacturers frequently mounted hit-and-miss engines on chassis with gearing and called them gasoline traction engines.

NOTES

Baker Notes

1. Robert T. Rhode, telephone conversation with Louis Abner Carson, August 4, 1998.
2. Blake Malkamaki, unpublished "North American Steam Engine List."
3. Hans J. Andersen, "A History of the Baker Company," *Iron-Men Album Magazine* July–August 1954, 19. Also, LeRoy W. Blaker "A. D. Baker History," *Iron-Men Album Magazine* May–June 1956, 14.
4. Hans J. Andersen, "A History of the Baker Company," *Iron-Men Album Magazine* September–October 1954, 4.
5. Robert T. Rhode, interview with Lillis Baker Cort, July 14, 1998.
6. Robert T. Rhode, interview with Rosabelle Krauss, July 2, 1998.
7. Robert T. Rhode, interview with Louis Abner Carson, July 6, 1998.
8. Andersen, July–August 1954, 20.
9. Obituary, *Iron-Men Album Magazine* May–June 1960, 26.
10. Horace Levengood, "A Trip to the Baker Factory," *Iron-Men Album Magazine* July–August 1985, 7–8.
11. Rhode, interview with Krauss.
12. Andersen, July–August 1954, 19. With the exception of the sentence containing the 13th footnote, the details in this paragraph and in the following two paragraphs come from Andersen. Similar details are found in LeRoy Blaker's "A. D. Baker History," *Iron-Men Album Magazine* May–June 1956, 14–15.
13. *Baker Threshing Machinery*, catalog #27, 3.
14. Rhode, interview with Carson.
15. Rhode, interview with Cort.
16. Rhode, interview with Carson.
17. Andersen, July–August 1954, 20.
18. Frank L. McGuffin, "Valve Gears: An Outline," *Iron-Men Album Magazine* September–October 1962, 3.
19. McGuffin, 3.
20. Jack C. Norbeck, "The MacDonald Thresher Company Limited," Iron-Men Album Magazine March–April 1983, 4.
21. John Hoover, "On the Cover," Iron-Men Album Magazine November–December 1987, 23.
22. Andersen, July–August 1954, 20.
23. A. D. Baker Company traction engine book, courtesy of Louis Abner Carson.
24. Andersen, July–August 1954, 20–21.
25. *A. D. Baker Company Photo Album*, 4.
26. A. D. Baker Company traction engine book, courtesy of Louis Abner Carson.
27. LeRoy W. Blaker, "The Baker Fan," *Iron-Men Album Magazine* March–April 1958, 5. See also Hollis Cortelyou's "The Battle of the Fans" and Harry Trego's "Baker Huber Contest of 1907 at Wichita, Kansas," *Iron-Men Album Magazine* July–August 1958, 13–15. Of special interest is Lyle Hoffmaster's "The Baker Fan," *Iron-Men Album Magazine* January–February 1964, 24–27. Hoffmaster goes into great detail to explain all facets of the fan's operation.
28. LeRoy W. Blaker, "The Baker Fan," *Iron-Men Album Magazine* March–April 1958, 6.
29. Blaker, "The Blaker Fan," 6.
30. See Marcus Leonard's "More about the Baker Fan," *Engineers and Engines Magazine* June 1959, 36–37. One of many useful ideas offered in Leonard's article is the insight that the Baker fan puts on resistance rather suddenly and that, to develop its full power, an engine must have a fast rpm prior to the resistance.
31. Claude P. Abbert, "The Baker Fan," *Iron-Men Album Magazine* January–February 1975, 11.
32. Robert T. Rhode, interview with Raymond H. Fork, August 10, 1998.
33. Rhode, interview with Fork.
34. A. D. Baker Company traction engine book, courtesy of Louis Abner Carson.
35. LeRoy W. Blaker, "Did You Know That . . . ?" *Iron-Men Album Magazine* May–June 1972, 3–4.
36. A. D. Baker Company traction engine book, courtesy of Louis Abner Carson.
37. Rhode, interview with Fork.
38. Robert T. Rhode, conversation with Kim Besecker and Dan Greger, August 7, 1998.
39. Rhode, interview with Fork.
40. LeRoy W. Blaker, "Did You Know That . . . ?"
41. Rhode, interview with Carson.
42. This section is based on Rhode's interview with Krauss.
43. Rhode, interview with Fork.
44. Robert T. Rhode, interview with Herb Beckemeyer, July 14, 1998.
45. Andersen, September–October 1954, 4.
46. Rhode, interview with Krauss.
47. Rhode, interview with Cort.
48. A. D. Baker Company sales books, courtesy of Louis Abner Carson.
49. Andersen, September–October 1954, 4.
50. *Farm Album* Winter 1948, 15.
51. Rhode, interview with Krauss.

Farquhar Notes

1. I standardized the spelling and punctuation in quotations from Farquhar's book. For a well-written, comprehensive article on the Farquhar firm, see Gail E. Knauer Anderson's "Company History: A. B. Farquhar" in the September–October 1992 issue of *Iron-Men Album Magazine*.
2. White, John Jr., *A History of the American Locomotive, Its Development: 1830–1880* (New York: Dover, 1979), 449.
3. Farquhar, vii.
4. Farquhar, viii–ix.
5. Farquhar, 2.
6. Farquhar, 20.
7. Farquhar, 4.
8. Farquhar, 5.
9. Farquhar, 6–7.
10. Farquhar, 14.
11. Farquhar, 16.
12. Farquhar, 10.
13. Farquhar, 11.
14. Farquhar, 12.
15. Farquhar, 18.
16. Farquhar, 19.
17. Farquhar, 25.
18. Farquhar, 28.
19. Farquhar, 30.
20. Farquhar, 20.
21. Farquhar, 31.
22. Farquhar, 31–32.
23. Farquhar, 33.
24. Farquhar, 35.
25. Farquhar, 36.
26. Farquhar, 21.
27. Farquhar, 27.
28. Farquhar, 24.
29. Farquhar, 37.
30. Farquhar, 38.
31. Farquhar, 39.
32. Farquhar, 41.
33. Farquhar, 42.
34. Farquhar, 43.
35. Farquhar, 45.
36. Farquhar, 47.

37. Farquhar, 51.
38. Farquhar, 53.
39. Farquhar, 54.
40. Farquhar, 69.
41. Farquhar, 55–56.
42. Farquhar, 67.
43. Farquhar, 56.
44. Farquhar, 57.
45. Farquhar, 57.
46. Farquhar, 58.
47. Farquhar, 59.
48. Farquhar, 62.
49. Farquhar, 63.
50. Farquhar, 64.
51. Farquhar, 70.
52. Farquhar, 71.
53. Farquhar, 73.
54. Farquhar, 75.
55. Farquhar, 80.
56. Farquhar, 90.
57. Farquhar, 92.
58. Farquhar, 81.
59. Farquhar, 82.
60. Farquhar, 83.
61. Farquhar, 84.
62. Farquhar, 86.
63. Farquhar, 87.
64. Farquhar, 96.
65. Farquhar, 89.
66. Farquhar, 104.
67. Farquhar, 105.
68. Farquhar, 105–106.
69. Farquhar, 107.
70. Farquhar, 110.
71. Farquhar, 121.
72. Farquhar, 120–121.
73. Farquhar, 121.
74. Farquhar, 203.
75. Farquhar, 275.
76. Farquhar, 279.
77. Farquhar, 281.
78. Farquhar, 122.
79. Farquhar, 123.
80. Farquhar, 128.
81. Farquhar, 145.
82. Farquhar, 146.
83. Farquhar, 234–235.
84. Farquhar, 151.
85. Farquhar, 153.
86. Farquhar, 154.
87. Farquhar, 156.
88. Farquhar, 158.
89. Farquhar, 283.
90. Farquhar, 141.
91. Farquhar, 217.
92. Farquhar, 159.
93. Farquhar, 172.
94. Farquhar, 174.
95. Farquhar, 232.

96. Farquhar, 182.
97. Farquhar, 183.
98. Farquhar, 190.
99. Farquhar, 244–245.
100. Farquhar, 276.
101. Farquhar, 283.
102. Farquhar, 285.
103. Farquhar, 293.
104. Farquhar, 300–301.
105. Farquhar, 254.
106. Farquhar, 256.
107. Farquhar, 256.
108. Farquhar, 257.
109. Farquhar, 228.
110. Farquhar, 313.
111. Farquhar, 314.
112. Farquhar, 303.
113. Farquhar, 217.
114. Farquhar, 220.
115. Farquhar, 223.
116. Farquhar, 316.
117. See http://www.ydr.com/history/comm1.htm and http://www.ydr.com/history/x1887.htm.

Heilman Notes

1. Johnson, Mary Rose Heilman, *William Heilman, Immigrant's Outstanding Achievements* (Ft. Lauderdale: Tropical Press, 1982). For the reader's convenience, I have standardized the spelling and punctuation within quotations from Heilman's memoirs. I would like to point out that Heilman's memoirs give his mother no name other than Mrs. Heilman. I want to thank the Alexandrian Public Library, 115 West Fifth Street, Mt. Vernon, Indiana, 47620, for making Heilman's memoirs available to me. I also want to express my appreciation to the Willard Library, 21 First Avenue, Evansville, Indiana, 47710, for providing 15 photocopied sources on William Heilman. I am grateful to the librarians at both institutions who devoted much of their time to gathering information for my research.
2. Heilman, 2.
3. Heilman, 3.
4. Heilman, 2.
5. Heilman, 3.
6. Heilman, 49.
7. Heilman, 3.
8. Heilman, 4.
9. Heilman, 5.
10. Heilman, 7.
11. Heilman, 5.
12. Heilman, 7.
13. Heilman, 11.
14. Heilman, 6–7.
15. Heilman, 10.
16. Heilman, 11.
17. Heilman, 12–14.
18. Heilman, 15.
19. Heilman, 16.
20. Heilman, 18.
21. Heilman, 17.
22. Heilman, 18.
23. Heilman, 19.
24. Heilman, 7.

25. Heilman, 20.
26. Heilman, 21.
27. Heilman, 24.
28. Heilman, 25.
29. "Modern History Sourcebook: Andrew Carnegie: The Gospel of Wealth, 1889" Aug. 1997. http://www.fordham.edu/halsall/mod/1889carnegie.html (accessed January 25, 2002). Carnegie's original essay was entitled "Wealth," and appeared in *North American Review* in June 1889.
30. Heilman, 28.
31. Heilman, 25.
32. Heilman, 27.
33. Heilman, 28.
34. Heilman, 31, 29.
35. Heilman, 30.
36. Heilman, 32-33.
37. Heilman, 35.
38. Gilbert, Frank M., *History of the City of Evansville & Vanderburg* [sic] *Co., Indiana*, reprinted 1988.
39. Heilman, 36.
40. Heilman, 38.
41. Heilman, 40.
42. Heilman, 41.
43. Heilman, 42.
44. Heilman, 43.
45. Heilman, 44.
46. Heilman, 48.
47. Heilman, 53.
48. Heilman, 55.
49. Heilman, 59.
50. Heilman, 60.
51. Heilman, 13.
52. Heilman, 49.

Kelly Notes

1. "E. S. Kelly, 78, Dies at Home," *Springfield Daily Republic* May 16, 1935, 12. *Yester Year in Clark County*, Ohio, Springfield: Clark Co. Historical Society, 1978, 29. Sections of this work were first published under separate titles in 1947 and 1948.
2. *Springfield Daily Republic*, 12.
3. *Yester Year*, 28.
4. *Yester Year*, 27. *Kelly-Springfield Today*, 3 Parts, 1987. Part 1. This work is part of a special series published by the Kelly-Springfield Company to commemorate corporation history.
5. *Yester Year*, 28.
6. *Yester Year*, 27.
7. *Yester Year*, 29.
8. *Yester Year*, 30.
9. *Kelly-Springfield Today*, Part 1.
10. McKinney, James P., "The Industries of Springfield, Ohio, and Environs," 1893, 27, *Kelly Springfield Today*, Part 1.
11. *The Industries and Wealth of Ohio*, New York: American Publishing and Engraving, 1891, 117.
12. *Kelly Springfield Today*, Part 1.
13. Maggard, James H, *The Traction Engine: Its Use and Abuse*, (Philadelphia: McKay, 1915), 17.
14. Maggard, 36.
15. Weber, Irving B., *Historical Stories about Iowa City* Vols. 1, 2 and 5. This work also goes under the title *Irving Weber's Iowa City*. Weber, Irving B. Transcript of telephone conversation with Dr. Robert T. Rhode, May 29, 1996. Weber read portions of this series over the telephone to Dr. Robert T. Rhode.
16. Weber, Vol. 2, 275.
17. Weber, Vol. 5, 142.
18. Eskin, Sandra. Transcript of telephone conversation with the author. May 28, 1996.
19. Weber, Vol. 1, 104.
20. *Kelly Springfield Today*, Part 1.
21. *Industries and Wealth of Ohio*, 117.
22. *Industries of Springfield*, 28.
23. Kelly, Maurice A., *The American Steam Traction Engine: A History of Trans-Atlantic Variety*, (Stamford, Great Britain: CMS, 1995), 49.
24. *Kelly Springfield Today*, Part 1.
25. *Kelly Springfield Today*, Parts 2 and 3.
26. *Springfield Daily Republic*, 1, 12.
27. *Kelly Springfield Today*, Part 2.
28. *Industries and Wealth of Ohio*, 117.

Owens, Lane & Dyer Notes

1. *The Republican-News* Greater Hamilton Ed., 48.
2. *General Machinery Corporation*, Hamilton: GMC, 1945, 10.
3. Lane, Clark. "Reminiscential," Unpublished memoir in the collection of the Lane Public Library, 6–7.
4. Norbeck, Jack, *Encyclopedia of American Steam Traction Engines*, (Sarasota: Crestline, 1976), 196.
5. *General Machinery Corporation*, 10.
6. *The Centennial Anniversary of the City of Hamilton, Ohio*, Ed. D. W. McClung, (Hamilton: n.p., 1892), 257.
7. *Owens, Lane & Dyer Machine Company's Traction or Road Engine*, Hamilton: n.p., 1874, 2.
8. *Owens, Lane & Dyer*, 1.
9. Schwartz, James E., *Lane Public Library: Commemorating the Years 1866–1997*, (Hamilton: Lane Public Library, 1997), 4.
10. *General Machinery Corporation*, 11.
11. Bogue, Allen G., *From Prairie to Corn Belt*, (Ames: Iowa State UP, 1994), 283–85.
12. *Centennial History of Butler County, Ohio*, Ed. Bert S. Bartlow, (Hamilton: B. F. Bowen, 1905), 746.
13. *A History and Biographical Cyclopaedia of Butler County, Ohio*, (Cincinnati: Western Biographical Publishing, 1882), 386.
14. *Centennial Anniversary*, 257.
15. *Republican-News*, 48.
16. *Centennial Anniversary*, 257.
17. *Centennial History*, 254.
18. *Centennial Anniversary*, 265. *Centennial History*, 254.
19. *Republican-News*, 48.
20. *Centennial Anniversary*, 257.
21. *A History and Biographical Cyclopaedia*, 386.
22. *Centennial Anniversary*, 258.
23. *Centennial History*, 254.
24. *General Machinery Corporation*, 11.
25. *Centennial Anniversary*, 258.
26. *General Machinery Corporation*, 11.
27. *Republican-News*, 48.
28. *General Machinery Corporation*, 12.
29. *A History and Biographical Cyclopaedia*, 358.
30. Kessling, Helen, "Faces Out of the Past," (Hamilton: Butler Co. Historical Society, n.d.).
31. Kessling, *A History and Biographical Cyclopaedia*, 396. *Centennial History*, 746.
32. *Centennial History*, 746.
33. *Centennial History*, 747.
34. *Centennial History*, 747–48.
35. Kessling.
36. *Centennial Anniversary*, 265.
37. *Centennial Anniversary*, 265. Kessling. *Centennial History*, 746.
38. *Centennial Anniversary*, 265. See also *History of Hamilton*,

Ed. Stephen Cone, n.d. Typescript copy in collection of Butler Co. Historical Society & Museum.

39. *Centennial History* , 746.

40. *Centennial History* , 748.

41. *Centennial History*, 746.

42. Kessling.

43. *History of Hamilton.* Ed. Stephen Cone, n.d. Typescript copy in collection of Butler Co. Historical Society & Museum.

44. *Centennial History.* 748.

45. *History of Hamilton.* Ed. Stephen Cone, n.d. Typescript copy in collection of Butler Co. Historical Society & Museum.

46. *Republican-News*, 48.

Scheidler Notes

To find the source of a quotation lacking a note, see the nearest note before that quotation.

1. *The Newark Advocate* April 30, 1903. Dr. Robert T. Rhode thanks Dr. Philip Payne for locating and assembling all newspaper articles cited here. He also thanks Karen Dickman, Office Manager, and Ella Hare, Office Secretary, of the Licking County Historical Society for their valuable help in researching McNamar and Scheidler.

2. *The Newark Advocate March* 3, 1887.

3. William T. Richards, *The Era of Steam in Licking County, Ohio: The Agricultural Aspect* 3rd ed. (Granville, Ohio, 1985). 12. Dr. Robert T. Rhode thanks Brian K. Volkmer, Director of the Institute of Industrial Technology, a museum based in the former Scheidler factory building, for making available this book and for sharing his theories about Scheidler's life and business.

4. *The Newark Advocate* April 30, 1903.

5. *The Newark Advocate* November 8, 1940.

6. *The Newark Weekly Advocate* August 28, 1890.

7. *The Newark American* February 24, 1882.

8. *The Newark Weekly Advocate* August 28, 1890.

9. *The Newark Advocat*e April 30, 1903.

10. William T. Richards, "History of the McNamar & Scheidler Engine Building, Newark, Ohio," *Engineers and Engines* July–August 1976, 23.

11. Richards, *Era of Steam in Licking County*, Ohio, 23.

12. Richards, *Era of Steam in Licking County*, Ohio, 3.

13. *The Newark American* February 24, 1882.

14. *The Newark Advocate* August 28, 1890.

15. *Engineers and Engines* July–August 1976, 24.

16. *The Newark American* February 24, 1882.

17. William T. Richards, "History of the McNamar Machine Works, Newark, Ohio," *Engineers and Engines* March–April 1976, 3.

18. *The Newark American* February 24, 1882.

19. *Engineers and Engines* July–August 1976, 25–26.

20. *Reinhard Scheidler vs. Jacob Tustin*, U.S. Circuit Court, November 1883.

21. Richards, *Era of Steam in Licking County, Ohio*, 4.

22. *The Newark American* April 8, 1881.

23. *Scheidler vs Tustin*, U.S. Circuit Court, November 1883.

24. William T. Richards, "Newark, Ohio: City of 5 Engines," *The Iron-Men Album Magazine* March–April 1955, 4.

25. Richards, *Era of Steam in Licking County, Ohio*, 9.

26. Richards, *Era of Steam in Licking County, Ohio*, 15.

27. *Engineers and Engines* July–August 1976, 26.

28. *The Newark Advocate* November 8, 1940.

29. *The Iron-Men Album Magazine* March–April 1955, 5.

30. *Engineers and Engines* July–August 1976, 26.

31. *The Newark Advocate* November 8, 1940.

32. Richards, *Era of Steam in Licking County, Ohio*, 10.

33. Richards, *Era of Steam in Licking County, Ohio*, 3–4, 15.

34. *The Newark Advocate* April 30, 1903.

35. Richards, *Era of Steam in Licking County, Ohio*, 10.

36. Richards, *Era of Steam in Licking County, Ohio* , 12.

37. Richards, *Era of Steam in Licking County, Ohio* , 16.

38. Richards, *Era of Steam in Licking County, Ohio* , 17.

39. Richards, *Era of Steam in Licking County, Ohio* , 13.

INDEX